Nations and Peoples

The Soviet Union

The Soviet Union

DEV MURARKA

with 30 illustrations and 3 maps

WALKER AND COMPANY

NEW YORK

To Girilal and Yamini
who were born in Moscow

© DEV MURARKA 1971

ALL RIGHTS RESERVED. NO PORTION OF THIS WORK MAY BE
REPRODUCED WITHOUT PERMISSION EXCEPT FOR BRIEF PASSAGES
FOR THE PURPOSE OF REVIEW

LIBRARY OF CONGRESS CATALOG CARD NUMBER: 79–120408

ISBN: 0–8027–2123–0

FIRST PUBLISHED IN THE UNITED STATES OF AMERICA IN 1971
BY THE WALKER PUBLISHING COMPANY, INC.

PRINTED AND BOUND IN GREAT BRITAIN

Contents

DATES

On 1 February 1918 (old style), Russia came into line with the rest of the world and adopted the Gregorian calendar, making that day 14 February 1918 (new style). For simplicity's sake this book uses the old style before that day, and the new style thereafter; both are given in one passage (p.46) to avoid confusion.

Preface

TO WRITE A BOOK about the Soviet Union is a foolhardy undertaking at any time. It is even more so doing it in Moscow while tied up with other professional duties. It was with great diffidence, therefore, that I took up the suggestion to write this book.

Russia is infectious: the more one knows about it the more fascinating it becomes. I have thoroughly enjoyed exploring the byways of Russian history and life in the course of preparing this book. In retrospect, I would not have liked to miss any of it, but this is not a scholar's book and I have no doubt that the more learned will be able to pick innumerable holes in my writing. I plead guilty to all these errors and omissions in advance.

Above all, this book is one man's exploration of Russian and Soviet history, his personal discovery of Russia's past and present. Such a personal vision is necessarily imperfect and limited in range, but even if one reader is encouraged after reading this book to interest himself more in the Soviet Union and its problems, my efforts will not have been in vain.

It only remains for me to express my gratitude to a host of friends, Russian and British, who have helped me in many ways to write this book. I have benefited enormously from their advice and criticisms. It is not their fault if I have not always accepted the suggestions made. I hope they will understand and not be offended if I do not mention all of them individually here. But I must make an exception or two and thank Mr Stephen England, who hopefully persisted in getting me to complete the book, and Mr Bill Scrimgeour, who spent part of his holidays correcting the final manuscript and ironing out the last traces of alien English which are bound to remain in any work by a non-English-speaking writer. My wife is frankly happy that the writing is over and will no longer keep me incommunicado on many an evening.

1   The Beginnings

THE HISTORICAL ROOTS of the Soviet Union and of the Russian people lie deep in the past but much about their real identity is uncertain. The geographical environment – the wind-swept steppe land, the spine-chilling cold of long winters, the frozen earth which yielded its fruit with only superhuman labour, the lack of natural protection which made Russia an ideal prey to invasions – all of this and more has shaped the character of the people, no less of the state, in the course of her long history.

The Soviet Union straddles the two continents of Asia and Europe, extending from longitude 20 degrees east to 170 degrees west. In the south it reaches the latitude of 35 degrees north and its northernmost point is 80 degrees north, within the Arctic circle. On the western frontier of the USSR lie Norway, Finland, the Baltic Sea, Poland, Czechoslovakia, Hungary and Rumania. Her southern frontier is determined by the Black Sea, Turkey, Iran, Afghanistan, China, and Mongolia. In the east lies the Pacific Ocean and in the north the Arctic Ocean. In the north-east the Bering Straits separate the Soviet Union from Alaska by a distance of only 35 miles.

The vast area which the Soviet Union occupies, 8,646,490 square miles, roughly 17 per cent of the inhabited surface of the earth, contains different climates, different soils, much of it still unproductive, covered with forests and ice. The three chief features of the landscape which have indelibly influenced the course of Russian history and the evolution of the Russian people are the steppe, the forest and the rivers; above all, the steppe, a great plain which stretches from Asia to Western Europe, 3,000 miles long from central Siberia to the Baltic and 2,500 miles broad from south Turkmenistan to northern Siberia.

In the early stages of Russian history wave after wave of Tatars, Mongols, and other hordes roamed across this Eurasian plain in an

9

attempt to break through to the west. Though in Kiev, Novgorod and other cities strong city-empires flourished between the tenth and the sixteenth centuries, the depredations of the invaders gave Russian life a nomadic flavour till the sixteenth century when the Slav people at last began to rally and consolidate themselves. It was a life of constant danger, movement, dreams and expansion. Something of that frontier feeling in Russian life still comes through.

Then there was the forest in which at any given time half the population sheltered rather than lived. The axe was the symbol of this life of battle with the wilderness as more and more people sought the sanctuary of the forest to escape from the pressure of nomadic invaders, from the oppression of chieftains and to seek a peaceful living amidst the surrounding chaos.

Lastly, the rivers. They became the road to colonization, the link which bound together innumerable settlements and which were to lay the foundations of successive kingdoms and help to create the Russian empire which lasted for two centuries, from Peter the Great early in the eighteenth century to the end of tsardom early in the twentieth.

The expanse of the Eurasian plain became the heartland of Russia and gave that urge towards the sea which many historians believe to be a distinctive and powerful feature of Russian history. The Russian frontier moved along the rivers and portages while the occupants, remaining behind, turned first to agriculture, then to mining and industry, slowly mastering their surroundings and absorbing the non-Russian elements of the population.

The true frontiersmen, though, were those who lived by hunting and fishing and who rolled back the wilderness in their constant search for game, furs, fish and honey, leaving others behind them to tame nature. At the outset the frontier was always pushed east and north. In the west there were strong kingdoms barring the way. In the south the Russian advance was held back till the sixteenth century by the warlike Tatars, who yielded only to the Cossacks, the most notable of all the breeds of hunter-frontiersmen. It was in the course of these centuries-long struggles, too, that Russia acquired that streak of anarchic individualism which accompanies the most authoritarian regimes in her history.

Much remains obscure or controversial about the earliest phase of Russian history. In the southern part of Russia traces have been found of palaeolithic and neolithic man. The origin of the Slav race too, which came to dominate Russia and Eastern Europe in historical times, is not known with certainty, but it is known that these people, a branch of the Indo-European family, were peaceful cultivators. They were still a dormant race when Greeks, Cimmerians and Scythians occupied the greater part of southern Russia, the Greeks along the coast line of the Black Sea and the Sea of Azov, the others in the hinterland. The Scythians gave way in the fourth century before Christ to a kindred, nomadic tribe, the Sarmatians, who spread up to the Danube.

In the second century AD the Sarmatians were invaded from the north by the Baltic Goths, who ultimately established the empire of King Hermanric. The river routes from the Baltic to the Black Sea now acquired a new significance and in later ages they were used by the Swedes and others trying to assert their supremacy over Russia.

In the second half of the fourth century the first Asian invasion of Russia took place. Baulked by the Great Wall of China, the Mongols struck westward. Their march was made easier by the natural track along their route which supplied them with fodder for their cattle and horses. They absorbed the conquered tribes and collectively came to be known as the Huns. They lived, conversed, and slept on horses, never changing their clothes till the torn shreds just dropped off. They gave Russia the first taste of the bitter struggle with nomads from Asia which was to last for centuries. Their most famous leader was Attila the Hun who, in 448, received an embassy from the Byzantine emperor Theodosius II in Hungary. He incorporated a large number of the Slavs into his short-lived empire. The Huns were defeated in France in 451 and two years later Attila died. The Huns disappeared from history thereafter but not before they had destroyed the Western Roman Empire.

Their legacy was a medley of tribes which figured in later Russian history for brief periods, such as the Bolgars, the Avars and the Khazars. After the disintegration of the Hun Empire the Slavs emerged as a great tribe settled over a vast area and holding the basin of the Vistula, Pripet, Dnieper, Desna, Bug and Dniester rivers. By the reign of Charlemagne the territory of the West Slavs (Poles, Czechs, Lusatians) was delimited by the river Elbe. The South Slavs, comprising the Slovenes, Croats, Serbs, Bosnians and Montenegrins, Macedonians and Bulgars, all speaking variants of the Slavonic language, settled in the region now known as Yugoslavia and Bulgaria. The East Slavs were the Great Russians, Ukrainians and Byelorussians.

It is likely that the Slavs originally came from the northern Carpathians although there is great controversy on this issue. The first mention of the Slavs is in the Byzantine and Gothic chronicles in the sixth century. Jordanes, the Gothic historian and bishop, and Procopius of Caesarea, a Byzantine historian, alluded to them towards the end of the sixth century. Between the sixth and the ninth century, the Slavs spread over the territory which has still remained Slav in our time. The only expansion after this period was by the East Slavs, but they expanded only eastwards, into Asia.

In the sixth century the East Slavs had spread out into the basin of the Don. Their social basis was the clan, with property held in common under their chief. They deified nature. These forerunners of the present-day Russians were conquered briefly by the Avars, who harnessed women to chariots and made the Slavs fight in the front line in their wars against Byzantium. Though the Avars vanished from history relatively soon afterwards, their tyranny hastened the process of dispersal of the East Slavs, some of whom took to the riverway of the Dnieper. Their long march, however, transformed their social organization. It became centred more on the family since small groups had to look after themselves during the march. Their first major settlement was Kiev on the banks of the Dnieper, named after a chief, Kiy. In course of time they occupied a whole system of waterways – the Dnieper, Pripet, Dvina, Lovat and Volkhov. Kiev was the southern centre of this area and Novgorod the northern.

Before Kiev was firmly established the East Slavs had to fight the Khazars, a people of Turkish origin, who established a kingdom on their eastern side and absorbed the considerable Slav population between the Sea of Azov and the Dnieper. They demanded and received tribute from Kiev. The Khazars were a remarkably tolerant people in religious matters and their Khakan (prince) adopted the Jewish faith.

In the second quarter of the ninth century, the Vikings came to Russia. They were to play a prominent role in the early period of Kievan Rus, but they had to contend with the Ugry (Magyars), related to the Finns, and the Pechenegs or Patzinaks. They were all fierce fighters. They fought the Khazars, they fought the Slavs and they fought each other. They overran the Khazar kingdom.

Ultimately the Magyars established themselves in the Danube valleys, which came to be known as Hungary. The Magyars thus permanently separated the South Slavs from the West and East Slavs.

The Pechenegs blocked the river-trade to the sea and Byzantium. The Slavs employed the Vikings to protect themselves and their towns. The Rurik of Russian history was a Viking chief who was in the service of the city of Novgorod and he established his supremacy over the city, and sent two of his brothers and a deputy to outlying posts. On his death he was succeeded by a kinsman, Oleg, who captured Kiev in 882. Kiev was to emerge as the first centre of Russian statehood and civilization.

Rurik, a foreigner, thus laid the foundations of the first Russian empire. Russia was to be ruled many times again by persons of foreign origin. Nevertheless it was the people, the Slavs, who in the long run determined the political and economic life of the state and this must be constantly kept in view. It was because of incessant strife in their midst that the Slavs invited the Vikings to establish order. As the old Chronicle says, 'Our land is great and rich but there is no order in it. Come, then, to rule as princes over us.'[1] Rus was the name given by the Vikings to the Slav lands, but within a century the Slavs had assimilated the Vikings. Oleg's grandson was given a Slav name, Svyatoslav.

Svyatoslav extended the boundaries of Kievan Rus further than at any time, either before or after him. The core of Kievan Rus was the economic unity of its territory, closely bound together by river-borne trade. The first task of the Kievan rulers was to impose discipline within the area, the second was to keep open the direct trade routes to Constantinople, and the third was to conclude commercial treaties with Constantinople. For this purpose numerous expeditions to Constantinople were led by the Kievan kings. It was on his retreat from one of these expeditions that Svyatoslav's army was surrounded by the Pechenegs; he himself was killed and his skull turned into a drinking cup for a Pecheneg Prince. Svyatoslav did, however, succeed in putting an end to the Khazar kingdon.

After a war of succession, Svyatoslav's third son, Vladimir, won a victory over Kiev, largely with the support of Novgorod. He was a savage, polygamous heathen who succeeded in converting Russia to Christianity. The legend is that he rejected Judaism 'for its sins' and Islam because it did not allow drinking and he believed that it was impossible to be happy in Russia without strong drink, a belief undoubtedly shared by the Russians to this day. To establish that he did not accept Christianity as a gift but as a conquest, he persuaded the two Byzantine emperors of his time, after threatening them with devastation, to give him their sister Anna in marriage. Vladimir's subjects followed the example of his conversion and Christianity was generally received willingly among the people.

The reign of his successor Yaroslav (1019–1054) was long and peaceful, and was noted for the final elimination of threat from the Pechenegs. A capable scholar, he encouraged translations from the Greek and the copying of manuscripts. He immensely enhanced the beauty of the city of Kiev by building a number of churches and monasteries. These monasteries became noted for their Russian chronicles, which provide the earliest source material of Russian history. The clergy also introduced canon law, modelled on Byzantine laws. It covered domestic matters and several categories of population. The first Russian legal code, *Russkaya Pravda*, was a modified version of Byzantine secular laws. It is notable for its detailed guidance about commercial dealings, which is a reflection of the importance of trade at the time.

Kiev also set the pattern of political organization in Russian society which was to last for several centuries. The real element of power lay in the princes' bodyguards. In the later period of Kievan ascendancy it split up into three segments. At the top of the hierarchy of classes came a group of elders who formed the Prince's council of advisers (this was the origin of the later, powerful, Council of Boyars). Then there were the junior officials and the household bodyguard. The kings' authority rested on their ability to fight and to manage the day-to-day affairs of the rudimentary administration. Then came the innovation of the town gathering (*veche*) which was later transformed into the local governing body. The power of the *veche* grew as the town populations increased. One characteristic feature of the period was a phenomenal growth in the number of slaves, as the princes and boyars turned to agriculture from commerce and trade.

Yaroslav's death was followed by another struggle for succession. Kiev was ruled by two more worthy kings: Vladimir Monomakh, an extraordinarily brave, wise and just man, and his son Mstislav I who died in 1132. After his death the decline of Kiev began, largely due to persistent feuds among the princes. Nevertheless, Kiev had earned its place in the evolution of Russia as a civilizing influence and the centre of the then existing Russian State. It was no less an admirable model in art and architecture.

Three factors brought about the disintegration of Kiev: the endless strife among the princes, the devastation wrought by the Polovtsy, a tribe of Kipchak Turks, and the consequent movement of population away from the chaos in Kievan territory. The *druzhiny* or private armies of the princes ruined every district by their fighting, and the squabbling princes failed to combine against the Polovtsy, who, as a chronicle laments, 'are carrying away our land piecemeal'.[2] In this atmosphere, the cultivators sought security. The only way open to them was to migrate and for this purpose a dense forest was the best refuge since large hordes of Polovtsy could not follow them there.

This migration took place in many directions, the most important of which was up the river Desna towards the Middle Volga. There the Russians met only a scattered Finnish population which offered no resistance. Ultimately the settlement of this region led to the rise of Muscovy, or Moscow.

This migration became the formative influence on the Russian peasant character, the backbone of society. The climate in this zone was severe, with no outdoor work possible for months on end. It formed the habit of working in great bursts with sustained effort. It also meant prolonged periods of lethargy. The lonely wandering through the forests produced an innate longing for society but it also made the Russians wary in dealing with people.

One reason why feudalism did not take root in Russia as it did in Europe was the persistent movement of population. The Russian princes' main problem was retaining labour, since even plentiful land was of no use if there were no people to work it. Only he who had manpower could be powerful and rich.

An example was Andrew Bogolyubsky, a grandson of Vladimir Monomakh. Born in 1111, he broke from Kiev and founded his new capital at Vladimir, not far from Moscow. Andrew was also a great builder and the result of his achievement is still to be seen in some magnificent churches and other remarkable architectural monuments in Vladimir, Suzdal and Rostov, now centres of tourist attraction. The supremacy of Vladimir, however, was shortlived, partly because of a long succession struggle but largely because

Vladimir was overcome by the rise of the Mongols and Tatars, a fact of supreme importance in Russian history.

From beyond the Altai mountains, near the great Gobi desert, a horde of Tatars under the leadership of Chingiz Khan, after overthrowing a Chinese governor, Ong-Khan, rode towards the grassland and steppes of the west. They first attacked the Polovtsy, with whom the Russians now joined forces for self-defence. On the river Kalka the joint forces of the Russians and the Polovtsy suffered a crushing defeat in 1223. The Russians fought bravely but were forced to surrender. Nearly all the princes and *bogatyrs* were wiped out and the Tatars built a wooden platform on top of their captives on which they wildly feasted, crushing the victims underneath. After this foray the Tatars went back. The Russian bishops appealed for unity in defence of Christendom but their appeals fell on deaf ears.

Another Tatar leader, Batu Khan, returned with a horde of 300,000 and, crossing into Russian territory, headed straight for Vladimir. After tough resistance they overran and sacked the city and continued their march westwards. They sacked Kiev in 1240 and next year laid waste Hungary and Poland. Their advance was only halted by the Czech King Vaclav and the Duke of Austria.

The motto of the Tatars was 'regret is the fruit of pity', and as conquerors they were absolutely ruthless. A traveller, Friar John of Plano Carpini, who saw Kiev six years after the sacking, testified that only two hundred houses were left there and that the countryside around was littered with skulls and bones.[3]

In 1242 the Golden Horde, as these invaders of Russia were called, established their headquarters at Sarai on the lower Volga. For nearly two and a half centuries they continued to torment Russia and Eastern Europe. Their only interest was to maintain their supremacy and to levy tribute. Their economic administration, though efficient, was destructive of the Russian economy. It has left its mark on the Russian vocabulary for taxation, which bears Tatar origins. The political consequences were even graver. As George Vernadsky concludes his study of the relationship between the Mongols and Russia, 'Autocracy and serfdom were the price the Russian people had to pay for national survival.'[4] The Mongol period of Russian history was a total calamity. It cut off Russia from Europe, and plunged her into darkness. Russia's first considerable encounter with Asia was a bitter one.

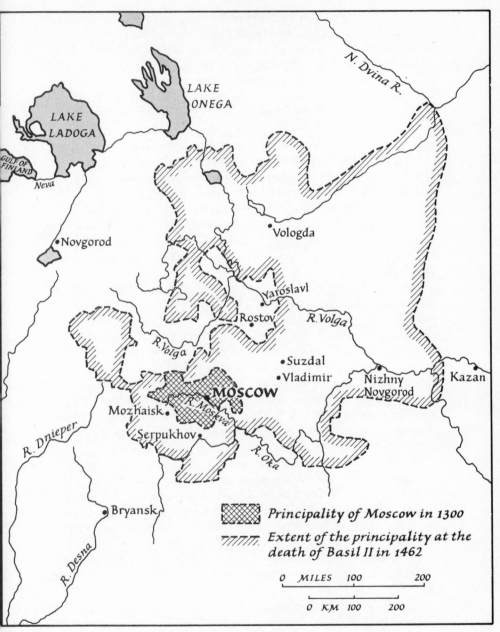

LAKE ONEGA

LAKE LADOGA

GULF OF FINLAND

Neva

N. Dvina R.

• Novgorod

• Vologda

Yaroslavl

• Rostov

R. Volga

R. Volga

• Suzdal

• Vladimir

Nizhny Novgorod

Kazan

MOSCOW

R. Moskva

Mozhaisk

Serpukhov

R. Oka

R. Dnieper

• Bryansk

R. Desna

Principality of Moscow in 1300

Extent of the principality at the death of Basil II in 1462

0   MILES   100   200

0   KM   100   200

Map of Muscovy

At first almost unnoticed, there now began the rise of Moscow. It is first mentioned in 1147. As a perceptive historian, Robert J. Kerner, has observed, 'The history of Moscow is the story of how an insignificant *ostrog* (blockhouse) became the capital of a Eurasian empire. This insignificant *ostrog*, built in the first half of the twelfth century on an insignificant river by an insignificant princeling, became, in due course of time, the pivot of an empire extending into two, and even three continents.'[5] But this insignificant *ostrog* had one advantage. It was on one of the main river routes frequented by the Tatar and other armies. Thanks to the flight of population from Kiev and Vladimir, Moscow also had a sudden access of manpower, which gave it an advantage over other regions, as did the removal from Kiev of the head of the Church. The Church was an influential and powerful body able to command the loyalties of the people, and unlike the political authority it was unified. Throughout the long nightmare of Tatar domination the Church kept alive the national consciousness of the people. It became an instrument for cohesion.

Moscow gained in power and its rulers imposed their authority, first on the surrounding countryside, then on rival cities like Novgorod.. Whilst consolidating their kingdom, the rulers of Moscow alternately appeased and defied the Tatars. The most enterprising turned out to be Dimitry Donskoy, grand duke of Moscow (1359–1389). He was confirmed in office in 1371 by the leader of the Golden Horde, Mamai, but he soon began to defy the Tatar overlords. Inevitable conflict followed and on 8 September 1380, Dimitry's armies inflicted a crushing defeat on the Tatars and routed Mamai's mammoth army in the Kulikovo plain near Moscow. The great victory is engraved in the Russian national memory.

The Tatar menace was by no means over, however, for almost a century later they made a final attempt to subjugate Moscow. By then the Golden Horde had weakened owing to internal dissension. Early in 1480 a huge Tatar army under the leadership of Khan Ahmad marched towards Moscow. Ivan III, who was on the throne in Moscow at the time, prevaricated; all summer the two armies faced each other and Ivan even made attempts to retreat. But on 19 November 1480 the Tatars left of their own accord. The Tatar nightmare was over.

Ivan III, who had married Sophia, a niece of the last emperor of Constantinople, declared himself the Sovereign of All Russia and the

Tsar or Caesar. It was the beginning of autocracy both in name and in reality. Ivan the Great, as he came to be known, extended the domain of Moscow far and wide. He died in 1505 and was succeeded by his son Basil III (1505–1533). Basil was tyrannical, and disliked even by the Boyars, the higher nobility, but he was successful in extending the domains of Moscow even further. He was succeeded by his infant son Ivan.

The reign of Ivan the Terrible (1533–1584) was a long one because he came to the throne at the age of three. His early period was a successful one but towards the end disasters overtook Moscow. Temperamentally Ivan was unstable, being given to extremes of self-indulgence and self-pity. During his reign the conflict between the monarchy and the Boyars became more pronounced. He called an assembly, *Zemsky Sobor,* representing all classes, which later emerged as a valuable instrument in the struggle between the Tsars and the Boyars, with which the hold of the Boyars was broken. In 1552, he laid siege to Kazan, broke the power of the Tatars completely and in 1566 annexed Astrakhan, thus extending the empire of Muscovy to the Caspian. Though in 1571 the Crimean Tatars and Turks made a successful assault on Moscow, burning, killing 800,000 Russians and carrying away 130,000 prisoners, they could not break the power of Moscow. Ivan the Terrible also inaugurated the notorious *Oprichnina,* a supreme police force responsible to and controlled directly by the Tsar.

Although his initial campaigns in the Baltic were also successful, Ivan later lost many of his conquests to Poland and Sweden. His later years were marred by the dreadful massacre of Novgorod, when he suspected the city of negotiating with Poland. He marched there in the winter of 1570 and in five weeks slaughtered almost the entire population. Families were thrown into the river, where soldiers in boats pushed them under the water. He killed his own son in a violent rage when the son protested against his father breaking into his apartments and insulting his wife.

But this demented genius had completed the work of Moscow rulers by creating a nation. Till then there had been only territorial units that lacked a fixed population. These barriers were broken down in the process of Moscow's emergence as the centre of an empire. Between the two Ivans, the Great and the Terrible, a nation was not only formed but welded together, sometimes by means which were spectacularly cruel, if effective. But a price was paid for it. A great Russian historian has remarked of this period that all was asked of the people and nothing was done for them.

Their fate was all the sadder in the period immediately following the death of Ivan the Terrible. It was as if the last ounce of energy had been drained from the people and they were powerless to combat their misfortune. This is the period (1584–1613) which has been always remembered by the Russians as the 'Time of Troubles'.

Ivan's second son Fyodor, who succeeded him, remained immature throughout his life. The real power lay with some of the Boyar families. For the first few months the regent was Nikita Romanov but he fell ill and was succeeded by Boris Godunov. He was an efficient ruler but widely distrusted. On the death of Fyodor, Boris was elected Tsar. He lived in constant fear of hostile intrigues and had the rival Romanov family exiled and nearly exterminated.

From 1601 to 1604 Russia was plagued by severe famines. There were also the claims of a pretender to the throne who insisted that he was Dimitry, the murdered son of Fyodor. The pretender was supported by Poland and some of the Boyars. More Boyars changed sides and following the sudden death of Boris Godunov in the midst of this struggle and the subsequent deposition and murder of his son Fyodor Godunov, the pretender came to the throne. But within a short time he was deposed by Basil Shuisky, another Boyar leader, who, as Tsar, was harassed by further pretenders. King Sigismund of Poland also planned to gain the throne for himself.

Through all these upheavals the people suffered. Life became insecure. There was widespread treachery and opportunism. The outstanding exception was the Patriarch Hermogen, an old man of eighty when he was appointed to the post. In fact it was the Church leadership which preserved a sense of unity and purpose, its authority considerably enhanced since the Patriarchate was created in 1589 with the blessing of the Patriarch of Constantinople. The Russian Orthodox Church now became autonomous, choosing its own head.

After nearly forty years of upheaval and turmoil an exhausted but united people decided to put a member of a Russian noble family, Michael Romanov, on the throne. He was crowned the first Tsar of the Romanov dynasty on 11 July 1613 in Moscow. The dynasty was to last exactly 304 years and to be overthrown just as it was ushered in, in social chaos and bloodshed.

Practically the whole of the Romanov era was to be dominated by the great issue of serfdom, its later years by the effects of the emancipation. In no other country did serfdom reduce the life of the majority of the people to such abject misery and degradation, in no other country were its effects so malign and deadly. Serfdom, indeed, became the cardinal foundation of Russian society and endured longer in Russia than anywhere else. It settled on the soul of Russia like a blight from which neither the victims nor the victimizers could find an escape.

The consolidation of serfdom was greatly hastened by the ravages of the Time of Troubles. The state as well as the gentry needed labour, for military and civil service and for work on the estates. Since the population had dispersed to escape the unbearable conditions, the impoverished gentry relied on the Tsars to give them a right over fugitive peasants. The crucial step which reduced the peasants to serfdom was the decree issued in 1649 by Tsar Alexis, which abolished the time limit for recapturing the fugitives. The peasants gradually came to be regarded as chattels, absolutely at the mercy of their master, even their private lives regulated by them. The peasant became worse than a slave.

The harshness of this order, which grew more and more rapacious with time, provided another theme of Russian history in the sixteenth, seventeenth and eighteenth centuries – the peasant revolts. In fact there grew up a more or less permanent body of people who placed themselves outside the law in order to escape the conditions of serfdom. Peasant risings surged up like sudden storms in the sea and were ruthlessly crushed by the state. Some of the leaders of these risings became folk heroes and their memories survived, as further stimulants to rebellion, in songs, poetry, and literature. One such hero was Stepan Razin, who was hanged in 1671 after four years of tempestuous campaigning against the Boyars and landlords. Another was Pugachev, who led peasant revolts in 1773–1775.

Serfdom also received the sanction of the Orthodox Church, which had gradually become identified with the state. What it had gained in secular power, it had lost in spiritual authority. There grew up an opposition group within the Church calling themselves Old Believers or Schismatics (*Raskolniki*). Persecuted both by the Church establishment and the state, the *Raskolniki* played an important role in many of the peasant rebellions.

The peasant revolts and disorders also weakened the *Zemsky Sobor*. Nominally it still continued to be consulted when a new Tsar was crowned but it had become primarily an assembly of landed interests and those bound by military service to the sovereign. It lost all independence. The state became more and more centralized, owing to the need to maintain and supply a large army.

The army was necessary not only for internal order but also for external security. Indeed the external dangers which faced Russia from the west played no mean part in exacerbating internal disorder and driving the population underground. It also meant continual wars and financial burdens. At the time the main enemies of Russia were Sweden, under her greatest king and general Gustav Adolf, in the north, Poland in the centre and Turkey in the south.

The prolonged upheavals in state and society, however, produced still other consequences. The Church, though it became the voice of the nation, also became more obscurantist and reactionary. It set its face against modern knowledge and external contacts. The most illuminating example of this dominant spirit in the Church was the bishop who declared, 'Abhorred of God is any who loves geometry; it is a spiritual sin.'[6]

This spirit was also matched by the public sentiment which learnt to view with suspicion everything which was alien. Though Russia was badly in need of the technical skills of the time, available only in Europe, those who were brought in to teach were resented and the very knowledge they had to impart was considered contaminated, anti-Slav and unpatriotic.

This is what invests the reign of Peter the Great (1682–1725) with such extraordinary importance. A remarkable man, he was still more praiseworthy as a catalyst for modernization, one might even say Europeanization of Russian society. His means were rough and cruel but he prevailed in the end. It is no reflection on Peter's greatness that almost all his reforms were consequences of military requirements, for the sake of greater order and for defence. He considered it his task to convert his subjects from 'beasts into human beings', from 'children into adults'.

Almost the whole of Peter's reign was taken up with the fight against the Swedes. Victorious at first, they were gradually beaten back as Peter modernized his army. It was Peter who gained the Baltic coast from the Swedes and laid the foundation of St Petersburg.

It was Peter who went to Europe and England in search of knowledge and teachers. It was Peter again who, after destroying the *streltsy*, the elite core of the old militia, created the regular army, and having created it, used it as a civilian army to maintain order in towns and provinces.

The maintenance of the army impoverished the population in the countryside. It impoverished the gentry no less. Peter abolished the traditional order of precedence by birth and instituted instead status by rank. And since rank was given as a reward for efficiency, army officers and civil servants became the new gentry. State service became compulsory for all, as did education for the class which aspired to state service. For marriages within this class, too, a certificate of education became essential. Peter also imported a large number of teachers and experts but he balanced this by sending out a number of Russians to study abroad. He founded the Academy of Sciences.

Peter took vigorous measures to create industries and to exploit natural resources and their by-products. He also introduced a new administrative structure, but this did not last long and was revised radically by his successors. His more lasting creation was the Senate, which began as an advisory body but ended up as the supreme court of appeal.

The growing volume of work forced Peter to reorganize the central ministries but they were not designated as such and were governed by a college bearing collective responsibility. With another innovation he abolished the post of Patriarch in the Church and formed a Holy Synod to govern it. To the Holy Synod was attached the office of an *Ober-Procuror*, a layman and the 'Tsar's Eye'. His job was to prevent the Church from opposing the throne. The Ober-Procuror did much to subjugate the Church to secular authority, and in the end to enfeeble and demoralize it totally.

Peter's reforms were not unmixed blessings. Taxation increased to a fearsome extent. The hold of serfdom tightened. The ranks of the fugitives swelled as peasants fled from the land to escape the misery and bands of robbers became common, particularly in the provinces of the south-east. The paradox was that though centralization of authority increased, it did not help the local authority to take more initiative and responsibility, which was what Peter wanted in spite of his own autocratic approach. His reforms were piecemeal, improvised and without any unifying pattern. For all his pains, Peter was paid with sullen hostility from every section of the population. The traditionalists, outraged by his modernism, exploited the general discontent for their own purposes.

His own son Alexis, the Tsarevich, became the focus of hope for the disaffected in high quarters. Alexis once fled to seek refuge with the Austrian emperor in Vienna but was brought back, confessed to the whole plot under torture and died of wounds inflicted by the knout. There was no court mourning for him.

Peter died in January 1725, worn out and suffering from the consequences of syphilis and of drunkenness. He left no successor and this caused years of distress in Russia. But for all his faults, Peter had dragged Russia to the threshhold of a new age, a Russia bearing within herself the heritage of the past and looking forward into the future.

It was no mean achievement.

1 Vladimir was the prince who converted Russia to Christianity in 989. This miniature shows (left) his envoys at the court of Emperor Constantine IX and (right) their return to Vladimir at Kiev.

2 The Moscow Kremlin on Palm Sunday, 1636. Mikhail Romanov, the first Tsar of the dynasty which was to last until the Revolution, leads a procession from the Saviour's Tower.

3 *The Old Testament Trinity* by Andrei Rublev. Rublev, who got his artistic training as a monk at the Monastery of the Trinity and St Sergius, painted this, his masterpiece, in 1411. It is one of the most famous of all Russian icons.

4, 5 Right: this eleventh-century Caucasian sculptured relief was found above a window of a monastery in Kubatchi, Daghestan, and illustrates the love of horses and riding shared by the people of this area. Below: an ancient military road running through the beautiful countryside of Georgia.

6–8 Left: Anton Chekhov, playwright and short-story writer, reads his play *The Seagull* for the first time to the actors of the Moscow Art Theatre in 1898. To his right the director, Stanislavsky, and Chekhov's future wife, Olga Knipper. Below left: Leo Tolstoy, author of the famous *War and Peace* and *Anna Karenina*, and perhaps the best-known of all Russian novelists, at work in his study. Below: Fedor Dostoevsky, an anti-rationalist and harbinger of the modern psychological novel, is an author whose works have greatly influenced world literature.

9–13 In 1905 strikes and demonstrations flared up in Russia, and in
October the workers staged a
demonstration in Moscow
(opposite, above). The front
banner carries the slogan *Workers
of the world, Unite!* This short-lived
revolution was but a prologue of
the real Revolution to come in
1917. Opposite below: a patrol car
in the early days of the February
Revolution. The Tsar, Nicholas II,
abdicated that year and was
interned at Tobolsk. Right: he and
his family enjoy the sun on the
roof of a conservatory. Lenin, the
leader of the Bolsheviks, then took
power. Below: he reports on the
international situation at the second
Congress of Comintern, 1920.
Below right: Trotsky, the
co-architect of the Revolution and
later Commissar for War.

14 After the death of Lenin, Joseph Stalin took over supreme power in Russia, and his personal dictatorship, marked by bloody purges and iron discipline, was to last until 1953. This photograph was taken in 1930.

2 The Tsardom – high noon and sunset

THE MISERABLE PERIOD after Peter the Great has been described by one historian as 'the period *par excellence* of a State without a people.'[1] Peter had created a new aristocracy based not upon birth but upon service to the state. In the confused years after Peter, when one ignoble Tsar succeeded another with lightning rapidity and imposed only their mediocrity on everything they did, the old aristocracy tried to regain its power, but the new governing class was too well entrenched. The new Tsars, many of them from Peter's marriage alliances with Germany, did not know the people and had to rely on the vast army of civil and military servants.

This new gentry saw to it that its class interests remained paramount. Only those on the register of gentry were allowed to have serfs. By an edict of Tsar Peter III in 1762, the gentry was freed from state service and thus became an ordinary aristocracy. This brought no relief to the serfs or to the peasants. Nominally the peasants had legal rights, though in reality there were none. The serfs became even more degraded. Their owners acquired the right to punish them, to send them to forced labour or to sell them, separated from their land and their families. Journals of the period are full of advertisements of serfs for sale, particularly girls.

The gulf between the upper strata and the lower widened. A tiny minority became westernized, rich and cultivated. The mass of the people remained poor, illiterate and deeply conservative in their outlook. It was as if two cultures were growing simultaneously without any contact with each other.

With Catherine the Great (1762–1796) style came to Russia. Catherine was a prodigious worker, a profligate lover and a brilliant intellect, but she did not understand the Russians. In some of the schools the pupils were caned on the hand if they uttered a Russian word. The gentry, freed from obligations of government service, lived materially on the borrowings from their land, earned by the blood, sweat and tears of the serfs, intellectually on the borrowings of Europe's ready-made formulae, which had little or no relevance to their environment at home.

Intellectually daring, Catherine was ineffective in putting her concepts to use. Her big idea was an Instruction (*Nakaz*), for consideration by a Great National Commission, to formulate a new law code. In December 1766 the Great Commission was duly convened in Moscow, but after discussions lasting for a year and a half, achieved almost nothing. It did, however, give vent to strong feelings on serfdom. Catherine herself was in favour of some degree of emancipation of the serfs but vested interests would have none of it. The other demand which surfaced was for local self-government. But Catherine wanted more centralization and got it, with particularly disastrous consequences for peasants in the Ukraine. She did, however, create some new institutions in the field of local government, which survived till the revolution.

Catherine's reign was noted for two things above all. First was the rising of discontented peasants under a Don Cossack, Emelian Pugachev, which terrified the gentry and was suppressed with great brutality. The other was the war with Poland and Turkey. This was a consequence of the forward policy in Europe which the successive Tsars had been following before Catherine. It was extended even further by her with the aim of acquiring a firm grip over the whole of Poland. She was helped by political intrigues and the rise to supreme position of one of the greatest of Russian generals, Alexander Suvorov. In 1772 Poland was partitioned between Russia, Prussia and Austria. Despite repeated attempts by the Poles to regain their freedom they were crushed each time and for some years after the Third Partition of 1795 Poland disappeared from maps altogether.

Meanwhile, in 1789, the French Revolution broke out and it alarmed Catherine. It frightened the Russian gentry, too, who had imbibed French ideas indiscriminately. The inevitable reaction of Catherine was to impose severe censorship and denounce free thought. Towards the end of her reign Alexander Radishchev published *A Journey from St Petersburg to Moscow*, a bitter social exposé of the living conditions for the poor, which marked the beginning of a great epoch in Russian thought. The book was suppressed and Radishchev was exiled to Siberia. The French Revolution thus had an unexpected sequel in Russia: it permanently split the autocrats from the democrats, conservatives from revolutionaries, and introduced a new ambivalence in Russian attitude towards Europe. *A Journey from St Petersburg to Moscow* itself became the touchstone of the Russian intelligentsia's attitude to their own country.

Catherine's embittered son Paul (1796–1801), father unknown, who came to the throne at the age of 42, was a prissy tyrant, glowing with the consciousness of his own divine right. To the Swedish Ambassador he remarked, 'Know that no one in Russia is important except the person who is speaking with me; and that, only while he is speaking.'[2] He proscribed the words *society* and *citizen* but considered himself a protector of the common man. He did, however, restrict the labour which a serf had to do for his master to half a week, which was an important step on the road to emancipation. But Paul was slightly mad and sent a Cossack army to conquer India. He was dangerously whimsical, like most Tsars, and specially enjoyed ridiculing his military officers. These included Suvorov, Russia's military genius, though Paul heaped the highest honours upon him when his services were required for the coalition against Napoleon.

Paul exiled and imprisoned a large number of people and it is said that married couples slept arm in arm lest the husband was taken away at night without his wife knowing. He came to an ignoble end, being strangled with a scarf in his own bedroom by high-ranking conspirators who enjoyed the support of his son Alexander, though it can never be known for certain whether Alexander was accessory to the murder plot or not.

One of the sensible things Paul had done at the outset of his brief but important reign, was to lay down the rules for future succession. People rejoiced at his death and Alexander I (1801–1825) succeeded him. It was the beginning of the high noon of Tsardom in Russia. With Alexander, Russia emerged as a European power, the foundations for which had been laid in the period of Catherine. Alexander also inherited all the accumulated social tensions of the past, particularly the ill-effects of the regressive measures of Paul. But hopes of substantive reforms were dashed as Alexander embroiled Russia in European affairs.

The great event of his reign was the contest with Napoleon, which brought Russia so much misery and so much glory. It also revealed that though the people hated tyranny, they hated foreign intruders even more, and centuries of accumulated resentment at the humiliation of Russia played its role in the defeat of Napoleon's invasion. It was the authentic people's war of the nineteenth century, and more than a century later the pattern was to be repeated on an even more heroic scale.

Alexander began well. He abolished torture, one of the first acts of his reign. He recalled the troops sent by his father on the hopeless task of finding a route for the conquest of India. He surrounded himself with liberals, with the express purpose of reforming Russia. But on the major problem, the abolition of serfdom, without which no reform could be of any avail, Alexander gave in because there was powerful opposition. His liberalism had feet of clay. Every difficulty made him retreat and in the end all that his reign produced was a measure of administrative reforms. But he did try to ease the lot of serfs in many ways and in theory made it possible for anyone to acquire land. His most fruitful step was to refuse to allow any more crown peasants to become serfs, a step which had important consequences and kept the question of serfdom a live issue till it was abolished in 1861.

Alexander joined the continental coalition against Napoleon, who had declared himself Emperor of France. He also had a good deal of trouble from Turkey, and Finland became a thorn in his flesh because he chose to occupy it and annex it as an autonomous Grand Duchy. After a period he joined Napoleon but this did not last long because their interests were not compatible and Alexander bitterly resented Napoleon's attempts to restore a measure of autonomy to Poland. Their play of mutual hate and admiration continued until Napoleon crossed the river Niemen with 600,000 men and began his march towards Moscow. He meant to restore contacts with Alexander and bring Russia back into an anti-English alliance. At great cost Napoleon reached Moscow but he waited in vain in the burning city for Alexander to come and sue for peace. Alexander stood firm and did not move from St Petersburg. Behind him stood the people of Russia, who were even more determined to defeat Napoleon utterly. In many ways Napoleon was his own worst enemy, but this does not detract from the complete triumph of Russia in this gigantic struggle. It made Russia feared in Europe in a mysterious, mystical sort of way.

Alexander himself crossed into Europe to liberate it from Napoleon and his people's victory served to increase his glory. He entered Paris in triumph on 31 March 1814. He was in favour of liberal constitutions abroad. When Napoleon re-established himself in Paris, Alexander organized a Holy Alliance against him. He kept his promise of giving Poland a liberal constitution and emancipated the Lettish and Estonian serfs of the Baltic provinces. But these reforms were not applied at home and various attempts to do so failed because Alexander could not bring himself to carry them out.

Nevertheless, the victory over Napoleon had an almost revolutionary effect upon Russia. Alexander, who had continued to dabble with the liberals and with liberal ideas, became an extreme reactionary. Repression increased in proportion to the spread of liberal and revolutionary ideas among the educated, and Alexander became all the more isolated and unpopular. He died from a chill on 18 December 1825.

Now followed a remarkable event which set the tone of Russian politics till the October Revolution in 1917. Alexander had accepted the renunciation by his brother Constantine, of any right to the throne, but he had not informed his next brother, Nicholas, of this. Upon his death, Nicholas proclaimed Constantine emperor in St Petersburg while Constantine, at the time Viceroy of Poland, proclaimed Nicholas emperor in Warsaw. This confusion was used by members of a revolutionary conspiracy, known as the 'Decembrists', to stage an uprising with the help of two thousand guards, shouting for 'Constantine and Constitution'. The rising was easily crushed but its victims became martyrs in the public eye.

To deal with the Decembrists became the first act of Nicholas on ascending the throne (1825–1855). It soured his whole reign and turned him into the drill-master of Europe. The one act to his credit was to help Greece liberate itself from Turkey but he did it unwillingly and had no love for the Greek rebels. After a rebellion in Poland, he took away what Alexander had bestowed and for all practical purposes Poland was incorporated into the Russian empire. Above all, education was discouraged in Poland.

Herzen, a leading Russian intellectual of the time, noted that Nicholas was '. . . handsome, but his good looks made you want to shiver . . . The eyes were the main thing. They were wintry eyes without warmth or pity.'[3] Appropriately enough, Nicholas was noted for the harsh censorship and police regime which he instituted. Both had existed before but Nicholas made them even harsher. The only field in which Nicholas made progress was in the codification of the existing laws, executed by the able Speransky in some sixty-six volumes.

Paradoxically enough, Nicholas's reign saw a marvellous flowering of arts and letters, particularly in the domain of literature. Some of the greatest names in Russian literature either lived during this period or came to their mature fulfilment then. Alexander Pushkin, beyond doubt the greatest poet in his language, who had traces of African blood in his veins, Lermontov, the great romantic poet, Krylov, the fairy-tale writer of genius, and the novelist Ivan Turgenev, were all writing during this period. There were many others besides. It is symptomatic of the times, however, that Pushkin and Lermontov perished in futile duels and all the best writing of the period expresses the futility of Russian society at that stage. It is symptomatic, too, that the typical heroes of the period were the 'superfluous men', people of talent but aimless, lacking strength of character.

This was the period when serious political and sociological thinking in Russia also began, greatly influenced by the revolutionary fervour in Europe following the French Revolution. Much admired were the contemporary German philosophers, but there also emerged a school of thinkers who were imbued with a Slavophile and mystical frame of mind. Katkov was the leading Slavophile, and a reactionary. Belinsky, Herzen and Bakunin were all westernizers and the most ardent of them all was Chaadayev, who had tremendous influence though his output was small.

Tolstoy and Dostoevsky, two of the greatest names in Russian literature, whose influence became world-wide, began their writing career during the reign of Nicholas though their major output belongs to a later period. Dostoevsky was sentenced to death for allegedly belonging to a secret revolutionary society but was reprieved while actually waiting to be shot. Such was the frightful and capricious way of Nicholas. His censors were equally whimsical. Turgenev, another well-known novelist, was also arrested and Belinsky escaped arrest only because he died a few minutes before the police arrived at his door.

When revolution broke out in France in 1848 and rapidly swept through Europe, Nicholas emerged as the gendarme of reactionary monarchy in Europe and helped the Hapsburgs to suppress the revolt in Hungary. He also became involved in the Eastern question and in a war with Turkey, where the Russian army had little success. The French and the British took the side of Turkey, and, to put Nicholas in his place, invaded the Crimea. Though their invasion was only successful after a number of years and an immense waste of lives, it exposed the corruption, incompetence and backwardness of the regime in St Petersburg. The colossus proved to have flaws, and in the end, only the Russian soldier emerged with enhanced reputation for his dogged bravery and heroism in one of the most wasteful wars ever fought in the nineteenth century. In the midst of the Crimean crisis, Nicholas caught a chill, and on 2 March 1855 he died. Though his reign produced scientists and scholars as well as so many of the great names of Russian literature, towards its close the intellectual climate grew suffocating. His death came as a relief to the intelligentsia, if not to the common man, whose life it affected very little.

The reign of his son, Alexander II (1855–1881), saw the emancipation of the serfs become a reality at last. Yet Alexander was no liberal. He took the measure partly because of the lessons of the Crimean War, which showed that, serfdom having become an anachronism in the modern world, Russia could not expect to be a modern state unless it was abolished. The emancipation was not a charter of liberty but a grudging concession to reality. Even so, it was a momentous step, for it was the question of emancipation which provided the leaven in the bread of political agitation against the autocracy of the Tsars. If, before Alexander II, the history of modern Russia can be described as one of serfdom, after him it can be characterized as a history of dealing with the consequence of emancipation.

Proceeding cautiously and in devious ways, but obstinately, the Tsar finally promulgated the end of serfdom on 19 February 1861. The legal statutes concerning this consisted of twenty-two enactments which were frequently amended in later years. The emancipation procedure itself was bewilderingly complex, necessitating reforms in local government and in the judiciary as well. Following the defeat of the Crimean War, the army was also reorganized and supplied with more modern weapons. The landed nobility, whose interests the Tsar intended to protect after the Emancipation Act in 1861, nevertheless suffered a gradual decline. The process continued until the revolution in 1917, after which this class vanished altogether.

NORTH SEA

ARCTIC

Arctic Circle

BALTIC SEA

FINLAND

POLAND

Niemen

ST PETERSBURG

Archangel

Brest-Litovsk

Minsk

Kiev

RUSSIA

Danube

RUMANIA

BESSARABIA

BULGARIA

Dnieper

MOSCOW

Nizhny Novgorod

Viatka

Kazan

Simbirsk

Perm

URAL MOUNTAINS

Ob

Rostov

Don

Volga

Tsaritsin

Yekaterinburg

Irtysh

Omsk

Toms

BLACK SEA

TURKEY

CAUCASUS

Tiflis

CASPIAN SEA

ARAL SEA

Lake Balkhash

Baghdad

Syr Darya

Amu Darya

Tehran

Tashkent

PERSIA

Samarkand

SIN K

MILES   0   500   1000

KM   0   500   1000

Map of Russia before 1917

For his reforms Alexander II is known as the Tsar Liberator, but his period is also highly important for growing political unrest, for an upsurge of industry, literature, music and the arts, and last but not least for Russia's growing involvement with Europe.

Alexander's reign opened with the Congress of Paris in 1856 to settle the Eastern question after the Crimean War. The Congress internationalized the Danube, forbade warships and fortifications in the Black Sea, persuaded Russia to renounce her religious protectorate over Christians in Turkey and to surrender the mouths of the Danube and portions of Bessarabia to Moldavia, part of the future Rumania. Nearby a quarter of a century later, at the Congress of Berlin in 1878, the settlement made at Paris was partly undone; Bessarabia returned to Russia but Rumania and Bulgaria emerged as states, with considerably greater area. During the intervening period the Russians had faced an insurrection in Poland which was crushed but left a bitter legacy of antagonism. They had fought a war successfully with Turkey which gave a strong boost to Pan-slav sentiment in the Slav world, including Russia, and thoroughly alarmed Bismarck in Germany. It led to the formation of the curious alliance of Russia, Austria and Germany after the assassination of Alexander II. He had demonstrated once and for all that Pan-slav sentiments did not always coincide with Russia's national interests.

Alexander II's reign also saw a tremendous upsurge in science and Russia during this period produced some of the most influential scientists of the nineteenth century. They include chemists like D. I. Mendeleev (1834–1907), the biologist I. I. Mechnikov (1845–1916) and the physiologist I. P. Pavlov (1849–1936). There were many more gifted people in other fields, such as history.

In the early 1860's a group of five highly talented musicians transformed Russian music and brought it near to the European tradition while maintaining its distinct national flavour. They were Balakirev, Cui, Mussorgsky, Borodin and Rimsky-Korsakov. The period also brought to the fore Russia's greatest composer, Tchaikovsky, whose symphonies are part of the Western musical repertoire and whose operas, particularly *Eugene Onegin,* based on Pushkin, are still revered in the Soviet Union.

In literature, despite a very strict censorship, the creative genius of Russia appeared at its best during this period. Not only Turgenev (1818–1883) came to maturity during Alexander's reign but Dostoevsky (1821–1881) and Leo Tolstoy (1828–1910), beyond any doubt the greatest fiction writers of the century not only in Russian but in any language, were also products of this period. Tolstoy's *War and Peace* is enshrined in Russian hearts as no other work of literature anywhere. From the beginning Russian literature had a pronounced sociological and radical bias which greatly aided the formation of a radical climate of opinion and politics. The more the repression, the greater was the radicalism since it virtually forced liberals to take up revolutionary positions.

The most celebrated case of all is that of Alexander Herzen, who ran the fortnightly journal *Kolokol* (The Bell) from London, in exile. Up to the Emancipation Act of 1861 he believed in reforms from above and hailed the Tsar for his decision, but soon he found that emancipation was not what it should have been and was bitterly disillusioned with the cruel suppression of freed serfs and peasants. A few months later he issued one of the most effective political slogans in Russian history; when denouncing the phoney emancipation he declared, 'The people need land and freedom (*zemlya i volya*)'. When the universities were closed down in November 1861 Herzen appealed to the students to go 'to the people', another potent and revolutionary notion which had an abiding influence on Russian radical politics. One radical position led to another and Herzen associated himself with the anarchist Bakunin's championing of Polish independence. Yet such was the temper of the times that soon Herzen was left far behind by the young radicals, who found him too genteel and humanitarian.

Revolution was in the air and there were extremist radicals like Bakunin, Nechaev and Tkachev who had considerable influence for some time. It was one of the followers of Nechaev, Zheliabov, who organized the assassination of Alexander II at Catherine Quay in St Petersburg on a wintry afternoon when the Tsar and his retinue were returning from the parade-ground on Sunday 1 March 1881. Alexander II was the victim of the great expectations which he had aroused but which he had not the imagination even to try to fulfil.

Political unrest was not confined to the intelligentsia alone. Some of it was carried to the rural areas, particularly because of a strong movement at one stage during Alexander II's reign when a large number of educated urban youth abandoned the cities and went to live in the villages among the people. The experiment was not a success because the village people were suspicious of the unwanted helpers from the cities, and their radicalism and sophistication offended the innate conservatism of the countryside. But it left its mark.

To this unrest were added economic factors. Russia had begun industrializing itself by fits and starts, and an important role in this was played by large-scale construction of railway lines during the reign of Alexander II. Though the Russian transition to capitalism was slower than in the west and often very painful, the advance was there. It was, however, held up not because of purely economic factors but because of *nekulturnost,* lack of cultural traditions and civilized social habits, which obstructed the entrepreneurs and technocrats of the period. But the process also created a proletariat or industrial labour force, which, poorly paid, badly housed and fed, swelled the ranks of the discontented.

The violent end of Alexander II was not the only symbol of the mighty upheaval which was to come. There was also the fact that the three architects of that earthquake were born during the last decade of Alexander's reign – Vladimir Ulyanov, the future Lenin, and Lev Bronshtein, the future Trotsky, in 1870 and Joseph Dzugashvili, the future Stalin, in 1879.

The brief reign of Alexander III (1881–1894) was one of black reaction and the last effervescence of monarchical absolutism. To the German Chancellor Bismarck's wish that 'Russia will preserve as long as possible the magic wand of absolutism', the Tsar's response was, 'May God will that every Russian, particularly our ministers, shall understand our situation as clearly as does Prince Bismarck and shall not strive to achieve unattainable fantasies and lousy liberalism.'

The instruments for carrying out the new policy were appropriate enough. There were three advisers on whom Alexander III relied heavily. Pobedonostsev, nominally the Procurator of the Holy Synod of the Russian Orthodox Church, was the most decisive influence in policy-making and at an early stage after Alexander III's accession to the throne persuaded him against any move towards even a mild form of representative political institutions. Another was Count Dimitry Tolstoy, a reactionary minister of education under Alexander II, who was now appointed Minister of the Interior and was noted not only for suppression of liberals and radicals in general but also for allowing anti-Jewish pogroms to be carried out at one time. The third influential executor of the court policy was Plehve, who became Minister of the Interior after Alexander II was assassinated. He was equally ruthless in suppressing every kind of dissent.

Strictest control was exercised on the press and publications through rigorous censorship. This was supported by conservatives like Katkov who claimed that 'the press in Russia, and perhaps in Russia alone, is placed in a position approaching complete independence. We know of no organ of the foreign press that could be called independent in the true meaning of the term.'[4]

This did not prevent dissent from becoming more pronounced, more radical and more sophisticated. Political groups vied with each other in attracting public attention through underground activity, and tremendous work was done by exiles based in Geneva, London and Paris, who published journals there and smuggled them back home.

Education was not only interfered with but restricted so that the lower orders could not take advantage of it. There was a purge of the student body, removing the undesirable elements. Worse still, discrimination was used against Jewish students so that many of them could not get higher education even if they could afford it. This went hand in hand with an aggressive Russian nationalism, which the authorities fostered, in the mistaken belief that it would prevent the radicals from gaining public support. There was also religious persecution, not only of non-Christians but also of Christian sects in conflict with the Orthodox Church. The Jews suffered most, economically as well as in religious matters.

The assassination of Alexander II changed the nature of revolutionary politics of the period, and Marxism began to seep in and command the attention of the intelligentsia to a greater degree. 'The People's Will', the organization responsible for the act, lost its appeal and elan, and its plot to murder Alexander III was discovered before an attempt could be made. Among those hanged for being connected with it was Alexander Ulyanov, elder brother of Lenin.

Of the political organizations the most important was the Land and Freedom group, more commonly known as the Populists, from which were to grow the later movements and parties of the era before the Revolution. These fed on the growing impoverishment of the peasants and the augmented ranks of urban labour, which was badly looked after. In some measure the revival was also due to the great famine of 1891–92 and the cholera epidemic which followed, because it prepared an audience for radical ideas. Yet, thanks to the inhuman police control, lack of any dangerous political involvements abroad and comparative absence of violent upheavals, an illusion of peace and calm was created. The storm lay just ahead.

Nicholas II (1894–1917) succeeded to the Tsardom upon his father's death on 20 October 1894. He was the last Tsar. Devoted to his wife and autocratic by training and inclination, he was least suited to the role which history placed on his shoulders. His personal reputation among the general public suffered a great deal because of his wife's propensity to be swayed by religious charlatans. The most pernicious influence was that of Rasputin, a Siberian peasant claiming mystical powers and with some kind of hypnotic ability to control the haemophilia from which the Tsarevitch suffered. The gross scandal caused by his behaviour and power over the Tsar led to his murder in December 1916. The political damage Rasputin did is incalculable. On 2 March 1917 (13 March, new style) the Tsar formally abdicated and on 16 July (29 July) 1918, some months after the Bolshevik revolution had established itself, the whole royal family was massacred in Yekaterinburg, now Sverdlovsk, in the Urals.

The two decades of his reign were the most dramatic of Russian history, possibly of world history. The inexorable march of events in the outside world, which involved Russia in a humiliating defeat and in the first world war, and the growth of radical political consciousness combined to seal the fate of Tsardom. By its rigidity, lack of imagination and insensitivity to the needs of the times, the royal family hastened the process.

In the confused chronicle of developments which took place in Russia at the time, several landmarks stand out. The first was the Japanese victory in the Far East in 1904–05. War between the two countries came about because of rivalry for the control of Manchuria and Korea and because of their incompatible interests in China. The Russians were obstinate in refusing to come to terms with Japan because they wanted a secure ice-free port in the Far East. On 5 February 1904, the Japanese broke off diplomatic relations with Moscow and a few days later attacked the Russian fleet at Port Arthur and Chemulpo. The Japanese were supported in their venture diplomatically and financially by America and Britain who feared Russia and resented Russian expansion in the East.

From the beginning the Russians lost heavily in fighting on land. Their operations were clumsily carried out and their supply lines did not function well. The final blow was given by Japan in naval engagements which ended most ingloriously for the Russians, particularly in Tsushima. The war was not popular with the people except for a few mystical reactionaries who talked about Russia's 'Asiatic Mission'. The Japanese victories alarmed all the Western powers, who became concerned with saving Russia's face against an upstart Asian power. A peace conference, convened on the initiative of America, met in Portsmouth, New Hampshire. The Treaty of Portsmouth was signed on 5 Sepember 1905 and under its provisions Russia made a number of concessions to Japan.

The humiliation deeply affected the course of domestic events. For the world it also signified the rise of Asia. Far away in India, a fifteen-year-old boy noted, 'Japanese victories stirred up my enthusiasm and I waited eagerly for the papers for fresh news daily . . . Nationalistic ideas filled my mind. I mused of Indian freedom and Asiatic freedom from the thraldom of Europe. I dreamt of brave deeds, of how, sword in hand, I would fight for India and help in freeing her.'[5] The boy, Jawaharlal Nehru, later became the first Prime Minister of independent India in 1947.

A Russian liberal of prescience prophetically remarked, 'The Japanese will not enter the Kremlin, but the Russians will.' They did.

The war shattered the economy and the burden was especially heavy on the country people. It felt even heavier because the war was unpopular from the beginning. The discontent caused by it merged with the rising tide of student revolt, terrorist assassinations of conservative government leaders like Plehve and Pobedonostsev and with vigorous Marxist, Populist and liberal agitation.

The Marxist movement had grown from the day Plekhanov formed the first Russian social democratic organization, 'Liberation of Labour', in 1883. Earlier he had parted company with the 'Land and Freedom' group. He can be justly described as the Father of Russian Marxism and under his guidance a whole generation of Marxists grew up. George Plekhanov had begun his political career with the Populists but came increasingly under the spell of Marxism as time went by. He formulated the basic strategy of the Russian Marxist road to revolution when he declared at the Foundation Congress of the Second International in Paris that 'the revolutionary

movement in Russia can triumph only as the revolutionary movement of the workers. There is no other way out for us, and cannot
be . . .' He thus broke with the political tradition of radicalism which
had always looked to the peasants for the salvation of the country and
its liberation from autocracy.

A new life came into the Marxist movement when Lenin and
Julius Martov joined it and formed the Fighting Union for the
Liberation of the Working Class in 1895 and by their tactics succeeded
in fomenting a wave of strikes. But Marxist groups and personalities
were still divided and an important step towards further unity was the
formation of the Russian Social Democratic Party at Minsk in 1898.
Lenin was under exile in Siberia then but he returned in 1900. Another
important milestone was the publication of *Iskra* (The Spark) which
was first printed in Stuttgart in December 1900. The editorial board
included Lenin, Plekhanov and other leaders of 'Liberation of Labour'.
But differences persisted and the second Party Congress met in 1903,
first in Brussels, from where it shifted to London because of excessive
Belgian police interference. The Congress consisted of forty-three
delegates, who agreed on a programme and a charter.

The keynotes of the programme were the overthrow of autocracy,
the organization of a democratic republic, an eight-hour day for the
workers, and the restitution of land to peasants who had lost it under
the Emancipation Act of 1861. It was amended in 1906 by the Fourth
Party Congress in favour of confiscation of large estates and their control by local authorities, and this revised programme remained until
1918. But there was also a programme of ultimate objectives, the maximum programme as it were, for a socialist revolution, the abolition of
capitalism and the establishment of the dictatorship of the proletariat.

Disputes over the programme and the role of the Party and control
of the policy-making organs caused dissension, and ultimately the
majority came to be known as *Bolshevik* and the minority as *Menshevik*,
from the Russian words for 'majority' and 'minority'. The struggle
between the Mensheviks and Bolsheviks remained a feature of the
movement till the Revolution in 1917, when the Bolsheviks emerged
triumphant from all their vicissitudes. There was a good deal of
to-ing and fro-ing by the leaders and rank and file through this period.
In brief, the Mensheviks were for a social democracy as a transitional
phase after the overthrow of Tsardom, while the Bolsheviks were
for a dictatorship of the proletariat from the outset. The character of

the Soviet state which was to be established after the revolution was determined by the Bolshevik outlook.

However, the Bolsheviks and the Mensheviks were not the only political groups and by no means the most influential at the time. There were also the Populists who, after being at a low ebb in the 1880's, came alive again and in 1900 founded the Socialist Revolutionary Party, uniting various segments of the movement. Many revolutionaries with a personal following joined the party. Doctrinally the Socialist Revolutionaries stood halfway between the Social Democrats and the Marxists. But an important element in the party was its terroristic organization, devoting itself to political murders. The party was much discredited because of internal strife and because Azef, the head of its terrorist organization for a long time, turned out to be simultaneously an agent of the security police.

There was also a liberal segment which was not united in a formal national organization but which found expression in the *zemstvos,* the local-government institutions which were elected on a limited franchise and which had certain restricted powers in economic and educational matters. For practical purposes the radical intelligentsia, consisting of teachers, doctors, nurses etc., found the *zemstvos* convenient and useful and a kind of constitutional movement also grew in these organs of local self-government. Eventually, officialdom came to regard extension of *zemstvo* powers as incompatible with autocratic government.

Meanwhile, from 1898 onwards, the Socialist Revolutionaries had begun a series of political assassinations, causing some unrest among the public. When Port Arthur, in the Far East, surrendered in December 1904 to the Japanese, it caused public indignation and perhaps contributed to a strike of workers in St Petersburg early in January 1905. On Sunday 22 January a huge procession of workers, led by a police agent and labour leader, the priest Gapon, marched with a petition to the Tsar towards the Palace Square, carrying icons and singing hymns. The hymns, however, were drowned by rifle fire. Hundreds died and thousands were injured. 'Bloody Sunday', as it came to be known, was entirely due to the ineptitude of the authorities; its consequences were far-reaching, and its echoes reverberated throughout Russia and beyond. The spark of revolution had been lit.

The government took some palliative measures which were totally inadequate. While ministers talked about popular representation in an advisory assembly, the greater part of liberal-radical opinion moved to demand a Constituent Assembly. Disaffection spread to the army and there were frequent cases of insubordination and mutiny. The most famous of all of these was the revolt of the battleship *Potemkin,* later the subject of a film epic by the Soviet director Eisenstein.

There was also a conservative and reactionary backlash. Encouraged by the authorities, some of the ultra-nationalistic elements carried out terrible pogroms against the Jews in which thousands died. In this situation the defining of the procedure for election to the State Duma, as the consultative assembly was known, acted like a red rag to the bull of radical opinion. Political tension reached a breaking point and on 26 October the St Petersburg Soviet of Workers' Deputies assembled for the first time. On 30 October the first number of its official organ *Izvestia* appeared.

By a coincidence, on that very day the Tsar signed a manifesto declaring Russia to be a constitutional monarchy and appointed as Prime Minister Sergei Witte, who promised to introduce fundamental civil liberties, and to make the State Duma a more powerful and representative organ. The enthusiasm for all this was not very great, and Trotsky accurately summed up the feeling when he wrote, 'Witte has come, but Trepov remains ... The proletariat knows what it does and what it does not want. It wants neither the police thug Trepov, nor the liberal financial shark Witte, neither the wolf's snout, nor the fox's tail. It rejects the police whip wrapped in the parchment of the constitution.'

But despite the fact that agitation swept the countryside and revolutionary fervour was at a high pitch, labour was weary of strikes and political activity. Witte sensed this and on 9 December he had the president of the St Petersburg Soviet arrested. The Soviet elected a presiding committee of three, including Trotsky, but the committee's call for non-cooperation and non-payment of taxes proved to be futile. There was an uprising in Moscow which was crushed. Mutinies in the army were also repressed, and the short-lived revolution of 1905 was over. It was but a prologue to the real revolution to come, and Trotsky prophetically summed it up: 'The revolution is dead. Long live the revolution!'

The period between 1905 and 1917, however, was one of weak constitutionalism alternating with autocratic severity. It was almost impossible for an old bureaucratic and authoritarian system of government to transform itself into a full-fledged democracy. The October declaration, moreover, provided flimsy ground for a democratic system to function on. All the concessions were hedged by the prerogatives given to the sovereign. Witte had, in the absence of liberal co-operation, to form a government consisting of high-ranking bureaucrats. From the beginning it was apparent that the opposition and the government intended to make different uses of the Duma.

Conservatives and liberals alike prepared for the elections. The most successful of these organizations were the Cadets, or the Constitutional Democratic Party, which played, for good or ill, an important role till the Bolsheviks took over. But when the first State Duma was inaugurated on 10 May 1906, Witte's government had already been dismissed by the Tsar. There was an immediate battle between the elected representatives and the Tsar, and the Duma was dissolved on 22 July, barely two months after the inauguration. On the same day Peter Stolypin was appointed Prime Minister.

The Second Duma lasted from 5 March to 16 June 1907, and it was notable for the decrease in the strength of the Cadets and the increase in the number of left-wing members, particularly since the Social Revolutionaries and Social Democrats decided to participate in the elections, Lenin having seen that a boycott was a wrong policy. But the government resolved to 'cook' the election laws and the third Duma from November 1907 to June 1912 was full of conservatives, the Social Revolutionaries having resorted to boycott again. The period of the Third Duma was one of conservative reaction and chauvinistic nationalism. These were the years of Jewish pogroms. It was also the time when important land reforms were carried out, directed towards the abolition of communal tenure, making land holdings compact, giving peasants ownership of land, and abolishing joint family ownership. Their immediate effect was to heighten the prevailing discontent since they increased the number of the landless and impoverished them further. Peter Stolypin, the Minister of the Interior who was responsible for these land reforms, was assassinated by left-wing revolutionaries.

These were also years of the greatest creativity in Russian literature and the arts. Writers like Chekhov and Maxim Gorky strengthened the realist school in literature, although they were writers of very different kinds. Chekhov, who died in 1904, had a great influence upon his contemporaries. There was high achievement, too, in painting and music, with the impressionist-realist school of painters of the 'World of Art' or *Mir Iskusstva* group, like Levitan, Korovin, Kustodiev and Grabar, and symbolists like Vrubel. The *Mir Iskusstva* group made an even greater contribution to the decorative arts, particularly theatre design, outstanding among them being Bakst, Benois, Korovin, Roerich and Kustodiev.

Two young composers, A. N. Scriabin and Igor Stravinsky, opened new vistas for world music while composers such as Serge Rachmaninoff added to the classical tradition of neo-Slavonic music. Innumerable instrumentalists and singers made Russian artists highly prized, such as Ziloti, Auer, Mischa Elman, Jascha Heifetz, the great violinist, and Fyodor Chaliapin.

In the theatre revolutionary work was being done by Stanislavsky and V. I. Nemirovich-Danchenko at the Moscow Art Theatre. The most daring of all theatre directors was V. E. Meyerhold. The Russian ballet also came into its own at about this time and has since retained its leading position in the world of Western art, although in the Soviet period there has not been much innovation.

Complex developments at home notwithstanding, Russia was getting deeply involved in European affairs, particularly in East Europe and Turkey. This unavoidably led to Russian participation in the Great War of 1914, in alliance with the British and the French against Germany and Austria-Hungary – a disaster which the old order in Russia could not survive. Early in the war, in August 1914, Russian forces suffered a shattering defeat at Tannenberg, followed a few weeks later by another disaster in East Prussia. In 1915 more disasters befell the Russian armies, with great loss of life and a vast number of wounded. Russian intervention had the effect, however, of saving Paris from German pressure and relieved the Italian army at a crucial stage in the war. Russian sacrifices also helped the Allies during the battles of Verdun and the Somme. By 1916 the Russian army had bled so much, and suffered so much from bad leadership, corruption and sheer incompetence that its will to fight had evaporated.

Back at St Petersburg the government kept changing like the scenery in a play with many episodes. The people were not only disheartened, they were on the verge of revolt. As the regime floundered, the revolutionary mood was strengthened by the mutinous troops, fighting a hopeless cause in appalling conditions. Ordinary peasants were heard saying, 'When ten or fifteen generals are on the gallows we shall begin to win.' To the chaos of the war were added millions of refugees from Poland, rising prices and chronic food shortages.

Strangely enough, Lenin had foreseen just such a situation, without daring to hope that it would come about. Back in 1913 he had forecast that 'a war between Austria and Russia would be a very helpful thing for the revolution'. But he also added that 'it is not likely that Franz Josef and Nikolasha will give us that pleasure.' They did, and more.

3　The Revolution

THE REVOLUTION that took place in February 1917 was more of a
spontaneous combustion than most revolutions are. The leaders
followed rather than led it. Lenin, living in exile in Switzerland, had
only a month earlier doubted whether 'we, the old' would live to see
the coming revolution. On 26 March Lenin, together with a number
of prominent Bolsheviks, left for Petrograd through Germany in a
sealed railway carriage.

It all began with a riot on 23 February in front of a bread shop and
quickly engulfed the whole population of Petrograd. Contagious
exhilaration spread through the country. What it felt like to live in
that dawn is described in his memoirs by Konstantin Paustovsky, the
great Soviet writer. He wrote:

> In the course of a few months, Russia spoke out everything she
> had kept to herself for centuries.
>
> Day and night, from February to the autumn of 1917, the country
> seethed from end to end like one continuous rowdy meeting.
>
> Crowds shouted in city squares, in front of monuments, in rail-
> way stations smelling of chlorine, in factories, villages, markets, and
> in every yard and stairway of every house which showed the
> slightest sign of habitation.
>
> . . . The noise rumbled, like the thunder of carts on cobbles, from
> crossroads to crossroads.[1]

The fourth Duma, which had been convened in November 1912
and was dominated by right-wing and conservative parties, was still
in session. It was prorogued on 26 February. The members of the
Duma, however, decided to remain in session and elected a provisional
committee charged with restoring order. On the same day and in the
same place – Taurida Palace – a Soviet of Workers' Deputies was

54

organized and was destined to play a significant role in the Revolution. The imperial government's authority completely collapsed. The Duma clamoured for the abdication of the Tsar. On 2 March the Tsar did so, in favour of Grand Duke Michael who refused the responsibility thrust upon him.

On 2 March a Provisional Government was also formed, which was committed to the convocation of a Constituent Assembly. The first Provisional Government was headed by Prince G. E. Lvov, a Cadet. The pace of events was too much for him and though he tried to maintain optimism in public, in private he confessed, 'We are tossed about like flotsam on the sea.'

The Soviet had more power in reality and its business was in the hands of an Executive Committee in which the Mensheviks were predominant. Alexander Kerensky (1881–1970), a member of the Labour group in the Duma, was the vice-chairman. The example of the Petrograd Soviet was copied by other cities and soon a conference of the Soviets was arranged but power really remained in the hands of the Petrograd Soviet. The slogan coined by the Kronstadt naval garrison, 'All power to the Soviets', gradually caught on. Both the Provisional Government and the Soviets moved to the left but the party which ultimately triumphed because of its tactical superiority and the brilliantly effective leadership of Lenin was the Bolshevik Party.

Lenin had an innate sense of how to grasp a situation and use it. On his arrival at the Finland Station in Petrograd on 16 April, where he was given a tumultuous reception, he raised the slogan, 'Long live the socialist revolution'. Next day he shocked an unbelieving gathering of Bolsheviks by presenting his vision of the revolution in the celebrated *April Theses*. The hard core of his argument was that the Provisional Government was not a revolutionary socialist government and that a transition must be made to a government of the proletariat and the peasants. It also placed greater faith in the work of the Soviets and rejected the defensive war which the Provisional Government and the left parties had been upholding.

The reaction of the Bolsheviks was overwhelmingly negative. As for the others, they laughed it off. Lenin had obviously gone out of his mind, they thought, and Plekhanov, now a right-wing socialist leader, wrote *On the Theses of Lenin, Or Why Delirium is Sometimes Interesting*. Lenin was unshaken. The sophisticated politicians did not perceive the momentous nature of Lenin's call for an end to the war and 'All land to the peasants'. The people, who did not have all this sophistication, did. The sophisticated also did not see any alternative, and party opinion changed in favour of Lenin in a couple of weeks. His programme was adopted by the All-Russian Conference of the Bolsheviks, held from 7 to 12 May. The strategy of long-term revolutionary action was contained in the slogan adopted by the conference, 'All power to the Soviets.'

Meanwhile, events in the army and the countryside were working for the Bolshevik viewpoint. The army was disintegrating fast. The countryside was ablaze with peasants taking over and destroying the big estates and dividing the land among themselves. The Provisional Government just watched helplessly and there was talk of making legal provision for peasant ownership of land but no effort to do so. The village assemblies, which continued to redistribute the land, paid no attention to what Petrograd did on this question.

Labour unrest also increased, aggravated not only by demands for better wages and conditions but also by the provocative action of rich industrialists who adopted the tactics of gradual closure of factories. In this they were encouraged by the Provisional Government.

A new coalition government took office on 18 May, consisting of six socialists and nine non-socialists. Prince Lvov was still Premier and Minister of the Interior, Kerensky was Minister of War and the Navy and Chernov, a socialist revolutionary, was Minister of Agriculture. Its programme was as useless, impracticable and contradictory as before. For instance, it talked of revising war aims in consultation with the allies, a practical impossibility. The Bolsheviks, outside the coalition, gained support. Early in May they received an invigorating additional dose of leadership when Trotsky arrived in Petrograd with his eloquence, his fiery zeal and tireless energy.

Kerensky, in touch neither with the conditions in the army nor with the feelings of the masses, prepared a military offensive in Galicia in support of the allied cause. The offensive failed, with disastrous consequences. When the disaster became known, an official statement on 22 July called it 'an immeasurable calamity that threatens the ruin of revolutionary Russia'. Kerensky had been appointed Chairman of the Provisional Government on 8 July and agreed with the newly appointed General of the south-western front, L. G. Kornilov, in taking harsh measures against deserters. It did not help matters at all.

A violent demonstration took place in Petrograd on 3 July, but it petered out. The Bolsheviks were not in favour of such militant action yet. The Provisional Government used the opportunity to crush the Bolsheviks and other left-wing opponents. *Pravda,* the Bolshevik organ, was closed on 18 July and warrants for the arrests of Lenin and others were issued on 19 July. Lenin went into hiding, and Trotsky was arrested.

Lenin arrived at the conclusion that the new set-up was counter-revolutionary and in the hands of the bourgeoisie, and must be over-thrown by force. He bided his time. From August onwards Lenin began to urge preparations for armed action. In the middle of September he wrote to the Central Committee from Helsinki, where he had been resting, 'History will not forgive us if we do not capture power now.'

But Lenin had an uphill struggle in convincing the leadership of the party that the time for insurrection had arrived. Finally on 10 October, he attended a meeting of the Central Committee in disguise and persuaded it to commit the party to an armed uprising.

The coalition headed by Kerensky, which was to survive till October, can best be described as a twilight government. During this period Kornilov raised the banner of revolt to establish a military dictatorship but was thwarted mainly at the instance of the Bolsheviks, who would not allow his troops to reach Petrograd and removed rail tracks. Kornilov surrendered and was imprisoned with other generals in Bykhov. The Kornilov affair hastened the downfall of the Provisional Government. Meanwhile, on 1 September it had already proclaimed Russia a republic. On 8 October Kerensky formed another coalition government.

The forces contending for political supremacy ranged over a wide spectrum, from the extreme right to the extreme left. The monarchist cause was lost after the abdication of the Tsar. After February those still in the running were the Cadets, who were a conglomeration of liberal-bourgeois interests, the right and left Socialist Revolutionaries, a host of smaller groups and the Bolsheviks. The Cadets stood for a republic on the European model without any radical economic programme. The Socialist Revolutionaries were the biggest party, though divided. Their strength was among the peasants, whose interests they represented. Their idea of the future was a kind of peasant socialism based on the village community.

Completely unrealistically, the right SRs held the view that Russia must continue to participate in the war on the side of her allies and only leave it when universal peace was attained. It made nonsense of their professed belief in the Revolution. The left SRs co-operated with the Bolsheviks on most issues between February and October.

The issue of war became a crucial one in the developing crisis. The masses did not want to continue the war, and the political groups opposed to it gathered public support.

On 16 October the Petrograd Soviet formed a Military Revolutionary Committee. Its ostensible purpose was to defend the Revolution, not to prepare an insurrection, but Trotsky was appointed its chairman. This enormously facilitated the preparation for the uprising and the great day was fixed for 6–7 November. On the morning of the 6th the Bolshevik Central Committee met to finalize the plan. Lenin, Zinoviev and Stalin were not present at this meeting, which took place at the Smolny Institute, and Trotsky was in charge of the over-all strategy for the night *coup*.

Kerensky, too, was waiting for the Bolsheviks to move. He told the British Ambassador Sir George Buchanan, who had been urging him to crush the Bolsheviks, 'I only wish that they would come out and I would then put them down.'

Early on the morning of 7 November the pro-Bolshevik troops and the Red Guard of armed factory workers – the real shock troops of the Revolution – went into action. They met with no resistance worth the name and took over one key point after another. The Provisional Government was thrown into the 'dustbin of history'. The population of the city was not even aware of what was happening. Late-night social life went on uninterrupted. The Revolution had happened.

'In the name of the Military Revolutionary Committee I announce that the Provisional Government no longer exists,' Trotsky declared to the Petrograd Soviet, perhaps a little prematurely since the Winter Palace held out for another twenty-four hours, but aptly. Drawing an analogy with Russia's favourite game, he called it 'mate in two moves'.

The Second Congress of the Soviets opened in the tumultuous aftermath on the night of 7 November and went on till the early hours of the morning. The Mensheviks and the Right Socialist Revolutionaries tried to turn back the tide of history and bitterly denounced the Bolsheviks, but to no avail. Trotsky, the practical architect of the victory, later evocatively recalled the supreme moment, the new dawn.

The session finally came to an end at about six o'clock. A grey and cold autumn morning was dawning over the city. The hot spots of the campfires were fading out in the gradually lightening streets. The greying faces of the soldiers and the workers with rifles were concentrated and unusual. If there were astrologers in Petrograd, they must have observed portentous signs in the heavens.

The capital awoke under a new power. The everyday people, the functionaries, the intellectuals, cut off from the arena of events, rushed for the papers early to find out to which shore the wave had tossed them. But it was not easy to make out what had happened . . . The political editorials, written before the seizure of the Winter Palace, exude a cloudless optimism. But the optimism of the right in an eventual defeat of the revolution was an illusion. Their moment had passed. All that awaited them were funeral rites.[2]

Kerensky, who had nothing but hatred and contempt for the Bolsheviks, had left on the morning of the Revolution in an American embassy car for Gatchina in a vain attempt to arouse the garrison there to crush the revolution. He never came back and died in exile in America in 1970. Other members of the Provisional Government were arrested.

The Congress of Soviets elected a Council of People's Commissars, which was all Bolshevik with Lenin as chairman. On the second and last day of its session it confirmed this. At this, the finest hour of his destiny, Lenin, a confirmed Marxist and atheist, crossed himself.

Power was in Lenin's hands and those of his comrades but it was not yet secure. The quest for security was going to be long and hard. Meanwhile Lenin instinctively kept the initiative. His first two pronouncements as Chairman of the Council of Commissars were on peace and land.

Peace was what Russia longed for. Land was what the peasant had waited for through centuries of Tsarist oppression. Lenin, on his very first appearance at the Congress, grasped the nettle. He first proposed a decree on peace, calling upon all belligerent peoples and their governments to begin 'immediate negotiations for an honest democratic peace'. It must be peace 'without annexations and indemnities'. It proposed an immediate armistice for three months. Secret diplomacy was no longer to be favoured and all secret agreements made by the Provisional Government were to be published. The decree was aimed as much at the Allied powers as at the Central powers.

Next Lenin proposed a decree on land. It abolished private owner-ship of large holdings without compensation. All land belonging to landowners, appanages, monasteries and the Church was to be controlled by local land committees and peasant Soviets, pending the final decision on the question by the Constituent Assembly. More-over, private ownership of any kind of land was abolished forever and it could not be bought, sold, leased or mortgaged in any way. All land became state property. The peasants had in any case been taking over big estates illegally. But the decree brought the Bolsheviks the crucial support of the Left SRs on the morrow of the revolution.

Civil War, intervention by America, Britain, France and others, and the difficult and painful peace negotiations with Germany lay ahead. The Revolution was over and consolidation had to take precedence, although the confusion created by the Bolshevik take-over persisted for some time and there was even apprehension that counter-revolution might triumph after all. Protection of the Revolu-tion, therefore, became the primary concern of Lenin and his followers and there was not very much to build upon. The country was in a chaotic state, the army had become a rabble, uncontrollable and unpredictable. There were always the right-wing parties to exploit the situation and army generals who were bent upon overthrowing the new order.

What followed was determined as much by circumstances as by Lenin, the undisputed leader of new Russia. A century of revolution-ary effort had gone into making the Revolution, and to justify itself it had to work. Defence and consolidation, therefore, became almost the ideology of post-revolutionary Russia. Marxist ideology as expounded by Lenin was there to act as a leaven. The problem, however, was to produce the bread, which was in short supply.

To deal with the external threat first, Trotsky, as Commissar for Foreign Affairs, sought to negotiate with the Allies. But the Allies refused to deal with him and moved their military missions to the headquarters of General Dukhonin, who was Commander-in-Chief and did not recognize the Bolsheviks. The Germans agreed to sign an armistice in December.

The negotiations for the Treaty of Brest-Litovsk dragged on until March 1918. They aroused tremendous passions among the Bolsheviks and their allies. The majority of the Bolsheviks were against accepting the terms proposed by the Germans. At stake was the future of the Revolution in Europe, as the antagonists of the peace terms saw it. They argued that a compromise by the Russian revolutionary regime would weaken the revolutionary forces in Poland and Germany, who appeared to be on the verge of throwing out the old regimes in their countries. Trotsky himself was for buying time, for 'neither war nor peace' in his own famous phrase. His object in the Brest-Litovsk negotiations was to prolong this state till revolution happened in Germany and Poland, when the problem would solve itself. The left Bolsheviks, among them Bukharin, however, were for a 'revolutionary war' against the German and Austrian emperors.

Eventually, on Lenin's personal intervention the humiliating terms of the treaty were accepted though opinion remained bitterly divided. Under the treaty Russia lost Estonia, Latvia, Lithuania and Russian Poland, which were taken over by Germany and Austria; the independence of the Ukraine, Georgia and Finland was recognized and Moscow had to evacuate the areas of Kars, Ardahan and Batumi in favour of Turkey. Over and above this severe loss of territory and population 6,000 million marks had to be paid as reparations. Russia was now virtually cut off from the Baltic and lost one-third of its best agricultural land. Lenin, however, rightly argued that to continue the fighting would mean an end to the Revolution. The Germans accepted the treaty in the mistaken belief that it would keep Russia in a state of chaos. The signing of Brest-Litovsk was a shock to those who believed in a world revolution. Faced with a choice between the idealistic quest for such an upheaval, and the safety of the Russian Revolution, they were compelled to opt for safety.

The four interventionist powers were seeking their own ends, apart from overthrowing the Bolsheviks. In December 1917 the British and the French had signed an agreement in Paris dividing Russia into spheres of interest. According to it the French were to predominate in Bessarabia, the Ukraine and the Crimea. The British were to have the Cossack lands, the Caucasus, Armenia, Georgia and Kurdistan. Both powers supported the White Generals who had raised banners of revolt. A French naval force landed at Odessa and the British sent troops to Batum and Baku, where there was oil. The first serious blow against the Bolsheviks was delivered, however, by the Czechoslovak Legion of some 30,000 which was marooned in Siberia. The legion threatened Moscow at one stage but in fact was successfully routed at Kazan, where Trotsky showed his mettle as an army leader, rallying the Red forces in defence of the Revolution.

British troops, advancing through Baluchistan and Iran, also occupied the Transcaspian area, while a White Russian government under British protection was set up in Turkestan. The three main enemies of the revolutionary regime were Admiral Kolchak in Siberia, Denikin in the south and Poland's dictator Pilsudski. Kolchak had Anglo-French support as well as that of the Americans. Early in 1919 he launched an offensive which swept almost all before it until it menaced Kazan. Trotsky, who had mobilized 30,000 officers of the former Tsarist army, rose to the occasion again and one of his protégés, Kamenev, also a former Tsarist officer and at the time commander of the eastern front, forced Kolchak back till his forces disintegrated and by the end of the year he was captured by the Red Army. He was shot at Irkutsk early in 1920.

About this time serious trouble began in the south. Apart from Denikin, the White Russian leader, there were local adventurers and thugs, like Makhno and Petlura in the Ukraine, who were spreading chaos. First under Stalin's leadership and then under Trotsky's, successive attacks by Denikin and his associates were repelled. He was succeeded by General Wrangel but by this time the British and the French had lost interest and withdrew from the Black Sea as well as the Transcaspian area. They also lifted their blockade in January 1921.

The next threat came from Pilsudski, who took Kiev in May 1920 and received a congratulatory message from King George V of England. But soon the Red Army got the upper hand and even made an unsuccessful bid for Warsaw. Early the following year a treaty was signed at Riga ending the war in the west. Even so it took almost two years before the anti-Soviet republics in various regions of the Soviet Union were finally brought under control and the last stronghold of the White Russians in Vladivostok was occupied by Soviet troops at the end of 1922.

As well as these military battles the Bolsheviks were also having political troubles from their allies, the left SRs, who considered Brest-Litovsk a betrayal of the Revolution and wanted to continue the war with Germany. In July they murdered the German Ambassador, Count Mirbach, in Moscow, to which the capital had been moved from Petrograd in March 1918. The right SRs who always were for continuation of the war murdered several Bolshevik personalities in August, and Dora Kaplan made an attempt on Lenin's life, firing three shots at him. Two bullets hit Lenin; he had a narrow escape and it took him a long time to recover from the wounds.

The attempt on Lenin's life was made on 30 August. The same evening, Sverdlov, a Bolshevik leader and President, called for terror against opponents; on 2 September the All-Russian Central Executive Committee (VTsIK) approved it, and Kaplan was executed. This was the beginning of the terror which eventually silenced all opposition in Russia and established the firm authority of the Bolshevik government. Intervention and civil war accentuated the trend towards greater discipline and control in which terror played an important role. Though it undoubtedly consolidated the new regime and state, terror became an habitual method which had unfortunate consequences later on as well.

The cumulative effects of a long period of war, followed by revolution and civil war, were also increasingly felt. Agricultural production fell sharply because of the policy of requisitioning surplus from the peasants to feed the cities. The farmers retaliated by producing barely enough for their own requirements. The sown area had declined by 1921 to fifty per cent of that in 1913. Cattle, sheep and pig stocks were also dangerously diminished and in fact there was a flight of the poor population from the cities to the villages, where the food situation was marginally better.

The conditions in industry were no better. Because of anarcho-syndicalist tendencies, industries were brought under state control more rapidly than intended. Wages were often paid in kind and production fell. The chaos due to civil war also tended to encourage a tightening of state control on economic and political life in every possible way. A black market of stolen goods from factories and shops flourished because the workers could not otherwise feed themselves. As a climax to it all, in 1920–21, came the terrible drought and famine in the Volga region which claimed five million lives. Banditry, robbery and peasant revolts were on the increase as well. War Communism was the term used to describe policies in this period.

Lenin sorrowfully told the Tenth Party Congress in March 1921,

'The poverty of the working class was never so vast and acute as in the period of its dictatorship. The enfeeblement of workers and peasants is close to the point of complete incapacitation for work.'[3] The political corollary was that the alliance between the peasants and the workers, on which the success of the Revolution and of the Bolshevik regime was based, was breaking down. Just how dangerous the situation had become was revealed by the Kronstadt mutiny which took place a few days before the Tenth Party Congress.

The sailors and soldiers who took part in it were recent recruits. They demanded more freedom for the peasants and aimed at breaking the monopoly of the Bolshevik party. They were supported not only by anarchists and Mensheviks but also by some Bolsheviks. When Trotsky's call for surrender went unheeded, the mutineers were crushed by loyal troops led by Tukhachevsky, with Trotsky supervising.

For some time Lenin had already been contemplating a change in policy to restore some measure of confidence to the peasant. These distressing events hastened the process. Lenin presented his policy, soon to be known as the New Economic Policy (NEP) to the Congress. The essence of the policy was to replace requisitioning with a graduated agricultural tax, first paid in kind and from 1923 onwards in money, and to allow the surplus to be sold in the market freely, thus restoring a market economy. This policy created a new class of *Nepmen* or small-scale producers, caterers and middlemen. The socialist state thus reverted to partial capitalism under the stress of events, even though the commanding heights of the economy, in Lenin's own phrase, were still in the hands of the state.

Lenin justified the new policy on political as well as economic grounds. If there had been a revolution in other countries, things could be arranged differently. But Russia was isolated and the diverging interests of the peasants and the workers had to be reconciled, and reconciled on the peasant's terms. He declared, 'In general the situation is this: we must satisfy the middle peasantry economically and accept freedom of turnover, otherwise it is impossible, economically impossible, for the proletariat to retain power in Russia while the international revolution is retarded.' There could be no answer to this impeccable logic. Lenin knew how to take two steps forward, and when necessary, one step backwards.

To be sure, the ideological retreat was made possible by claiming that it was not of a permanent character, but it was not of a short duration either. For good or ill it endured, more or less in its original form, till 1928, four years after Lenin's death. The NEP, however, gave rise to tremendous tensions within the party, which was unprepared for such an ideological turnabout. This tension was exacerbated by a decision of the Tenth Congress to forbid the functioning of any group as a group within the party; the prolonged and acrimonious debate that accompanied the whole period of the NEP often developed into a personal debate between antagonistic leaders. This had no small effect on Lenin's health and for the worse. He was worried by many trends which had appeared since the halcyon days of the Revolution. He was wont to express his opinions strongly on some of these, and to the end was busy formulating remedial measures.

Lenin's health had been failing for some time and his capacity, if not determination, for work was visibly lessening. On 26 May 1922 he had a stroke. He was afflicted with partial paralysis of the right leg and right arm and a speech disturbance. When doctors tried to comfort him, Lenin said, 'No, this is the first bell'. He never really fully recovered from this stroke. He had others and after a long illness, during which he always kept straining himself with overwork – he even went back to the Kremlin for a period – suffered the final stroke on 24 January 1924 and died within half an hour at 6.30 p.m. The extraordinary life which changed the shape of the world came to an end at the early age of 53.

A post-mortem revealed that for years he had been suffering from progressive sclerosis of the brain. The Health Commissar of the time, Semashko, wrote, 'Sclerosis of the blood vessels of Vladimir Ilyich's brain had gone so far that these blood vessels were calcified. When struck with a tweezer they sounded like stone. The walls of many blood vessels were so thickened and the blood vessels so overgrown that not even a hair could be inserted in the opening. Thus, whole segments of the brain were deprived of fresh blood.'[3]

Lenin's body, after all internal organs and body fluids had been removed, was embalmed and placed in a mausoleum in Red Square, which is still a place of pilgrimage for the Soviet people. What Lenin, a simple, modest man in his personal habits, would have thought of such religious veneration, we can only guess.

Vladimir Ilyich Ulyanov was born on 22 April 1870 in Simbirsk, a small town on the Volga. Theirs was a respectable family. His father, an Inspector of Schools, died a few years after the birth of Vladimir. From his youth Vladimir took an interest in politics and this interest deepened when one of his elder brothers, Alexander, was hanged in St Petersburg for plotting to assassinate the Tsar. Vladimir was then seventeen and the event made a tremendous impact on his mind. He cried and pledged, 'I'll make them pay for this! I swear it!'

Vladimir Ulyanov adopted the name of Lenin when his revolutionary activities began and he had to escape from Siberian exile and the police. A good part of his early life was spent in exile abroad – Poland, Germany, England and Switzerland. His dedication, his zeal and his learning, combined with a superb ability to argue his case in words as well as in print, soon made him a natural leader of the growing Marxist faction in the Russian politics of the time. He towered head and shoulders above the others in the revolutionary movement and became its natural leader.

Lenin was a Marxist but he did not hesitate to bring the doctrine up to date, to adapt it and use it for the cause of the Russian Revolution, making some important ideological contributions of his own. Undoubtedly he was the most profound thinker among the revolutionary leaders of his time.

The secret of Lenin's success lies not only in his determined pursuit of the objective he had set himself but in his extraordinary ability to judge a situation and to take the plunge. His arrival in Petrograd when the Revolution had already begun, his intuitive grasp of the significance of what was happening and what was needed and his ability to communicate this not merely to intellectuals, politicians and party workers but also to the ordinary people was the stuff out of which greatness is made in history. His speech on arrival at the Finland Station, in the charged atmosphere of the time:

> I am convinced that when they talk to you sweetly, when they promise you a lot, they are deceiving you and the whole Russian people. The people needs peace; the people needs bread; the people needs land. And they give war, hunger, no bread – leave the landlords still on the land . . .

was the most damning of all indictments of the ineffective Provisional Government as well as the most inspiring of all the calls to arms made in the course of the Revolution.

Of humility Lenin had little, but simplicity, fellow-feeling and sympathy he had in plenty. He could be the most deadly of enemies when crossed in the path of the Revolution he believed in, but he could not be vicious and mean as Stalin was.

Lenin's great reconciliation with Trotsky on the eve of the Revolution and the complete trust with which he let him take care of the Civil War after the Revolution, show the statesman in him.

Lenin will be primarily judged by the heritage he has left the world – post-revolutionary Russia. It can be argued that this heritage has been distorted, that Lenin's insistence on the monopoly of power by the Communist Party, his insistence on discipline at all costs, might have been necessary in the initial period of the Revolution but that the fetish made out of it by Stalin was perversion. This would be to ignore that the system of political organization which Lenin built could not but lead to some of these consequences.

Lenin himself seems to have been groping for a new path towards the end of his life, but by then it was physically impossible for him to prevail in any significant way. The disregard of his warning about Stalin had fateful consequences, as we shall see. But in his last years Lenin did ask himself the searching question, 'What else could we have done?' Even to Lenin the choices available were not very many. Besides, the Revolution has still not run its course and it is premature to declare it either a complete success or a complete failure.

What is undeniable is that the Russian Revolution, with its unique emphasis on the need for political action to control and direct the economy for the benefit of society at large, has become the source of inspiration for that part of the world which is still struggling with dire poverty. Its consequences are still reverberating down the corridors of history, even if the model is no longer inimitable. It is unquestionably Lenin's achievement, his contribution to the twentieth century.

4   The Stalin Ascendancy

AN EVEN MIGHTIER TUMULT lay ahead. The NEP was a palliative, not a permanent cure, and it was on the back of the confusion created by the NEP that Stalin rode to power and gained an absolute hold over the state and party machine. The crisis was as much the result of failure of expectations as of the external circumstances in which the Soviet Union found herself. The dilemma which faced the leaders was as grave as it was simple. Although the adoption of the NEP had brought success and the economy had revived to some extent, it showed no promise of abolishing poverty and fulfilling the hopes of material welfare which the Revolution had aroused. Besides, ideologically, the policy of the NEP was as near to reviving capitalism as could be imagined.

If production was to increase, capital and machinery had to be found. The state of Soviet relations with the outside world and the hostility it generated among the leading capitalist countries of the time ensured that no financial or technical help could be expected from them. There was some kind of rapprochement with Germany, but it was totally inadequate for the creation of the industrial society to which the Soviet leaders aspired. Internal savings, on the other hand, could be generated only if living standards and the consumption level were kept down. Under the NEP it was not possible since the middle peasants, on whom the NEP placed so much reliance, could not be persuaded to sacrifice their immediate interests for the sake of promises for the future. Even if they found the promises attractive, the state of the economy did not encourage them to believe in their redeemability.

Stalin's answer to the quest for a solution was forced industrialization. In other words, socialism in one country was possible even if it was surrounded by hostile capitalist nations. The only available alternative, the theory of permanent revolution, was too nebulous and impractical since it implied waiting for the world revolution before the Soviet Union could attempt a transformation of its own. The debate which followed the application of the NEP was passionate, bitter and of tremendous consequence for the country.

The economic after-effects manifested themselves soon enough. The beginning of the end of the NEP came with a decision by the Fourteenth Party Congress, which met in 1925, that it was possible to build a complete socialist society in Russia and the main task of the party was to strive to make it a reality. There can be no denying that the vision which Stalin evoked was magnificent and inspiring. It also fulfilled a psychological need felt by the masses. The people did not, perhaps, care much whether backward Russia was to set an example to the rest of the world but they were at one with Stalin when, in 1931, while the Soviet Union was in the throes of the first Five Year Plan, he fervently declared:

It is sometimes asked whether it is not possible to slow down the tempo a bit, to put a check on the movement. No, comrades, it is not possible! The pace must not be slackened! This is dictated to us by our obligations to the workers and peasants of the USSR. This is dictated to us by our obligation to the working class of the whole world.

To slacken the pace would mean to lag behind; and those who lag behind are beaten. We do not want to be beaten. No, we do not want to . . . (Russia) was ceaselessly beaten for her backwardness. She was beaten by the Mongol Khans, she was beaten by Turkish beys, she was beaten by Swedish feudal lords, she was beaten by Polish-Lithuanian *Pans*, she was beaten by Anglo-French capitalists, she was beaten by Japanese barons, she was beaten by all – for her backwardness. For military backwardness, for cultural backwardness, for political backwardness, for industrial backwardness, for agricultural backwardness. She was beaten because to beat her was profitable and went unpunished. You remember the words of the pre-revolutionary poet: 'Thou art poor and thou art plentiful, thou art mighty and thou art helpless, Mother Russia.'

. . . We are fifty or a hundred years behind the advanced countries. We must make up this lag in ten years. Either we do it or they crush us.

The sentiments which Stalin expressed illuminate, as nothing else can, the secret of the success of the drive for industrialization, even if the cost in men and resources was monstrous. It appealed to an innate sense of fear, and to the nationalism and pride of the Russian people. As posed by Stalin, the success of industrialization was not merely a question of welfare but of the survival of the Soviet Union. Everyone was interested in that.

Behind the simple-sounding appeal lay weightier reasons which were left unsaid at the time. But after the war Stalin was to explain that they knew that a war was coming and the country must have the industrial sinews to defend herself. It is perfectly true, of course, that the Soviet Union would not have survived the onslaught of Nazi Germany but for the basic industry created by the industrialization programme. But Stalin's explanation put a gloss on a policy which was far from faultless in the manner in which it was carried out.

Among other reasons, the crisis of the NEP was caused by agriculture. It was one thing to create a vast number of land-owning peasantry, another to expect efficient agricultural production. Moreover, the wealthier peasants, or kulaks, were unwilling to supply grain to the cities at cheap prices. In the long run an increase in the power of the kulaks also meant that no radical economic measures were possible since the kulaks as well as the smallholding peasants would have resisted such a course.

The dilemma was simple if brutal. If a planned economy was the aim, the vast agricultural sector could not be left out of it for that would have made nonsense of planning altogether. Since the peasants were unwilling to volunteer for such controls, the solution devised was to collectivize them. Stalin maintained that not to do so would have led to a collapse of the whole economy. The problem could not be postponed since the 1927 Party Congress had decided to go ahead with planning and creating a socialist industry and to restrict capitalism in the countryside – which meant collectivization. But the programme was a moderate one. No one at the time foresaw the breakneck speed and total ruthlessness with which the programme would be enforced. The object of the scheme was to encourage the poor peasants to merge together, while the rich peasants were to suffer disability in the form of higher taxes. The first Five Year Plan was launched in 1928, and its strong bias in favour of heavy industry reacted upon the pace of collectivization as well.

The method which Stalin ultimately adopted was characterized by N. Valentinov, a Menshevik, who worked for some time in the Soviet planning organs, as 'primitive socialist accumulation by the methods of Tamerlane'. It was not an unjust description.

The end of the NEP in the countryside was signalled by decrees passed in June and July 1929 in the RSFSR and the Ukraine bringing in a new system of grain procurement. The battle against the peasants took two forms: first, the enforcement of a delivery quota upon all peasants, with a specially heavy bias against the rich peasants; and second, the forcible collectivization of all farms. The aim now was one hundred per cent collectivization and it became intertwined with the process of 'dekulakization'. At the start there was a strong tendency among the poor peasants to divide the loot from the rich peasants' or kulaks' property among themselves but this was stopped because it was feared that it might make the process of collectivization harder. As for the fate of the kulaks, Stalin did not give a damn. As he put it, 'When the head is off, one does not mourn for the hair.' The kulaks were not even permitted to join the collective farms, and disappeared as a class.

Worse still, not only was the term 'kulak' no longer used for a rich peasant but those peasants who opposed collectivization in any way were condemned as 'ideological' kulaks. Another category was *podkulachnik* (sub-kulak), the peasant who sympathized with the kulaks. These categories were subject to repression, deportation and worse. This was not done without resistance from the peasants, which took many forms, above all of voluntary destruction of property and livestock. The orthodox, establishment novelist and subsequent Nobel Prizewinner, Mikhail Sholokhov, has described the atmosphere realistically:

Stock was slaughtered every night in Gremyachy Log. Hardly had dusk fallen when the muffled, short bleats of sheep, the death squeals of pigs, or the lowing of calves could be heard. Both those who joined the kolkhoz and individual farmers killed their stock. Bulls, sheep, pigs, even cows were slaughtered, as well as cattle for breeding. The horned stock of Gremyachy was halved in two nights. The dogs began to drag entrails about the village; cellars and barns were filled with meat. The cooperative sold about two hundred poods of salt in two days, that had been lying in stock for eighteen months. 'Kill, it's not ours any more . . .' 'Kill, they will take it for meat anyway . . .' 'Kill, you won't get meat in the kolkhoz . . .' crept the insidious rumours. And they killed. They ate till they could eat no more. Young and old suffered from stomach-ache. At dinner time tables groaned under boiled and roasted meat, everyone had a greasy mouth, everyone hiccoughed as if at a wake. Everyone blinked like an owl, as if drunk from eating.[1]

No wonder then that there were riots and peasant uprisings. No wonder that in Kazakhstan, for instance, almost the entire sheep population was slaughtered or died of fodder shortage. Many of the Kazakhs also died in the process, as shown by the censuses of 1926 and 1939 which revealed a decline of over 20% in the number of Kazakhs.

For a brief period in 1930 Stalin called a halt to this campaign and accused the officials of being 'dizzy with success'. It was not entirely their fault and in any case the responsibility was Stalin's own, but worry about right and wrong was not a powerful trait of Stalin's character. Moreover, Stalin resumed the campaign for collectivization by a decree on 30 June 1930. He knew what he was doing in waging a war against the peasantry. His explanation, given in reply to Sholokhov's complaint about excessive cruelty by officials in his region, made this clear. Stalin said, '. . . the honourable cultivators of your region, and not only your region, committed sabotage and were quite willing to leave the workers and the Red Army without grain. The fact that the sabotage was silent and apparently gentle (no blood was spilt) does not change the fact that the honourable cultivators in reality were making a "silent" war against Soviet power. War by starvation, my dear comrade Sholokhov.'

Instead, the peasants were starved into submission by Stalin. Not until after his death was their plight given serious thought and not till 1965 were really effective measures taken to deal with the problem of agriculture, the Cinderella of the Revolution. Yet it must be admitted that to break the power of the peasantry was a necessary part of the Revolution, even if one deplores the methods used. The excesses of collectivization no doubt deserve unqualified condemnation, but it also must be considered whether a gentler remedy than collectivization did exist. Given the premises of industrialization, it is extremely doubtful.

Famines during the period of collectivization are an integral part of the story although even now they are not officially admitted. One of the ablest of commentators on the Soviet economy, Alec Nove, has estimated on the basis of the census figures that between 1932 and 1939 some ten million people disappeared demographically, i.e. the normal rise in population did not materialize as it should have. Of these a substantial number were peasants, although account also has to be taken of those who disappeared in the political purges.

Disaster in agriculture, however, had compensation in another field – industry. The first Five Year Plan aimed at industrializing the country rapidly. In fact, encouraged by the success of its implementation in the first year, Stalin then aimed to fulfil the plan in four years, and it ended on 31 December 1932 instead of in September 1933. Moreover, its targets were revised upwards in the intervening periods. The expeditious implementation of the plan was also influenced by a desire to rid the country of dependence on foreign sources for machinery. This imposed its own pattern of priority in favour of heavy industry, a priority which was maintained in all subsequent plans and specially in the second Five Year Plan, which was affected by the threat of Hitler's growing power in Germany.

The great achievements of the first plan were the huge metallurgical plants in the Urals region, notably Magnitogorsk. The plan targets were, of course, unrealistic and not completely fulfilled but at the end of the Plan the national income had nearly doubled, industrial production had more than doubled and even production of consumer goods nearly doubled. Coal output also nearly doubled as did electricity production, but it failed to reach the level of the contemplated fourfold increase. Though pig-iron production doubled, steel production was only 5·9 million tons compared with 4 million tons in 1928. The most impressive rise was in machinery production, which more than trebled. On the other hand, handicrafts and production by small workshops declined. The official statistics of the period are still suspect but there is little doubt that on the whole the plan succeeded.

The success was all the greater if account is taken of the chaotic conditions and the shortage of skills, raw materials and even proper tools. Yet it is undeniable that the people were fired by enthusiasm and zeal, and they worked in primitive conditions to perform miracles of construction and engineering. Though critics of the achievement have tried to make out that all this was the result of forced labour, that is a gross exaggeration. Some projects were undoubtedly dependent on an abundant supply of cheap labour, and forced labour was used, for instance, in the construction of the Volga–White Sea canal. But by and large, all witnesses of the period testify to the immense fire of endeavour which was lit by the industrialization programme, paradoxically because the targets set for it sounded so improbable and the means to achieve it were so limited. Enthusiasm naturally waned in later years but by then planning had become more organized. The self-sacrifice willingly accepted by the people at the start succeeded in laying the foundations for the Soviet Union's emergence as a great industrial power by the time war broke out in 1939. The achievement was all the more striking since the rest of the world was passing through a severe depression at the time and the contrast immensely enhanced the prestige of economic planning in general: its influence is to be seen not only in the economic methods of the western countries, albeit to a limited extent, but in the under-developed countries who accept planning as a method even if they do not bring the same tenacity of purpose to it, fortunately, as Stalin did.

Owing to the paucity of consumer goods, falls in agricultural production and inflation, the living standard of the people as a whole went down during this period, though Stalin tried to disguise this by insisting upon the slogan, 'Life has become better, comrades, life has become more joyous.' He had a twisted sense of humour.

The benefits to the people were of course not entirely imaginary. The welfare activities of the state were established and expanded during the same period. Education, medical services, sick-pay benefits, paid holidays and facilities for sports – these were genuine improvements in the life of a people who had never known it under the old order. It helped to mitigate the hardships of the inhuman endeavour which was imposed upon them.

Many of the shortcomings of the industrialization drive can be explained by inexperience and sheer ignorance. The political purges and terror which came in the wake of the success of the first Five Year Plan cannot be explained away like that. From beginning to end they served but one purpose, to strengthen the personal dictatorship of Stalin over the party and the country. They left a blot upon the Soviet system from which it is still recovering.

Behind it was the titanic struggle for power which began between Stalin and Trotsky during the last years of Lenin's life. The differences between them were ideological as well as temperamental. Though Trotsky was the co-architect of the October Revolution with Lenin, extremely popular and recognized abroad, he was not popular with the Bolshevik leaders or with many of the influential members of the party. Because of his association with the Mensheviks up to the time of the Revolution and because of his ideological independence from Lenin, he was considered something of an outsider. They did not want him to succeed Lenin as the supreme leader.

Stalin exploited this feeling and managed to isolate him by skilful manoeuvres and by joining forces with others who considered themselves rivals of Trotsky for power. The tragic irony was that neither Trotsky, nor Kamenev, Bukharin and the others who supported Stalin in his initial struggle against Trotsky, considered Stalin to be a candidate for leadership. Till the last moment Trotsky refused to believe that it was Stalin who was his enemy. When he realized it, it was too late to do anything about it. After all, Trotsky had been a party to the suppression of Lenin's testament – written a short time before his death – in which he had severely criticized Stalin and asked the party to search for a new leader and to take away Stalin's powers. The existence of this testament was denied publicly by Trotsky and Krupskaya, Lenin's widow, under pressure from the top party leaders. It was only made public in 1960.

The ideological differences arose from the conflict between the theory of socialism in one country, which Stalin developed, and Trotsky's idea of a permanent revolution. But serious ideological differences apart, Stalin had been in conflict with Trotsky since the beginning of the Revolution, jealous of his brilliance and popularity, particularly among the young and the army. Trotsky was accused of intending a Bonapartist coup. By clever manoeuvres, and helped by the fact that Lenin was dead, Stalin succeeded in isolating Trotsky, while Trotsky hesitated because he was afraid of splitting the movement at a critical time. In the spring of 1924 Frunze, Trotsky's opponent in military matters, was appointed as Deputy Commissar for War. In April 1925, Trotsky was finally removed from the post of Commissar for War and for all practical purposes his pre-eminence was over. At that time Kamenev and Zinoviev were allied with Stalin.

Following Trotsky's eclipse, Zinoviev and Kamenev broke with Stalin and early in 1926 formed an alliance with Trotsky. Kamenev was removed from the Politburo and so were Zinoviev and Trotsky.

In November–December the three dissidents and a number of their followers were expelled from the party. Trotsky was sent into exile early in 1929, never to come back, and was brutally assaulted by an agent of Stalin on 20 August 1940, in his Mexican hideout. He lingered on for another twenty-four hours in a state of coma before succumbing to the injuries. Throughout the long period of exile, he had been hounded by Stalin's agents from one country to another, and the Americans did not permit even his dead body to be brought to the United States for funeral ceremonies. Some 300,000 people filed past his body during the five days of the lying-in-state. The lonely outcast was not forgotten, even though he continued to be reviled after his death.

All revolutions have their tragedies and certainly the Bolshevik Revolution had its ample share. But none was greater than that of Trotsky. History has been singularly unjust to him. In his own country he was denied the acclaim due to him for his share in the success of the Bolshevik revolution; in his later struggle with Stalin he was not always in the wrong, even if he was not always in the right.

The truth is that no matter how much the official versions of history in the Soviet Union denounce him as a traitor to the cause and misrepresent and falsify his actual role in the creation of the Soviet state, his incomparable greatness as a vital and immense personality, a writer, organizer and leader, a Marxist idealist in the classical sense of the term cannot be denied. All the same he had a streak of ruthlessness, and he was wrong about the basic premise on which he differed with Stalin – that socialism cannot be built in one country.

Trotsky's failure was also partly due to his own ineptitude and slowness in dealing with Stalin, who was altogether too cunning for him. Some day perhaps it will be possible, even for the Russians, to tell the truth about him and accord him his historical place. Till this happens, the enigmatic figure of Trotsky will continue to haunt the history of the Russian Revolution. Trotsky at least had the vision, courage and generosity to say of the Stalin period, even before it was over, that it would be seen years hence as 'an episodic relapse'.

The exile of Trotsky was the signal for Stalin's total ascendancy. He now proceeded to isolate the other elements of opposition to his policy. Bukharin, editor of *Pravda,* Rykov, Chairman of the Council of Commissars, and Tomsky, the trade-union chief, were next to go. By the end of 1930 they were either expelled from the Politburo or dropped from it. If the opposition from Trotsky and his associates could be labelled leftist, since they stood for more radical policies, the opposition from Bukharin, Rykov and Tomsky could be described as rightist, since they were against upsetting the alliance with the peasants, and were thus opposed to forced collectivization. They stood for caution.

The twists and turns of all the participants in this struggle for power were too numerous to be recounted here. The complicated history of the period is made even more complex by the absence of authentic information, since the Soviet archives have not been opened and the published documents and histories in the Soviet Union continue to be afflicted by the gloss put on the events by Stalin and his successors.

Trotsky's exile was a misleading indication of Stalin's political methods. His harsh treatment of the kulaks was more characteristic, but what followed was even more ghastly and terrible. The year 1934 began with the Seventeenth Party Congress, the congress of the victors, to celebrate the success of the first Five Year Plan and the liquidation of the kulaks. It ended with the assassination of S. M. Kirov on 1 December in Leningrad. Kirov was a rising star in the party firmament and there have been some indications that at the Seventh Party Congress a secret move was afoot either to restrain Stalin's powers or to replace him with Kirov. It is highly probable, therefore, that Stalin had a hand in his murder and this signalled a return to political terror without any precedent in history. It began with a thorough purge of all possible dissident elements in the party.

In the middle of 1936 the big purge trials began. Leaders like Kamenev, Zinoviev, Bukharin and scores of others were brought to court on trumped-up charges, sentenced to death and shot. The amazing thing is that they all confessed to the 'crimes'. These confessions did not stand the test of credibility, consistency or even plausibility. They were, however, accepted by the courts, which had become mere rubber stamps for decisions already taken by the security service. Not only political leaders perished in this wave of terror, but writers, artists, bureaucrats and army leaders like Marshal Tukhachevsky, Chief of the Red Army, and Admiral Orlov, Commander-in-Chief of the Navy – all trod the same path. Some were shot, others died in the prison camps set up specifically for political prisoners.

Fame was, of course, a disadvantage for survival, whether it was national fame or only local, but obscurity was no guarantee either. Ordinary people were rounded up and marched to prison camps, to extinction without trial. The knock on the door at night was more often than not a summons to oblivion. Even the executioners were not spared. The security people who carried out the operation were themselves swept away repeatedly to make way for new ones, whose role was to impart new vigour to the whole gory business.

An agonized silence fell over the heart and soul of the people. They were afraid to talk to each other, even to their nearest and dearest, and could not entirely trust even friends. There was an orgy of mutual denunciations, of false accusations. The tragic thing was that many accepted it in the belief that it was the right thing to do for the sake of the Revolution and the party; many perished believing that Stalin was not to blame and with his name on their lips.

Those outside endured the hardship of living; those inside the prison camps bore the brutality of living. Such is the human spirit that many survived, and lived to tell the tale, when occasionally allowed to do so. What the existence in the camps was like at its mildest is well caught in the ironic style of Alexander Solzhenitsyn in the conclusion of *One Day in the Life of Ivan Denisovich*:

> Shukhov went to sleep fully content. He'd had many strokes of luck that day: they hadn't put him in the cells; they hadn't sent the team to the settlement; he'd pinched a bowl of kasha at dinner; the team-leader had fixed the rates well; he'd built a wall and enjoyed doing it; he'd smuggled that bit of hacksaw-blade through; he'd earned something from Tsezar in the evening; he'd bought that tobacco. And he hadn't fallen ill. He'd got over it.
>
> A day without a dark cloud. Almost a happy day.
>
> There were three thousand six hundred and fifty-three days like that in his stretch. From the first clang of the rail to the last clang of the rail.
>
> The three extra days were for leap years.[2]

The number of people who vanished is put at ten to fifteen million by Andrei Sakharov, a highly respected Soviet nuclear physicist. Others have put it higher.[3] If one takes into consideration relatives of those directly involved, the tragedy in terms of numbers alone was big enough. It probably did not leave a single family unaffected.

Its political effects were even worse. The purge was used to get rid of all the leading old-time Bolsheviks in high places who were associated with Lenin's period and who had crossed Stalin's path in some way. Thus apart from Stalin, few of the Politburo members of Lenin's time survived the purges. A large proportion of the Central Committee members and candidate members were also dealt with in a similar fashion. It brought forth new people, technocrats and bureaucrats, who were almost solely dependent upon Stalin for their careers. Political dissent in the inner ranks of the party and government thus completely disappeared. The masses were silenced by the continuing terror, the constant calls for more work and their isolation from the outside world. The purge of the army ranks weakened it, one of the reasons why in the early stages of the war Hitler's armies swept all before them and reached the gates of Moscow.

While the internal turmoil of the Soviet Union persisted from 1928 onwards, Europe also underwent an upheaval of a different sort. The great depression and the subsequent rise of Nazism in Germany created a new political situation which affected the Soviet Union directly. Though the intervention of the Allied powers had failed, and one by one all the leading states had proceeded to recognize the Soviet regime, hostility towards it remained ill-concealed. As a military power, the Soviet Union was an unknown quantity, but as the recognized leader of a revolutionary movement, it was feared and Moscow's hand was seen in every place and every political movement of any radical nature. Some substance was lent to this claim because of the tight hold which Stalin had over all the communist parties, whose policies zig-zagged according to the convenience of Moscow.

Survival and recognition, these were the two main continuing preoccupations of the Soviet Union during the post-Lenin years until the Second World War. But equally important were the economic objectives, more trade and possible financial help. The quest for loans was on the whole unsuccessful and Soviet relations with Britain had many ups and downs during this period. The breaking off of diplomatic relations and the unilateral annulment of the Anglo-Soviet Trade Agreement by London in May 1927 shook Moscow badly. The subsequent attempt by Britain to form an alliance with France, Germany and Poland against the USSR made matters even worse. Diplomatic relations, however, were resumed a year later. By this time the depression was beginning to affect the world economy and Britain was anxious to sell goods to the Soviet Union. Moscow, of course, always relied upon division among the Western countries to prevent them from presenting a solid front on this and other problems.

In this context Soviet-German relations assumed an interesting pattern. Though the Brest-Litovsk Treaty had been repudiated by both sides shortly after its conclusion, it did take Russia out of the First World War. Unhappy with the harsh terms of the Versailles peace treaty, to which the Soviet Union was not a party, the Germans were bound to turn to Moscow and they were not unwelcome. On 16 April 1922, an Easter Sunday, the Soviet Union and Germany signed a treaty at Rapallo, a seaside resort in Italy. As a treaty it was innocuous enough. Under its terms Moscow waived indemnities from Germany and established better economic relations. At a time when Britain and France were being equally antagonistic to the Germans and the Russians, it was something of a diplomatic triumph for the Soviet Union to normalize relations with Germany so swiftly and so easily, and something of a set-back to the Entente powers.

It was judged more harshly by the British and the French, who called it a piece of treachery by Germany. *The Times* indignantly described it as an 'unholy alliance' and wanted to teach both the countries a lesson. Neither the contents of the treaty nor its value justified this reaction, for it simply exposed the weakness of Soviet and German positions. Lenin had diagnosed the German situation more acutely when he said that while the German bourgeoisie felt a real hatred towards Bolshevism and repressed it in their own country, the international situation compelled them to seek an alliance with Russia. Rapallo was not even an alliance, it was an anti-Versailles front.

Far more important was the Berlin Treaty signed in April 1926, which guaranteed the neutrality of Germany in the event of an attack on the Soviet Union. Trade between the two countries expanded till Hitler came to power in 1933 and military co-operation was of some importance. In return for providing training and testing facilities for the German army, the Russians received technical advice in sophisticated armaments. This co-operation was kept very secret.

One of the most significant factors in German-Soviet relations at this period was the hostility between Moscow and the Social Democrats in Germany. The Russians loathed the German Social Democrats more than anybody else in that country and did everything possible to keep them out of power there. This had fateful consequences because the unceasing hostilities between the Social Democrats and the Communists helped Hitler to gain power.

Hitler considered the goal of German foreign policy exclusively in terms of conquering territory in the East, i.e. the Soviet Union. The Nazis out-did everybody else in their anti-Soviet propaganda. A sample of the kind of material they spread was the story that the body of the bishop of Voronezh had been cooked to make soup which the monks of a local monastery had been compelled by the Cheka to eat. Though, on the surface, relations remained correct after the advent of Hitler, the Russians were uneasy and put an end to military co-operation in June 1933. These uncertainties persisted until 1938.

On the broad international front the Soviet Union was now less isolated, if not trusted any more than before. In October 1933 President Roosevelt sent a message to the Soviet Government seeking normalization of relations and after swift negotiations, diplomatic relations were established between the two countries on 16th November. Yet only a year before, Henry L. Stimson was telling some of the delegates at the Geneva Disarmament Conference, 'Never! Centuries will go by before America recognizes the Soviet Union.'[4]

The Russians knew, of course, that the real menace was Germany and their strategy was to ward off Hitler as long as possible. The Soviet Union, therefore, constantly manoeuvred during this period to promote a variety of security pacts, some bilateral and some regional, including a Pacific region pact because the fear of Japan was also growing in Moscow. The Soviet Union also joined the League of Nations in 1934. The crisis, however, did not abate. One of the major reasons for the Soviet's lack of success was Britain's consistent policy of appeasement of Germany; this came to a climax after Hitler's annexation of Austria in the notorious Munich Agreement on 28 September 1939 which legalized Hitler's conquests, and which, according to the British Prime Minister Chamberlain, was to bring 'peace in our time'. It directly led to the German annexation of Czechoslovakia in March 1939.

It thoroughly alarmed Moscow, which had lost faith in a number of agreements and pacts, such as the 1935 Franco-Soviet Treaty of Mutual Assistance. Stalin was also beginning to recover from the domestic preoccupations which had occupied him for most of the thirties. He thought that with the collapse of any political resistance to

Germany by Britain and France, Hitler would move towards his cherished target, the East. Perhaps Stalin did not know how soon this move would come, and if he did, he chose to ignore it in the hope that he could buy time. In any case, despite bitter anti-Soviet propaganda by Germany, Stalin had carefully begun to prepare a way for a rapprochement with Hitler as the price for the continued security of the Soviet Union. This tendency was reinforced by the conflict between the Soviet Union and Japan which had broken out in 1938 in the Far East. He continued to try for some solid agreement with the French and the British but their response was at best lukewarm.

There followed the famous Nazi-Soviet Non-Aggression Pact, which was signed in Moscow on 23 August 1939. Under its terms the Soviet Union was to have got a share in Poland and it ensured Soviet neutrality against a German invasion of Poland. It came like a bolt from the blue in the tense atmosphere then prevailing. The pact was hastened undoubtedly by the stalling tactics adopted by Britain and France towards making any agreement with Moscow. Stalin came to believe that the two powers were unwilling to be involved in a war with Hitler and any agreement signed with them, without cast-iron guarantees, would deflect the brunt of Hitler's attack upon the Soviet Union.

Much ink has been spilled on the immorality of this pact. The left everywhere was shocked and considered it an act of betrayal, and this feeling was shared by many communists as well, though all Communist Parties loyally supported Stalin's about-turn. Yet it is equally unfair to blame Stalin for it exclusively. While the pact is indefensible ideologically, as a measure of *Real-politik* it had its merits. It gave the Soviet Union a breathing space although, in their zeal to defend the action, Soviet commentators have exaggerated its benefits. Within twenty-one months Hitler attacked the Soviet Union all the same. Stalin, obsessed with the fear of encirclement, was only guilty of having lost his nerve after holding out for so long, and rushing into a pact with Hitler.

On 1 September 1939 Hitler marched into Poland. World War Two had begun and the Soviet Union was out of it for some time.

5 The Patriotic War – and after

STALIN CAN BE more justly accused of forcing the line that it was a capitalist war in which the communists should have no part. By now, of course, even Stalin was convinced that war would come to the Soviet Union and in an effort to improve the Soviet defensive position he invaded the Baltic states and incorporated them into the Soviet Union. He also imposed some strategic concessions upon Finland, an act which nearly ended in disaster because the Finns fought bitterly and successfully for some time before giving in. The Winter War, as it came to be known, between Finland and the Soviet Union was fought from November 1939 to March 1940. It did little to enhance the reputation of the Red Army. The first months were catastrophic for the Soviet forces but in the end their overwhelming superiority in manpower prevailed and a peace treaty was signed between the two sides on 12 March 1940.

One of the nightmares of the Soviet leader was fighting on two fronts simultaneously, with Japan in the east and Germany in the west. Relations between Tokyo and Moscow were never good. There had already been fighting between the two countries, but in the battle along the Khalkin-Gol River, the Japanese were defeated in the autumn of 1939. After long negotiations, a neutrality pact was signed on 13 April 1941, which relieved the pressure on Moscow greatly although suspicions about the real intentions of Japan remained throughout the war.

Internally, economic discipline was tightened and resources were diverted to arms manufacture. Stalin received many warnings from reliable sources, including Winston Churchill, and Soviet intelligence agents of the high calibre of Richard Sorge, about the exact date of the invasion, but he ignored them.

On 22 June 1941, Hitler hurled his forces against the Soviet Union. Europe, which Stalin had sought to keep away from Russia, burst in, shattering the walls of self-imposed isolation. The German advance was rapid and by October they had overrun most of the Ukraine and reached the outskirts of Moscow and Leningrad. It was the tactic of *blitzkrieg*. Heavy bombing in advance reduced population centres to heap of rubble and, in the wake of this destruction, Hitler's tank and motorized infantry divisions moved with lightning speed, sweeping all resistance before them. Surprise, shock and movement were the three elements before which the Red Army collapsed. It was neither prepared for it nor properly equipped and Soviet losses were huge.

Once the shock had been absorbed, the war assumed a steadier pattern. The Soviet Government reacted by reorganizing the command structure of the Red Army and promoting new Generals like Zhukov, Rokossovsky and Koniev. Priority was given to removing all industrial assets from the path of the invaders to the eastern regions of the Soviet Union, beyond the Urals. Despite the German bombers, this operation was carried out with great success amidst chaotic conditions and it made quick rearmament possible during the war. The Soviet Union also hastened to sign a Mutual Assistance Pact with Britain and negotiations were opened with the Americans for full-scale Lend-Lease aid, which materialized after Japan had attacked Pearl Harbour in December 1941.

Yet a transformation had already taken place in the minds of the Russian people. Stalin took his time about it; for a few days he was probably as bewildered as everybody else, but when he spoke on 3 July 1941 he grasped the nettle, and his speech on the radio brought faith to the people. Russians who lived through those times still recall the electric effect it had on the masses. From his opening words, 'Comrades, citizens, brothers and sisters, fighters of our Army! I am speaking to you, my friends!' to his instructions to pursue a policy of scorched earth, leaving nothing useful behind for the enemy, to march onward to victory, his speech was calculated to arouse the deepest feelings of patriotism.

The Germans had made it their objective to capture Moscow by Christmas 1941, and in November they launched a tremendous offensive to achieve it. But despite the panic and disorder which their retreat had caused, the Russians did not give in and the offensive failed. It was not only the first failure of the German Army during the whole course of the war so far, but psychologically it put new heart into the Russian resistance. From this moment on, the Germans were doomed. The symbol of the Soviet will to defy and defeat the arrogant enemy was Stalin, who refused to vacate the Kremlin though the government was evacuated.

The Russians were to suffer many defeats in later years, particularly the fall of Rostov in the summer of 1942, but it made little difference to their spirits. After the fall of Rostov Stalin issued an order of the day which was read to all army units everywhere. 'Not another step back,' was the firm command to all of them. More ruthless reforms were also made in the army to cope with some loss of nerve caused by the Rostov affair.

What aroused the deepest hatred against the Germans were the cruelties and tortures committed by them in the occupied areas. Winston Churchill's apocalyptic vision of Russia, in a broadcast on the very day of the German invasion, came to be only too true: 'I see the ten thousand villages of Russia where the means of existence is wrung so hardly from the soil, but where there are still primordial joys, where maidens laugh and children play. I see advancing on all this in hideous onslaught the Nazi war machine . . . I see the dull, drilled, docile, brutish masses of the Hun soldiery plodding on like a swarm of crawling locusts.' It is doubtful if, since the dawn of history, any nation has inflicted more bestial cruelties upon another than the Germans did upon the Russians. It is also doubtful if any nation has ever risen more magnificently to the challenge.

The key event of the war, which turned the tide against the Germans, was the battle for Stalingrad on the Volga, lasting from August 1942 to 2 February 1943. The Germans devastated the city and made every effort to capture it. At times the situation became really critical but the Russians, defending it bitterly and fighting from every house and every room in the city, prevailed in the end, and on 31 January General von Paulus surrendered to the Russians, The German Sixth Army had been almost completely annihilated and Hitler never recovered from this catastrophe. For the Soviet people Stalingrad became a legend, inspiring them throughout the rest of the war and giving them the first real smell of victory.

Another notable event of the war was the siege of Leningrad. Even in a war noted for human suffering, the endurance of the people of Leningrad remains sharply etched on the pages of history. Here were three million people, surrounded by the German troops with all supply lines cut and not enough food in the city to last even for a month. Though they managed to keep the Germans out, a fearful famine resulted. The siege began on 8 September 1941 and was not lifted till January 1943. By February 1942 supplies were reaching Leningrad across the ice of Lake Ladoga, but in the critical months of winter in 1941–42 close to a million people died as a result of the famine, many of them suffering from post-famine physical conditions. A Soviet historian of the Leningrad blockade, Pavlov, has provided a grim account of the actual conditions in the city during those memorable months.

> Death would overtake people in all kinds of circumstances; while they were in the streets, they would fall down and never rise again; or in their houses where they would fall asleep and never awake; in factories, where they would collapse while doing a job of work. There was no transport, and the dead body would usually be put on a handsleigh drawn by two or three members of the dead man's family; often, wholly exhausted during the long trek to the cemetery, they would abandon the body half-way, leaving it to the authorities to deal with it.[1]

In 1943 the Germans made their last big-scale attempt to defeat the Soviet Union. In the early summer a well-prepared German offensive was launched against the Kursk-Orel salient, but it was beaten off with heavy losses and spelt an end to any hope of victory which Hitler might have still entertained. From then onwards the advance of the Red Army became irresistible and only came to a halt outside the smouldering Reichstag in Berlin. The Soviet Union had not only survived, but had emerged indisputably as a great power. The price paid had been heavy, nearly twenty million killed, another twenty million deaths indirectly due to the war, a vast area reduced to rubble and desert, and the formidable task of reconstruction ahead.

Germany surrendered on 7 May 1945, but Japan was still at war with the Western powers. Free of danger from Europe, and unwilling to be left out of the victory over Japan, the Soviet Union declared war upon Japan on 8 August. Two days earlier the Americans had exploded their nuclear bomb upon Hiroshima and the next day dropped one on Nagasaki, and the war in the Far East came to an end with the formal surrender of Japan in September 1945.

86

The conduct of the war had remained with Stalin from the very beginning. As Chairman of the State Committee of Defence, set up on 30 June 1941 with Molotov, Voroshilov, Malenkov and Beria as members, he was responsible for all major decisions, political and economic. The war almost erased the bitterness of the collectivization campaign and cemented relations between the party and the people. Except for occasional setbacks, the atmosphere was relaxed and free of the political terror which had prevailed before the war. Though the army leaders were allowed complete freedom about day-to-day military matters, the party's political control remained firm, if supple.

Victory, however, dissolved the unity which had held the Allies together. On the Russian side, despite Lend-Lease, enthusiasm for the Allies had never been very high. Stalin had met nothing but frustration in one of the major objectives of the wartime alliance – the opening of a second front by Britain and America. He argued that this would have diverted some thirty to forty German divisions from the Soviet front and saved Russia from bearing the whole brunt of the Nazi war effort. The second front, though promised in 1942, and again in 1943, actually did not materialize till 6 June 1944. By that time the Russians were already on their way to Berlin and Stalin always suspected that the delay was deliberate and that Churchill in particular wanted the Soviet Union to be bled by the Germans.

At the various conferences held by the Allied leaders, Stalin, Roosevelt and Churchill, during the war, at Teheran towards the end of 1943 and at Yalta in February 1945, the differences between them became visible. At the Potsdam Conference in July 1945, after the death of President Roosevelt, they became quite acute, with his successor, President Truman, in an aggressive mood. All this tended to make Stalin even more suspicious of the Allies. The seeds of the Cold War were sown at these gatherings. The differences were primarily about the East European countries, where the Russians wanted to establish regimes which were friendly and which would ensure Soviet security, while the West was interested in resurrecting old regimes, mostly hostile to the Soviet Union. But an added source of bitterness for Stalin was the abrupt termination of Lend-Lease for Russia by Truman immediately after the war in Europe had ended, just when Stalin was looking forward to using it for the mighty reconstruction of the economy which lay ahead. Even the U.S.

Secretary of State, Edward Stettinius, called it an 'untimely and incredible' measure. The differences continued to grow rapidly and brought about the Cold War which was to last till Stalin's death and after. Of course, Stalin was not blameless either because some of his policies had aggravated it.

The magnitude of the task of reconstruction was immense. The western half of European Russia, almost the whole of the Ukraine and Byelorussia were devastated. Twenty-five million people were homeless, nearly 2,000 towns and tens of thousands·of villages were destroyed. There was a shortage of men and materials. Stalin was now more determined than ever before that the Soviet Union must not remain backward industrially. He gave orders for the setting up of an ambitious fourth Five Year Plan and, in the perspective of fifteen years, talked of fantastic targets – 60 million tons of steel a year, 500 million tons of coal and 60 million tons of oil. In the event, the fourth Plan was over-fulfilled in most industrial sectors, and by 1960 even in steel, coal and oil the targets aimed by Stalin were surpassed. At the time, however, Stalin's figures sounded a wild exaggeration.

Reconstruction was not achieved without a price. The people, who looked forward to a relaxation of conditions after the war, had to tighten their belts again. By 1950, however, Soviet industrial structure was stronger than before the war and thus the Soviet Union could face the arms race, which was beginning, with greater confidence. A leading role in the successful execution of the Plan was played by Voznessensky, with his immense experience in running the war economy, but he, along with many others, was arrested in March 1949 on false charges and shot a little later.

There was no corresponding improvement in the agricultural sector and the lot of peasants continued to be as miserable as before the war. Reorganizations of agriculture continued, and one of these changes, amalgamation of smaller collective farms into larger ones, was largely carried out on the initiative of Khrushchev, who had been called to Moscow from his post as the Ukrainian party leader and Premier in 1949 and was emerging as one of Stalin's two important deputies as Secretary of the Central Committee. The other was Malenkov.

Another important element was influencing the policies of the Soviet leader. In all the East European countries, Communist regimes had come to power with Red Army support, except in Yugoslavia where the local party leader, Josip Broz Tito, had created his own splendid partisan movement and had come to power as the nationally acclaimed leader of his people. Stalin maintained a tight grip on his East European allies. As the Cold War sharpened, it became even more a fixed objective of Soviet foreign policy to preserve the rule of communism in these states so that they should act as a kind of protective barrier against the rest of Europe. This concern was further accentuated by the Anglo-American bid to rearm Western Germany as a defence against further Soviet expansion into Europe.

Stalin's quarrel with Tito, which broke out in 1948 and led to Yugoslavia's expulsion from the Communist camp, exacerbated the Cold War. Worried about ideological infection at home and in East European countries as well, Stalin went back to the conservative, hard-line policy of the pre-war days, complete with purges. Many East European leaders lost their lives, while the luckier ones spent a long time in prison, like the present Polish leader Gomulka. In the Soviet Union itself, those suspected of any opposition to the regime or its policies were terrorized and often liquidated. The heavy hand of persecution fell particularly severely upon Jewish elements in the party and Government ranks. They were accused of cosmopolitanism, of having contacts with the international Jewish community and being influenced by alien ideas. The establishment of the state of Israel, the obvious Jewish sympathy with the new state and the desire of many to emigrate there, as well as the fact that a large number of Jewish elements in the Soviet occupation forces in Germany deserted so as to be able to settle in Israel, lent some flimsy credibility to these measures.

Particularly harsh was the discipline imposed upon artists, intellectuals and writers by Zhdanov, the Central Committee Secretary in charge of ideological affairs. He was the unwavering propagator of the school of Socialist Realism in the arts and a warrior against formalism. He was also an enemy of objectivism in scholarly studies and one of the leading supporters of Lysenko, the biological charlatan. The mark of Zhdanovism is still felt in the Soviet arts and sciences, though Zhdanov died in 1948.

Another notable event of the last period of Stalin was the rise of Communist China under Mao. Stalin had not foreseen the success of the Communists in China and though he maintained, on the whole, correct relations with the new regime, it created new problems in the

89

sphere of foreign policy since China could not be subjected to the control which he exercised upon other Communists regimes in East Europe. The Korean war, a few years later, became another source of acute tension in international affairs. Stalin's persecution mania was scaling new heights now. By 1952–53 there were clear signs of a new purge in the offing and in December 1952 it was announced in the papers that, some time before, nine doctors had been arrested and accused of the murder of Zhdanov and of plotting to murder Stalin. Of the nine doctors, seven were of Jewish origin. They were tortured and 'confessed' to their crimes. Khrushchev later revealed that a bigger purge by Stalin was intended, to take care of the surviving members of the old guard such as Molotov, Mikoyan and Voroshilov. It has also been suggested that Beria was among those selected for liquidation; it is significant that he has never been accused of being connected with the 'Doctors' Plot', though a tendency has grown up lately to blame him for all the more hideous crimes of Stalin.

Whatever the truth, the purge never came to anything because Stalin died of a brain haemorrhage on 5 March 1953. It was the end of an epoch in the history of the Soviet Union and of the Communist movement. It was also a watershed in the history of the post-war world.

Stalin was a constructive monster. The image of his misdeeds, his bloody purges and totalitarian discipline has eclipsed his achievements in creating a modern, powerful state from a backward, primitive country. Stalin, the greatest falsifier of history, has also become a victim of falsification. The Soviet people can neither forget and forgive him, nor live comfortably with his memory.

Essentially, Stalin was a conservative whom circumstances threw up in a revolutionary milieu, and he became not only a leader but an exploiter of the Revolution. Morally his methods were thoroughly repugnant, but in retrospect he must be given credit for having had the right strategy. The contradiction between a revolutionary economic and social policy and reactionary political methods was the source of tension in Stalin's rule of the Soviet Union. This tension became all the greater because he brutalized the system of the one-party state to the maximum extent possible. He debased Marxism.

It will also not do to blame Stalin's lieutenants, such as Yagoda, Yezhov or Beria, for his misdeeds or praise them for his achievements.

That such a view is now being propagated in official historiography in the Soviet Union simply postpones the day when a fairer, if harsher, judgement will be delivered upon him.

The slick public-relations job done on behalf of her dead father by Svetlana Stalin (Alliluyeva), therefore, is at best a daughter's piety for her parent, at worst a perversion of history. He was a mean, vindictive man who, nevertheless, was instrumental in saving the Russian Revolution from dissipating itself or falling victim to external pressure. Stalin, in other words, was at once the tragedy and the salvation of the Revolution.

6 The Khrushchev phase

STALIN'S TIMELY DEATH saved the Soviet Union from another terrifying purge. But he was sincerely mourned by the people, for whom a landmark in their lives had disappeared. In a mood of intense grief mixed with relief and great anxiety about the future a vast crowd filed past him as he lay in state. Somehow it was symbolic of Stalin's blood-soaked rule that in the ensuing stampede many were killed. His body was placed in the mausoleum in Red Square by the side of Lenin.

On the same day, 7 March 1953, a new leadership was proclaimed, and Malenkov was appointed Chairman of the Council of Ministers as well as General Secretary of the Party. Within a week, however, he was relieved of the party post by the Central Committee. It was not till September that his rival for power, Nikita Khrushchev, was elected to the post of First Secretary. It signified the re-entry of the Central Committee of the Party as a decision-making body in the choice of leaders and in deciding upon major policies. The phrase 'collective leadership' became fashionable in the political vocabulary of the times.

One of the first acts of the new leaders was to announce, on 4 April 1953, that the Doctors' Plot was a fabrication from beginning to end. The confessions obtained from them were the result of torture. All the doctors were released, except two, who are presumed to have died from ill-treatment under arrest.

A most sensational development followed shortly afterwards. On 10 July 1953, the arrest of Beria was announced. He was charged with putting the Security Police above the law and beyond the control of the Party and government and with conspiring to seize power. Together with some of his close associates he was executed after a trial. The security Police were subsequently divided into a Ministry of Internal Affairs (MVD) and a Committee of State Security (KGB) and placed firmly under the control of the Party and the government. The terror was thus taken out of political life but some legacies persisted for a long time and fear did not entirely evaporate.

Momentous changes were to take place, affecting the very roots of Soviet life, though little sign of them was immediately evident. Just as Stalin's changes had been brought about from above, the changes by Khrushchev were also to be accomplished from above, though initially in this case they came about through genuinely collective decisions by the leaders. These internal developments also affected the course of Soviet foreign policy and her relations with the outside world. The changes came about not in any planned or systematic manner but often through force of circumstances, and their very haphazardness gave rise to much tension. Economics and agriculture became the primary concern of the leaders but their policies were affected by the struggle for power, which continued for some time even after Beria had been removed; for though Khrushchev remained in the ascendant for a long time, he was not entirely free from pressures from his colleagues and opponents as Stalin had been. Nevertheless, the decade after Stalin bore the distinct mark of Khrushchev.

To understand what happened it is necessary to see the situation as Stalin left it. This was a mixed heritage but altogether too powerful to be ignored. The Khrushchev period in Soviet history can be defined as one long attempt to come to terms with Stalin's legacy. That the problem remained unresolved even at the end of it was due as much as anything else to the weakness of efforts made in this direction.

The immediate task before Stalin's successors was to put the affairs of the Party in order and to reassert its supremacy over the government. This may sound paradoxical since Stalin always did things in the name of the Party. In fact, however, he was his own master and paid scant attention to the Party or to anything else. Party Congresses were not called for an excessively long time. The gap between the Eighteenth Party Congress and the Nineteenth which met in October 1952, and which was the last held under Stalin, was 13 years. The Central Committee met very infrequently and the Politburo, too, was given short shrift. Stalin also enhanced the authority of the government as a counterbalance to the Party.

Therefore, although membership of the Party had increased and it had become a mass Party, real power was in the hands of the responsible officials either in the Party or in the government. This, combined with centralization within the Party and its penetration of the government, fostered a bureaucratic approach in all matters. The paradox was that while the Party's power was in theory more widely diffused, it was nullified by the personal authority of Stalin. In other spheres, the Party's control was still rudimentary, particularly in agriculture, since organization of the Party in the countryside had not had the success expected of it.

It was not unnatural for the new leaders to seek popularity, and the economic policy which emerged at first was consumer-orientated. There was a need for urgent improvement in the quality as well as the quantity of consumer goods, for better housing and better services. The problem of the villages and agriculture was a headache in itself. But since leadership at the top had little time to become stable and a power struggle was still on, this kind of orientation itself became a matter of dispute at the highest level.

In the public mind Malenkov was identified with the new liberal policy. Retail price cuts were announced as early as 1st April 1953. The price cuts were no doubt welcome since they amounted to ten to fifteen per cent, but they made little sense when no increase in supply had taken place. A new black market sprang up to fill the gap between supply and demand. Other budgetary measures also increased the supply of money in the hands of the people. These measures were specifically taken by Malenkov and once he was ousted, they were not repeated.

Nevertheless, attempts were made to increase the supply of consumer goods and in 1953 the rate of increase in the production of consumer goods was faster than that in other goods. These measures rekindled the permanent debate about priorities between heavy goods and consumer goods, always lurking below the surface in Soviet economic policy decisions. This debate played some part in the removal of Malenkov from the post of Prime Minister on 8 February 1955, when Bulganin was elected by the Supreme Soviet to succeed him.

Khrushchev, meanwhile, had begun to concentrate on agriculture – his speciality. The revelations he made to a Central Committee plenum shortly after Malenkov had outlined his industrial policy to the

Supreme Soviet, about the shocking condition of Soviet agriculture as compared with the rosy pictures painted by Stalin, served several purposes. They brought agriculture into the focus of public attention, and also served as a pretext to attack some of the ministries concerned with agriculture, which were the responsibility of Malenkov. It was about this time, too, that Khrushchev launched the idea of ploughing up virgin lands on a big scale as a means of increasing food production, a scheme which played a substantial role in his rise to power. Above all, Khrushchev strengthened the role of the Party as against the government as a decision-making body.

Malenkov's authority primarily rested on the government apparatus. In his speech he did not attach great importance to the role and supremacy of the Party. Khrushchev, on the other hand, was at home within the Party and had experience of controlling its machinery. By lauding the Party Khrushchev was gathering support for himself. In this tactic he succeeded, as the subsequent demotion of Malenkov proved.

Khrushchev's espousal of the case for agricultural development brought him into conflict with Malenkov. Khrushchev balanced it by taking up the cause of heavy industry as well. In these manoeuvres he was helped by Malenkov's belief that with the acquisition of the hydrogen bomb Soviet defence expenditure need not be increased since the possession of the bomb by the two super-powers acted as a mutual deterrent. This was not a popular view with the army. Khrushchev opposed it too, thus gaining allies on a wide front in the Party and the government. The struggle for supremacy between him and Malenkov was barely concealed. In the end, Khrushchev proved to be the better tactician.

The changes in economic and agricultural policies were radical although hidden by old-fashioned arguments. Economic changes were accompanied by a general relaxation everywhere inside the country. Beria's apparatus of terror had been tamed after his fall and made subservient to the will of the Party. Many of the prisoners still languishing in Stalin's labour camps were released and declared innocent. This, too, created an air of expectancy.

During the short period of his ascendancy Malenkov also set a new tone in foreign policy, undoing some of Stalin's policies. He had to proceed cautiously at first, for not all the changes were to the liking of the old guard within the highest Party circles or inside the ranks of administration and Party officials. Although Khrushchev exploited this innate resistance to change in his struggle with Malenkov, his policies were in fact not so different. Having got rid of Malenkov, he was to adopt his policies wholesale and apply them cautiously. He only waited until his bases of power were secure within the Party and then gave his opponents a push which scattered them to far-away corners of the country and to the political wilderness.

In his Party post Khrushchev had not been idle. To one important post after another he brought his own nominees, many of them associated with him during his years of power in the Ukraine. With Malenkov's defeat in 1955, he was able to remove some influential people from the Party secretariat and this cleared his path to fill the Central Committee with reliable men who supported him. The army was not excluded from this process, and a number of generals, associated with Khrushchev in the Ukraine and elsewhere, were brought to the fore. Khrushchev himself made a tour of the length and breadth of the Soviet Union, which made his personality familiar to all and sundry, particularly Party officials, and his was a likeable personality.

By the time the first Party Congress after Stalin, the famous Twentieth Party Congress, came to be held in February 1956, Khrushchev had established his visible ascendancy, had brought about a degree of reconciliation with Yugoslavia, and by his travels to India, Afghanistan and Burma had projected a new image of Soviet foreign policy, of 'peaceful co-existence'. He was still, no doubt, worried about Malenkov but did not bring matters to a head.

For in the Twentieth Congress he was preparing a great shock and surprise for the Party and for the world. Everything else that happened at the Congress was obscured by one thing – the dethronement of Stalin. Mikoyan cast the first stone on the third day of the Congress, when he criticized Stalin by allusion. A week later, at a closed session where no foreign delegate was present, Khrushchev delivered his truly historic speech – a savage indictment of Stalin and his methods of purge. It stunned those present.

Giuseppe Boffa, at that time Moscow correspondent of the Italian Communist Party paper *L'Unità*, has described the effect it had on one of the Russian delegates. 'One of them told me later', Boffa wrote, 'that he ran home, took his skis, left the city, and wandered through the woods till late at night, trying to get tired, to be numb, and not to think at all. The next day he still hadn't recovered'.[1] Overnight, Stalin's body was removed from the Mausoleum.

The speech was never made public in the Soviet Union but its text became known to almost anyone who cared to know about it. At Party meetings it was widely publicized and explained. It was leaked to the outside world as well. By any standards the performance given by Khrushchev was a remarkable and courageous one, in many respects a foolhardy one too. If his enemies expected him to be damaged by it, they were not wrong but Khrushchev confounded them all by recovering and even deriving credit from it. There were no lights and shades in Khrushchev's denunciation of Stalin. The portrait he drew was one of unrelieved blackness, of a leader who was not only fallible but vicious in a personal way, callous in the extreme, and not even in command of his full faculties at the time of the gravest crisis in Russia's history, the invasion by the Nazis. The speech threw light on many murky and unsavoury chapters of Stalin's career. It revealed how Stalin became more and more 'capricious, irritable and brutal'. Many horrific details of the way Stalin treated some of the leading members of the Party came out for the first time. Khrushchev also insisted that, had Stalin not died when he did, people like Molotov and Mikoyan would probably not have survived. The pattern which clearly emerged from this speech was one of Stalin's insane jealousy for any old Bolshevik.

Postyshev's famous retort to Stalin who asked him, 'What are you actually?' – 'I am a Bolshevik, Comrade Stalin, a Bolshevik' – and for which he paid with his life, showed this clearly. In his speech Khrushchev commented, 'This assertion was at first considered to show a lack of respect for Stalin; later it was considered a harmful act and consequently resulted in Postyshev's annihilation and branding without any reason as a 'people's enemy'.[2]

Elsewhere in the speech Khrushchev made the significant assertion about Stalin that, possessing unlimited power, 'he indulged in great wilfulness and choked a person morally and physically. A situation was created where one could not express one's own will'.[3]

Strong as the indictment was, it was only partial. By and large Khrushchev dealt mostly with the cases of Stalin's crimes against the Party members. He left the issue of broader mass terror aside. Even in condemning Stalin's actions against Party members, he gave the unmistakable impression that the condemnation did not include action against such prominent opponents of Stalin as Trotsky, Bukharin and Kamenev, who had been hounded to death.

Though the speech made a great impact at the time, it soon became evident that the exposure of Stalin was one-sided and partly even unfair. Even so, it set the tone of the succeeding unsatisfactory post-Stalin period. Its consequences for the Soviet Union were staggering. The framework which Khrushchev laid down in 1956 is the one within which the Soviet Party still functions though naturally some changes have taken place, progressive as well as retrogressive.

Even before the Congress, a quiet process of rehabilitation had been going on. Some of the survivors were drifting back from the camps to which Stalin had relegated them. After the Twentieth Congress the process became accelerated and the tempest unleashed by de-Stalinization became deeper though on the surface there was not much to show.

Khrushchev's speech was no spontaneous outburst. It was a deliberate political choice, audacious as well as necessary. He admitted later that something like a fever swept the communist countries, including the Soviet Union, but insisted that 'it had to be done'. Of course, Khrushchev was not striving to arrive at an objective historical judgement about the role of Stalin in Soviet history. He was using anti-Stalinism to bring some sanity, some security to the tortured masses and to explode their mystical belief that Stalin was *sans reproche* despite all that had happened. He was also trying to gain popularity for himself and refurbish the image of the Party.

In the autumn, the storm broke on the western flank of the Soviet Union. First in Poland and then in Hungary the people took de-Stalinization as a signal to undermine the Communist rule which had been imposed upon them during the war. The Party leaders there had generally been even more Stalinist than Stalin himself and were extremely unpopular. The Russians were worried on two counts. They feared that these countries would break away from the Communist camp altogether. They were also worried that this defiance might prove infectious and encourage people at home to challenge the authority of the Party. These events, moreover, threatened Khrushchev's position as a leader.

His response was characteristic. On 19 October 1956, he descended on Warsaw accompanied by Molotov and Kaganovich. The Central Committee of the Polish Party was about to meet to demand the removal of Marshal Rokossovsky, a Soviet citizen but Defence Minister of Poland since 1949. It also wanted to elect Gomulka as the new party leader. Khrushchev threatened and cajoled but the Poles did not give way. They got away with it partly because they showed impressive imperturbability in the face of Moscow's threats to use force, partly because on 23 October the Hungarian revolt flared up and this was more serious for the Russians. The Soviet leaders had no option but to intervene unless they were prepared for the disintegration of Eastern Europe as their sphere of influence. The Western powers tacitly recognized this and refrained from any intervention in Hungary, although a tremendous fanfare of abuse and invective was unleashed against Khrushchev in particular. Curiously enough, the upshot was to establish the Communist regimes in Poland and Hungary on a firmer basis and even make them acceptable to the people.

The events provided the anti-Khrushchev elements within the Soviet leadership with a chance to rally against him. The showdown came in June 1957. At a meeting of the Presidium on 18 June Molotov launched an attack on Khrushchev and had the support of the majority of the members. It would have been the end of Khrushchev but for the fact that he prevailed in calling a meeting of the Central Committee to decide the issue of leadership. The Central Committee was packed with Khrushchev's men. Khrushchev also received help from the military, Defence Minister Marshal Zhukov being particularly active in bringing Central Committee members to Moscow in army planes from all over the country. The plenum began on 22 June and the whole issue was bitterly argued for days. On 4 July it was announced that Molotov, Malenkov, Kaganovich and Shepilov had been removed from their posts and expelled from the Central Committee. Other anti-Khrushchev leaders like Bulganin, Voroshilov and Pervukhin still retained their government and Party posts but eventually retired. Khrushchev had won against heavy odds.

In one sense the victory of Khrushchev made little practical difference. Even before it, he had been strong enough to push through some of his agricultural reforms. He was admittedly more constrained in the industrial sphere but such constraint as there was, was removed now. Khrushchev, however, never intended to return to the orthodox Stalinist methods in either case. As for the consumer goods versus capital goods controversy, Khrushchev revived ideas propounded by

Malenkov. More consumer goods had become not only a political but an economic necessity.

In the sphere of agriculture Khrushchev's policy went through several stages and ultimately led to his downfall. Nonetheless, as a result of his innovations the Party began to take the problem of agriculture seriously for the first time. The importance of this should not be minimized. Khrushchev's policies were not a total failure, as was made out after his fall. Indeed, during his first years they were quite successful.

To go back a little, Khrushchev had started off by increasing the prices for compulsory procurement and over-quota deliveries of agricultural goods. These affected grain, potatoes, vegetables, meat, dairy produce and sunflower seed, the last an important source of cooking oil. This was accompanied by a reduction in procurement quotas so the farms were paid the higher over-quota price for a greater proportion of their sales to the state. At the same time a variety of other material concessions were made to the collective farms, which helped to improve their finances and incentives. A new liberal policy towards the private plots of the farmers was also followed, allowing them to sell produce for their own profit, and thus inducing them to produce more.

Much more important for agriculture was provision for greater output of tractors and other machinery as well as availability of more building materials. This was accompanied by the enforcement of greater discipline so that the farmers did not spend an undue proportion of their time on their own plots, neglecting the collective land.

The most important changes were made in the organization of the Machine Tractor Stations upon which the farms depended for their machinery. The Machine Tractor Stations (MTS) were the hiring agents for farm machinery as well as means of political control over the farms. To begin with, the quality of their service was improved. In 1958, after the fall of Malenkov, when Khrushchev began to implement his ideas on agriculture even more vigorously, the MTS were abolished. In 1958 also a new uniform price structure for procurement was introduced, with zonal variations, and this did away with the bad effects of two levels of prices, for quota delivery and over-quota delivery, which left the poor farms poor and made the rich farms richer.

As a consequence of these reforms agricultural output rose considerably between 1954 and 1958. An important contribution to this rise in output was made by bringing under cultivation virgin and fallow land in northern Kazakhstan, the southern parts of Siberia and parts of European Russia. It is estimated by Alec Nove that between 1953 and 1956 the area of cultivated land was increased by 35·9 million hectares, an area equivalent to the total cultivated land of Canada. This was done by mobilizing the young people to go and settle there or to give free time to cope with harvests. It became a tremendous campaign. Most of the newly cultivated land was turned into state farms. Nove comments: 'World history knows nothing like it.'[4]

Much was also done to bring some order into the structure of wages and prices. Social services were reorganized and vastly expanded. In May 1955 a State Committee on Labour and Wages was set up. It thoroughly revised the wages structure, laid down standard pay scales and reduced differentials, abandoned incentive schemes which involved very high payments. Above all it severely modified the excessive reliance on piece-rate methods of payment in industry. The reforms went on throughout the Khrushchev period and one of the Committee's main achievements was to fix minimum wages. As a result the low-paid workers gained.

There were many improvements in social benefits, too. The working week was reduced, working hours per day were cut to seven, paid maternity leave was prolonged to 112 days, tuition fees in secondary and higher institutions were abolished, criminal laws against changing jobs and absenteeism were repealed and great improvement in pensions was decreed, with a minimum of 300 old roubles (30 new roubles) per month. Most important of all, a great drive for an increase in housing construction was launched which had visible effect within two years. This drive has continued ever since on an intensive scale. The prices of foodstuffs as well as wholesale industrial prices were lowered, but prices of potatoes and vegetables were increased since they were ridiculously and unrealistically low.

Expansion and improvement in education and health services took place on an impressive scale. Emphasis was placed on training more teachers and opening new schools. There was a reduction in the cost of medicines and efforts to provide hospitals with more equipment, though the standard of hospital services continued to be rather poor on the whole where amenities were concerned.

The symbol of Soviet success and scientific achievement was the launching of the first Sputnik on 4 October 1957. In the outside world it rehabilitated the reputation of Soviet science and created confidence in Soviet technology. Even otherwise, industrial achievement during this period was impressive as a whole. But despite these successes troubles were piling up for Khrushchev on the industrial and, where it hurt most, on the agricultural front.

He was not wholly to blame. He had inherited a cumbersome planning system from Stalin which was overcentralized, allowed little scope for day-to-day decisions by the local factories, and was exclusively geared to quantity rather than quality. For instance, steel plants would not accept orders for thin sheets since it was more conducive to plan fulfilment to produce heavy sheets. Besides, the planners themselves were often in the dark about what was available and what was possible. Therefore, their plans were based on what was required rather than on what was capable of achievement. Moreover, planning had become complex since it was no longer orientated merely to produce heavy goods at all costs but had to take the requirement of consumer goods, housing, education and other needs seriously. Bureaucracy flourished; the economy suffered.

Khrushchev railed against this bureaucracy. He introduced a number of new organizational reforms designed to combat it. They only produced more bureaucracy, more paper work and defeated the very purposes for which they were designed. A great deal of the trouble also came from the multiplication of these measures, which Khrushchev often introduced without deep analysis or proper perspective. The changes were far too many to be listed here.

In agriculture, the main trouble was that too much was sacrificed for short-term advantage and the defects of too many changes, too frequently made, told upon production. The new *Communist Party History* published early in 1970 blamed Khrushchev for too much subjectivism, too much neglect of expert advice. It declared, 'he thought that to improve the conditions of agriculture, organizational and administrative measures would suffice, that it was only necessary to change the structure of agricultural organs.'[5] Thus, though Khrushchev sought to release the farms from the burdens of the past, he did not pay sufficient heed to their vital requirements. In 1963, because of extremely bad weather, the crop was well below the level of 1958. This caused widespread discontent and anger against

Khrushchev and led ultimately to his fall. Ironically enough the crop in 1964, the year he went out of power, was one of the best in history, but it came too late to help him politically.

The domestic scene was not the only one which changed rapidly during this period. Even more remarkable was the transformation which took place in Soviet relations with the outside world, with China, with America and with the southern Asian and Arab countries and the ex-colonial world in general. The first signs of this change came soon after the death of Stalin when in August 1953 Malenkov, as Prime Minister, inaugurated a new foreign policy and made friendly gestures towards Turkey, giving up all the territorial claims against her made by Stalin. Similar gestures were also made towards Iran and India and even towards the west. The tone was surprisingly mild and conciliatory. Far more interesting was the gesture for contacts with Yugoslavia, a heretic outcast from the Communist camp.

The rising in East Berlin in June 1953, which had to be crushed by Soviet troops, was an ample warning of the disastrous state of affairs in Eastern Europe. Without much fanfare the burdens imposed on the East European countries during Stalin's time were gradually lightened. There were important changes in relations with Peking. Instead of being treated with cool detachment, as they were by Stalin, the Chinese leaders were now courted and steps taken to provide China with more aid. Closer and warmer ties were forged. Meanwhile, with Russian encouragement an armistice to end the Korean war was signed in July.

Towards the USA the feeling was still ambivalent. The Soviet outlook on Europe was dominated by the unsolved German question. When the Federal Republic of Germany joined the North Atlantic Treaty Organization in 1954, Moscow was alarmed. The Russians were also disturbed by the fact that though the newly elected Republican administration in America came to terms with the Communist powers to bring an end to the war in Korea, it was militantly anti-Soviet in Europe. John Foster Dulles, the American Secretary of State, constantly emitted blood-curdling cries of a holy war against communism. Whether these frightened Moscow or not, they certainly frightened the West European countries, which did not want to embark on such an extreme course. Britain and France, the two leading European countries, were also rather preoccupied at the time with the problems of decolonization.

The Soviet response was to organize the Warsaw Pact, consisting of all the East European countries, but real decision-making remained safely in the hands of Moscow. The Russians, however, were unable to prevent the rearmament of West Germany. One consequence was that the division of Germany into two states became more or less permanent and tacitly recognized as such. Both sides waxed eloquent about the unity of Germany but no one was seriously interested, least of all the West German Chancellor Konrad Adenauer.

Foreign Ministers of the big powers met to discuss the German problem, Berlin and Indo-China. There were summit conferences galore. Khrushchev had meetings with Presidents Eisenhower and Kennedy. There was plenty of hustle and bustle on the diplomatic front throughout the decade of Khrushchev's stewardship of the Soviet Union. But though it contributed to an easing of tension, to greater and freer trade between the communist and non-communist countries, it established clearly that the Soviet Union and the United States were competing powers, not complementary allies. Whenever a political crisis arose, the two big powers were on the opposite sides of the fence.

One exception was in 1956, when Britain, France and Israel invaded Egypt after President Nasser had nationalized the Suez Canal as a reply to the provocative American reversal of their decision to help with the construction of the Aswan Dam. The Russians went all out to back him diplomatically and financially. The crisis provided the Soviet Union with a tremendous opportunity in the Middle East. The Suez crisis, however, underlined the fact, which was reinforced by the Hungarian crisis, that though the two super-powers could glower at each other, the new balance of forces established by possession of nuclear weapons ensured that they were not willing to rush to a head-on clash.

Though the Americans disapproved of the invading countries and co-operated diplomatically with the Soviet Union in the United Nations, it was only for tactical reasons. The same lesson can be drawn from the outcome of the Cuban crisis in 1962, a far more serious affair, when Washington strongly objected to construction of Soviet missile bases in Cuba, challenged Moscow to withdraw or face destruction of the island at least, and won. The Russians dismantled their bases. This episode also eroded the authority of Khrushchev at home.

Khrushchev's most serious foreign policy problem was not America but China. After a honeymoon period following the death of Stalin, relations between the two countries began to deteriorate. The reasons were partly ideological, partly practical. The Chinese looked askance at new liberal trends in East Europe as well as in the Soviet Union. They wanted priority for their needs at the expense of a better standard of living in the older communist countries. They also wanted a share in the nuclear technology and co-ordination of foreign policies to suit the Chinese viewpoint. In effect, they were seeking a permanent veto over Soviet policies, domestic as well as foreign.

No Soviet leader could have agreed to it. Khrushchev certainly did not. At first the dispute was kept hidden and Khrushchev tried his best to keep it so. To settle these differences on the ideological plane, gatherings of all the communist parties were held in Moscow in 1957 and 1960 from which the Yugoslavs were excluded at Chinese insistence. Khrushchev agreed to their exclusion as the price for the appeasement of China. He himself made a visit to Peking in July 1958 to talk things over with Mao Tse-tung. Mao only lectured him on his incorrect ideological perspective. He went to Peking again in October 1959 after his visit to the United States and talks with President Eisenhower at Camp David. This only confirmed the Chinese in their opposition to his policies.

In 1960–61 the Soviet Union withdrew its technicians and stopped project aid to China. When Khrushchev attacked the Chinese in June 1960 at the Rumanian Party Congress in Bucharest the dispute came out into the open and although for some more time the two sides continued to use Albania and Yugoslavia as proxies in their polemical battle, the illusion could not be kept long. The walk-out of the Chinese Prime Minister Chou En-lai from the Twenty-Second Congress of the Soviet Communist Party in October 1961, after an open clash with Khrushchev on the question of Albania, made it clear that the schism was no longer containable.

By 1963 the split had become irrevocable, the Chinese charging the Russians with denouncing the technical assistance agreement signed in 1957 and refusing in 1959 to hand over samples of an atomic bomb. They introduced new elements in the dispute – claims over vast tracts of Soviet territory in the Far Eastern region on the ground that they were taken over by Tsarist Russia under 'unequal treaties'. The Chinese were also about to explode their first atomic bomb and this made them even more intransigent. It was in these circumstances that Khrushchev conceived the idea of another international communist conference. The objective he had in view was to secure a condemnation of the Chinese from the movement as a whole and thus not only prove the hegemony of Moscow over the world communist parties but also to cast out Peking from the communist fraternity. The particular target of Soviet polemical attacks was Mao Tse-tung, whom the Russians held solely responsible for the breach. A preparatory meeting was fixed for 15 December 1964.

Khrushchev, however, met with resistance from the communist parties on a wide scale. Some of them like Rumania and, of course, China and Albania, simply refused to attend. Others put forward objections of their own. A dispute between Peking and Moscow enlarged their area of freedom but they were loth to push the schism to such a point that they had to choose between the two in an irrevocable way.

Thus the politics of the Sino-Soviet dispute up to the fall of Khrushchev was to a certain extent dominated by the issue of the conference. The Chinese derived immense satisfaction from the fact that Moscow's call was being resisted so widely and so strongly. Peking was also encouraged by splits in many communist parties, which the Chinese did their best to foster. In most non-ruling parties pro-Chinese factions formed and in some cases broke away to set up rival communist parties of their own. Khrushchev's tactics of rushing headlong into a collision with China looked like misfiring though the matter was not put to a final test because the reins of leadership were taken away from him before the scheduled date of the preparatory meeting.

Frustration in the quarrel with China, frustration in making any advance in solving European problems, and mounting disappointment and resentment at home eventually convinced Khrushchev's colleagues that he had better go. At the Twenty-First Party Congress in January 1959 he had outlined a programme of economic construction which he claimed would bring the Soviet Union on a par with the United States in gross and per capita production. The claim was too wild and the delegates to the congress knew it. In the event, the economy took a turn for the worse. Scarcity of meat and other food products was growing and their prices were raised to cut down demand. These measures were universally unpopular.

Personal factors also worked against him. He was getting old, seventy in April 1964, impatient, irritable and impossible to work with. Personal whims and obsessions now ruled him more than anything else and he began neglecting, even offending, his colleagues and influential sections of the Central Committee. Early in October he was persuaded to go on a holiday to the Black Sea coast. On 13 October he was called for an urgent Praesidium meeting in Moscow. He had little inkling that it was to ask for his resignation. They accused him of gross incompetence in dealing with the economy and particularly with agriculture. Khrushchev insisted the Central Committee should decide the matter and defended himself angrily and vehemently.

The Central Committee members were, however, won over to the side of his opponents. When it met, the verdict against Khrushchev was confirmed and the next day it was announced that Khrushchev's resignation on grounds of ill-health had been accepted by the Central Committee. Leonid Brezhnev was elected the new First Secretary of the Party and Alexei Kosygin was appointed Prime Minister. Once again the two posts, leadership of the Party and leadership of the government, were separated. There was no new upheaval, only a move to tidy up the mess which Khrushchev had made.

The faults of Khrushchev were many and enormous. He was irresponsible in a way few political leaders ever could be. But the deceptive ease with which he carried out his historic task obscures just how dangerous it was. The people cursed him for the temporary shortage of daily necessities, forgetting that under Stalin these conditions were permanent. In a sense Khrushchev was the victim of rising expectations, which he had himself done so much to encourage by his foolhardy talk of overtaking America.

Another important factor in his unpopularity with his own countrymen was his inability to cope with the intelligentsia. He offended the scientists by continuing to provide protection and support for the charlatan-biologist Lysenko. He offended the writers, painters and artists by his ignorance and by his crude methods of disciplining them when such discipline was neither necessary nor desirable. The truth was that even though he dethroned Stalin from his pedestal, he could not totally disassociate himself from all that had gone before. The hangover from Stalinism thus reduced the force of de-Stalinization. This was his personal tragedy as well as a national one.

One thing is certain. We still live too close to the Khrushchev period to be able to put his shortcomings and achievements into perspective. Future historians may give him higher marks for his services to the Soviet Union than is currently fashionable. And yet it is a measure of Nikita Khrushchev's political accomplishment that he, and countless others on a lower level, are living in comfortable retirement, serenely watching the sunset of their lives without fear. This is the difference between the Stalin period and the Khrushchev phase, for which he cannot be too greatly praised.

7 The post-Khrushchev period

TO THE VAST MAJORITY of the Soviet people from all walks of life the fall of Khrushchev came as a welcome relief. This astonished a disbelieving world outside, bemused by the personality of Khrushchev, but for the Soviet people he had become a leader who had failed to deliver the goods. The successors of Khrushchev were not thinking in terms of any radical departure from his basic policies; they simply wanted a more effective way of dealing with the problems which had accumulated. The new watchwords in conceiving and executing any policy were 'efficiency' and 'businesslike'.

One of the immediate tasks for the new leaders was to allay misgivings caused by the removal of Khrushchev and to mollify the feelings of many of the foreign Communist Parties who were highly critical of the manner in which he was dismissed. Many of the East and West European Communist Party leaders made a beeline to Moscow to find out what had happened behind the scenes and why. They were all perturbed to a greater or lesser extent, and some of them even issued official statements expressing their 'surprise and emotion' at his removal. The Chinese congratulated themselves and the new leaders, while the Albanians openly rejoiced at his fall, believing that the new leaders would modify their ideological approach to suit them. They were mistaken.

At a rally in the Red Square on 19 October in honour of the three Soviet cosmonauts who had together orbited the earth in the spaceship Voskhod (Sunrise), Brezhnev took the opportunity to assert publicly that Soviet policies would remain unchanged and would be based on the principle of peaceful co-existence. But he pointedly asserted that the Party would follow the course of 'collective leadership'. This was an indirect attack on Khrushchev who had wielded power in his later years with complete disregard to the sensibilities of his colleagues. The latest official history of the CPSU has since revealed that the October Plenum of the Central Committee which removed Khrushchev took a formal decision that in future the posts of Prime Minister and General Secretary of the Party should not be held by one person.[1]

The only major initiative in the foreign policy field taken by the new leaders was to seek a rapprochement with China. Chou En-lai, the Chinese Prime Minister, visited Moscow to attend the October Anniversary celebrations which came conveniently soon after on 7 November. With his every gesture he conveyed the impression of having come as a conqueror, a twentieth-century Chingiz Khan taking the measure of the Kremlin leaders. He sat through Brezhnev's policy speech at the Palace of Congresses looking bored and listless. The Russians were not willing to surrender their ideology and national interests to China, but they were reconciled to a peaceful co-existence with Peking, as perhaps Khrushchev was not. Chou's visit, therefore, came to nothing. Another attempt was made by Kosygin when he made two calls in Peking on his way to Hanoi and Pyongyang in February 1965 and had conversations with Chou and a meeting with Mao Tse-tung. But the Chinese remained irreconcilable. The new leaders in Moscow, however, put an end to the polemic against China in their press even though Peking papers and radio continued to make bitter attacks on them for being heirs of Khrushchevism and revisionists.

But generally in the first year the new leaders focused their attention on internal developments. Their first step was to change the haphazard system of party organization which Khrushchev had introduced. Within a month of their assuming power the party units were reorganized on a territorial basis, instead of being divided into agricultural and industrial branches. This move had the additional merit of appealing to party officials at all levels who had found the Khrushchev system chaotic. It was rather symbolic of the mood of restoration which was beginning to prevail.

The next important step was taken in the agricultural sphere. Agriculture was suffering from a number of chronic maladies. It was not exactly neglected during the Khrushchev era but the remedies applied were unsystematic. Indeed, Khrushchev himself was dedicated in his own way to improving the overall lot of the peasants, but he failed to understand the magnitude of the problem. Between 1959 and 1964 grain production increased by only ten per cent.

At a Central Committee Plenum held in March 1965 a number of measures were announced to improve agricultural performance. The most important of these was a vast increase in capital investment in agriculture, in State farms as well as collective farms. Another large sum was also set aside for the construction of farm premises and purchase of agricultural machinery. Some reforms were promised for a later date but in fact were quickly carried out, such as writing off the agricultural debt of the collective farms and changing the tax basis for them. State purchase prices of grain were increased and about six weeks later the purchase price of meat was also raised. Thus agriculture as a vocation was made materially more rewarding. It was also acknowledged by the leaders that much needed to be done to improve the material welfare of farmers and farm labourers.

The need for reforms was even more pressing in the industrial sector. In January 1965 the Soviet Government decided to go ahead with an experiment started during the last few months of Khrushchev's power. It announced that four hundred factories, mainly in the consumer goods sphere, would switch over to a system of production, based on meeting public demand and not solely upon directives of the planners. The profit made would be used to give bonuses to workers, thus there was a direct link between the bonus given and the profit earned.

More comprehensive reforms of an organizational nature followed towards the end of the year. The Regional Economic Councils established by Khrushchev were abolished and industrial ministries re-established. The original idea behind abolishing the ministries was that they had turned into self-contained entities, disregarding the broader interests of the economy. But the Regional Councils did not live up to the expectations because they in turn became territorial economic entities. The Central Committee resolution, passed at a Plenum held in September, explained that, 'although management of industry based on the territorial principle somewhat broadened the possibilities for inter-branch specialization and co-ordination in industrial production within the confines of economic areas, it has impeded the development of branch specialization and of rational industrial links between enterprises situated in different economic areas'.

The main problem was, of course, to find a correct balance between a centrally planned economy and local initiative.

Other important organizational changes were the abolition of the Supreme Council of the National Economy and the Republican and Regional Economic Councils. Their place was taken by the State Planning Commission under the chairmanship of Nikolai Baibakov, with the rank of a Deputy Prime Minister. These organizational measures, combined with others, and efforts to introduce some measure of autonomy at enterprise level were believed to contain the key to successful rationalization of the whole economy, including agriculture.

The atmosphere of these early days was on the whole optimistic, relaxed and sober. It appeared that the country was undergoing a renovation and the people were having a well deserved rest after the dizziness of the Khrushchev spell. At the political level, too, there was no victimization. A few people in influential posts, who were close to Khrushchev, were quietly demoted to unimportant posts. Some, like Baibakov and the agriculture Minister Matskevitch, who had earned the displeasure of Khrushchev, were brought back to perform important tasks. Other more obnoxious elements of the past, like the notorious Lysenko, were also speedily relegated to limbo without much fuss.

Moreover, to wipe out any lingering affection which there might have been for Khrushchev, the new leaders took several popular measures immediately. For the peasants the most beneficial was the lifting of restrictions on the size of their private plots, imposed by Khrushchev in 1961–62. Flour, which had not been obtainable during the last months of Khrushchev, was made available retail in big cities. Even the non-conformist writers and artists were assured of being left alone (they had felt particularly aggrieved and outraged by the attacks Khrushchev had made on them in 1963) but this lasted only a few months.

Soon a tendency towards a hardening of the ideological line became noticeable. It was partly a reaction against the methods of de-Stalinization which Khrushchev had used and which had become discredited, and it was partly due to a widespread feeling among party officials that the arts were getting out of control and must be brought within an acceptable ideological framework. The conservatives, who had never reconciled themselves to the liberals or the way in which the liberal writers were left alone after the advent of new leaders, were waiting for an opportunity to reassert themselves. The only person in a position of authority who spoke up for a liberal attitude towards the arts was the editor of *Pravda*, A. M. Rumyantsev, appointed after the fall of Khrushchev. On 21 February 1965, he wrote a long article in *Pravda* declaring that artistic creation is possible only in an atmosphere of research, experimentation, free expression and the clash of opinions, that science, literature and arts demand the existence of different schools and tendencies and that their development could not be stimulated to order or by bureaucratic control. He returned again to the theme, but in a more cautious manner, in September. Within a fortnight he was replaced by another editor much to the pleasure of the conservatives.

The conservative cause had another unexpected windfall about the same time. Two Soviet writers in Moscow were arrested a few days after the publication of Rumyantsev's last article. Andrey Sinyavsky, a writer and literary critic, and Yuli Daniel, a translator, were charged with publishing their writings abroad under the pseudonyms of Abram Tertz and Nikolai Arzhak. These writings were regarded as 'anti-Soviet'. The news of their arrest soon leaked out and stirred up protests on their behalf. The authorities hesitated for several months but eventually decided to put them on trial to make an example of them to other dissident writers. The reaction abroad and the great fuss made about the matter probably contributed to the stubbornness of the authorities.

The trial, which took place in February 1966, inevitably became a *cause célèbre* and did great harm to the Soviet prestige in the world. For one thing, it discredited the liberalism which had been evident after the new leaders took over. The conduct of the trial itself was not of a manner to inspire confidence abroad. The substance of the matter was perceptively summed up by the British Communist Party leader John Gollan who wrote in *The Daily Worker*:

The atmosphere created by comments in the Soviet press before the trial, and its reports of the trial itself, have played into the hands of anti-Soviet elements in the West. The Soviet press attacks on the accused before the trial assumed their guilt. So did the TASS version of what went on in court. Since no full and objective version of the proceedings of the trial has appeared, outside opinion cannot form a proper judgement. The accused have been found guilty, but the full evidence for the prosecution and the defence which led the court to their condemnation has not been made public. Justice should not only be done, it should be seen to be done. Unfortunately this cannot be said of this trial. The handling of this affair has done a greater disservice to the Soviet Union than have the works of Sinyavsky and Daniel which in any case were not widely known . . . until they were given prominence by the Soviet press attacks on them. Many who sincerely wish the Soviet Union well, will look on this episode and its consequences with deep concern.[2]

In so far as Sinyavsky was a well-known and respected figure in Soviet literary circles, whose literary criticism regularly appeared in the liberal monthly *Novy Mir*, it enabled the conservatives to insinuate that the whole of the liberal section of the writers were guilty of such 'mental treason'. The passionate protests made on behalf of the two sentenced writers by many well known figures in Soviet literary and academic circles, the letters addressed to the Central Committee and the Party leaders were ignored in the face of the conservative campaign to discredit and discipline the liberal wing.

The resurgence of conservatism was not confined to the arts alone. In the political field it soon became visible as the process of de-Stalinization came to a halt. There was not in any sense a rehabilitation of Stalin but more and more stress was now laid on the favourable aspects of Stalin and his unsavoury aspects were increasingly ignored. There were no more disclosures about the purges and no official encouragement was given to anti-personality-cult writings. On the contrary, all such literature produced during the Khrushchev phase came under attack. Above all, emphasis shifted to the constructive aspects of the Stalin period, in which the Party and its deeds appeared correct and were glorified. This was a process favoured by the Party officers but it aroused resistance among the intelligentsia because they were afraid that it would lead to re-Stalinization, to the full-scale rehabilitation of the dead monster, and all the consequences which would follow from such an ideological recognition.

Many believed that the formal rehabilitation would take place at the Twenty-third Party Congress which was to be held towards the end of March 1966. On the eve of the Congress, some of the foremost scientists, writers and intellectuals in the Soviet Union addressed a letter to Brezhnev in which they expressed their anxiety at these trends and warned that, 'We believe that any attempt to whitewash Stalin involves a threat of serious strife within Soviet society . . . No explanation or articles will induce the people to believe in Stalin. They will, on the contrary, only foster anger and disorder.'[3] The Twenty-third Party Congress, however, did not discuss the matter and although no overt attempt was made there to glorify Stalin, there was no criticism either.

Altogether the Twenty-third Congress turned out to be a tame affair with no new departures in any direction. It served to confirm, however, that within the collective leadership the balance of forces had been stabilized and that political upheavals at the leadership level were most unlikely. The Congress also gave an unmistakable impression that the political climate favoured conservatism at the expense of the liberals. Neither Alexander Tvardovsky, editor of *Novy Mir* and a prominent representative of the liberal wing, nor Vsevolod Kochetov, editor of *Oktyabr* and a militant conservative, were elected members of the new Central Committee. But while no liberal writer took the place of Tvardovsky, Kochetov's place was taken up by G. Markov, an even harsher critic of the liberals. However, it made little immediate practical difference to the arts because after the Congress both major sectors of the writers and artists went their own way and *Novy Mir* continued to publish the more restrained of the creative liberal works. An uneasy truce prevailed.

Amidst all these preoccupations on the home front, foreign policy took a back seat. But a world power like the Soviet Union can no more keep itself aloof from international complications than the small nations can avoid pressures from the big powers. Although in theory there was no departure from Khrushchev's foreign policy, in practice there were perceptible changes, in substance as well as style. The changed context in which the Soviet Union's policy makers had to operate also hastened this process. Khrushchev had started off by making as many friends as he could when the choice was not a very wide one. Therefore, during his period the Soviet commitment to the non-aligned countries of Asia and Africa was a militant one.

With the abatement of the Cold War, Moscow now felt the need for a wider rapprochement with its neighbours, irrespective of their ideology. There was also the urgent need for checking growing Chinese influence. Therefore, a quiet strategy of withdrawal from over-commitment in areas which did not directly affect the Soviet interests was put into operation. The biggest test for this policy came when, in the autumn of 1965, fighting broke out between India and Pakistan. Khrushchev had been committed to the support of India on Kashmir, the ostensible cause of fighting, but the Russians now adopted an attitude of careful neutrality on the substance of the issue, without making India feel that they had let her down. This increased Pakistani confidence in the Soviet's good intentions. Even before the fighting there were signs of warm ties having been established between the Pakistani leader Field-Marshal Ayub Khan and the Soviet leaders.

In the stalemate which followed the bitter but short war, both the countries found the Soviet offer of a joint conference at Tashkent, the capital of Uzbekistan, a convenient way out. The meeting opened on 4 January 1966, presided over by Prime Minister Kosygin, who gave a performance of suave, brilliant diplomatic skill and patience in persuading the two antagonists to come to terms. The Tashkent Declaration signed on 10 January enabled the two countries to retreat gracefully from untenable positions they had taken up and it even raised hopes for an eventual rapprochement between them, though these were disappointed. The Tashkent conference was, above all, a singular triumph of Soviet diplomacy and prestige. It was a culmination of a stage in her policy towards newly liberated Asia and it unmistakably underlined the fact that Soviet influence in Asia could no longer be ignored. True, the conference did not succeed in resolving the basic Indo-Pakistani differences and their relations remained very cool, but it defused a great crisis, frustrated Chinese manoeuvres towards encouraging Pakistan and India to fight to the bitter end and effectively demonstrated that despite their great involvement with the Indian sub-continent, neither Britain nor America was in a position to prevent a disaster there since they had forfeited the goodwill and trust of both sides by their overt or covert partisanship. The Russians reaped the reward. Soviet diplomatic gains, however, were qualified to some extent because Pakistan did not entirely move away from China and when, after the enforced resignation of Ayub Khan, General Yahya Khan succeeded him, he reverted to even closer contacts with China. In India, too, growing Soviet ties with Pakistan caused irritation and suspicion, and put some strain on officially friendly relations between Moscow and New Delhi.

Nevertheless, the Tashkent Conference remained a highwater mark of Soviet diplomacy in Asia. On the eve of the conference Sukarno had been overthrown, preceded by an unsuccessful Communist attempt at a coup d'état. This was a set-back for Moscow inasmuch as for nearly a decade the Russians had cultivated Sukarno and poured a vast amount of aid into Indonesia. Even before the fall of Sukarno, Moscow had become disenchanted with his policies because most of the aid was wasted and Sukarno had increasingly aligned himself with the Chinese and had involved Indonesia in the expensive and foolish policy of confrontation with Malaysia. But his fall and the decimation of the Communist Party of Indonesia which followed, left Moscow without the support of a major state in South-East Asia.

The events in Indonesia accelerated the Soviet search for wider contacts in the area and over the next couple of years good relations were established with Malaysia, hitherto rather shunned by the Russians. The Soviet diplomatic efforts in South-East Asia in the post-Sukarno period underlined a new trend which had emerged soon after Khrushchev's exit. It showed renewed Soviet determination not to bow out of an area where competition with the Chinese and the Americans was tough. Soviet interest in the region had always been variable in the past, partly because of distance and partly because of accessibility. But evidently under Brezhnev and Kosygin the role of South-East Asia in Soviet policy was reassessed and it was realized that the region, apart from its intrinsic importance as a buffer to Chinese influence, was also the soft underbelly of South Asia, where Soviet interests were of paramount importance. The effort to rejuvenate Soviet presence in South-East Asia has, therefore, been one of the most significant new departures in foreign policy by the Soviet leaders since Khrushchev.

A more serious matter was the development taking place in the Middle East where Soviet involvement had grown immensely since the Suez crisis of 1956. By May 1967 it was clear that another war between the Arabs and the Israelis was inevitable. The Russians became alarmed, although there is some doubt now whether the Soviet evaluation of the situation was based on very accurate or sound information. Moscow obviously underrated the Israeli capacity to inflict harm upon the Arabs and overrated the Arab capacity to resist Tel-Aviv's military might.

Whatever the reasons, the war came. The Arabs suffered a shattering defeat under the Israeli blitzkrieg which began on the morning of 5 June 1967, with wave after wave of Israeli planes striking at Egyptian, Jordanian, Syrian and Iraqi airfields. Within a week all was over and the Israelis conquered large stretches of Arab territory. The Six Day War, apart from humiliating the Arabs, cost the Russians a great deal. Most of the Arab military equipment destroyed by the Israelis was supplied by the Soviet Union. Naturally, there was exasperation in Moscow at this colossal waste and contempt for the utter inefficiency and lack of fighting qualities among the Arabs. Israel won admiration for its courage and bravery, although such sentiments were not publicly expressed.

The Russians had not wanted war and they did not participate in it, but in a sense it was a blow to Soviet prestige as well and challenged the hard won Soviet position in the Middle East. The Russians had already warned publicly that Israel might start a war, and at a dramatic meeting between President Nasser and the Soviet Ambassador at 3 a.m. on 3 June, even persuaded the Egyptian leader to give up any idea of a pre-emptive strike against Israel. After the war, Soviet diplomacy had two tasks: to persuade Israel to give up the gains of the war and to restore Soviet prestige among the Arabs as well as to strengthen the position of Nasser.

In the first objective Moscow failed. Although Mr Kosygin himself attended a session of the United Nations to rally support for the Arab cause, he failed in this attempt because of strong American and West European opposition. In the second objective Soviet success was greater. The Soviet Union began an immediate airlift of arms to Egypt and Syria and also took steps to train the Egyptian army and reorganize its officer corps. As a result of these measures, and because the Americans remained totally committed to the Israelis and upheld their position against any withdrawals save in exchange for Arab recognition of Israel, Soviet influence in the Middle East was consolidated even further. The Soviet support for the Arabs never wavered because it was felt that in the long run, no matter how strong Israel was, the Arabs had a good chance of becoming victorious and even Arab fighting qualities would improve with more training and stricter discipline. The main worries for Moscow were the absence of any unity among the Arabs themselves, the extremist position taken by countries like Syria and another Israeli attack before the

Egyptians were ready to face it. For practical reasons, Soviet policy remained and still remains centred upon Nasser, whom the Soviet policy-makers see as totally incorruptible among the Arab leaders, a progressive and a moderate. They know that their real competition is with America and not with Israel, and want to keep the Middle East as their sphere of influence even if it costs them a great deal.

For the Soviet Union, however, even bigger trouble lay ahead much nearer home. In East Europe, which had remained quiescent since the Hungarian uprising of 1956, there were new signs of radicalism. Soviet relations with Rumania had deteriorated during the last years of Khrushchev. In the quarrel between Moscow and Peking, Bucharest had found suitable means to enlarge its independence from the Soviet influence. Khrushchev had handled the Rumanians rather clumsily. The Rumanians now went a step further and began to take an independent line in foreign affairs. During the Middle East crisis, unlike the Soviet Union and other East European states, they refused either to condemn Israel or to break off diplomatic relations with Tel-Aviv and for a long time refused to hold Warsaw Pact manoeuvres on their territory. In 1969 Rumania became the first European country to be visited by an American President and so eager was Bucharest for this visit that the opening date of the Rumanian Party Congress was delayed by one day to accommodate Nixon. The Russians, however, continued to tolerate Rumanian deviations with rather sour amusement. What was more relevant for them was that internally Rumanian policy remained orthodox.

The Russians could not take developments in Czechoslovakia so lightly. For one thing, Czechoslovakia was an important buffer between the Soviet Union and West Germany. Another, the nature of the challenge which came from Czechoslovakia was such that it questioned the very roots of the Communist Party's authority to govern a country. The Russians feared that if Czechoslovakia were allowed to get away with it, the authority of communism not only in East Europe but in the Soviet Union itself would be undermined.

Up until the beginning of 1967 Czechoslovakia had remained stolidly Stalinist under the rule of Novotny, the only East European Communist leader, apart from Ulbricht of East Germany, to survive unscathed the Stalinist and the Khrushchev era. But early in 1967 stirrings of change began, first among the intelligentsia, then in the party rank and file. By the end of the year Novotny's authority had evaporated and even the Soviet leaders could do nothing to keep him in power. Novotny's plans for a military coup were leaked to his opponents. On 5 January 1968 Dubcek, a relatively unknown Slovak, was elected to the post of the First Secretary of the Czechosloval Communist Party, though Novotny remained President for a few more weeks. In March Novotny resigned and his place was taken by Svoboda. A fever of political reforms and changes swept through Czechoslovakia with the tacit approval of the new leaders. Without censorship the press became free and outspoken.

At the outset, the Soviet leaders had acquiesced in the changeover to Dubcek and their attitude to him was positive. They had either failed to realize the extent of Dubcek's commitment to reform or believed that he would in the end keep a balance between freedom and control in the orthodox sense as Moscow interpreted it. The publication of the Czechoslovak party Action Programme in April with its promises of a new style of democracy more akin to the western conception of democracy, startled the Russians who were beginning to worry about the political trends there. From the end of April to the occupation of Czechoslovakia by the troops of the Soviet Union, Hungary, Poland, Bulgaria and East Germany on 21 August, there were endless polemics in the Soviet press against the liberal course of events there.

In the rapidly evolving situation there were many moments of hope and relief when the impression was created that the differences were settled between Moscow and Prague. At a number of meetings between the Czech leaders and other Warsaw Pact members and at meetings between the Soviet and Czech leaders, repeated attempts were made to reconcile Moscow and Prague. In the end all these attempts came to nothing. But the occupation of Czechoslovakia raised many problems and these continued to plague Soviet policy towards East Europe for a long time afterward. To begin with, even after the occupation it did not prove easy to dislodge the new leaders of Czechoslovakia, who had won enormous public support and esteem. Although Mr Dubcek was arrested and brought to Moscow with some of his colleagues, and rather roughly treated by the Soviet security guards, he returned from Moscow as the acknowledged leader. The whole Soviet course in Czechoslovakia was a great tragedy for both countries and for communism, too deep for words.

Allegedly, military action against Czechoslovakia was taken because it had become a danger to the security of the Communist camp, because the West Germans were said to be active there. This was just a blind. The real fear of the Soviet leaders was that the example of Czechoslovakia would prove to be infectious and thus undermine their political authority inside and outside their own country. This fear, though greatly exaggerated, may not have been without some foundation. But the obnoxious doctrine of limited sovereignty of members of the Warsaw Pact, which soon came to be known as the Brezhnev Doctrine, was a strangely outrageous contribution to Marxist thought. In a fashion the Czechoslovak problem was solved because within a year or so Dubcek was stripped of his authority and Czech leaders more amenable to the wishes of Moscow were installed in his place. Soviet troops remained in Czechoslovakia on a permanent footing. Even the Western countries, which made a lot of noise about Czechoslovakia, just kept on making noises and did nothing, either before or after the crisis, which could have deterred the Russians either from taking such action or doing so again.

Externally, all things considered, the long-term effects of Soviet action were not too bad for the Russians. For a while, there was stiffness in their relations with Washington and that is about all. Within a few months, diplomatic relations returned to normal between the Western countries and the Soviet Union. Moreover, the events in Czechoslovakia established clearly that the Russians had a free hand in this region which they considered to be their sphere of influence. As for East Europe itself, the Czechoslovak events defined the boundaries of their ideological freedom from the Soviet Union and made it clear that any policy of outpacing the Soviet Union in liberalization was fraught with danger.

Czechoslovakia also showed that the Soviet leaders were hesitant and divided among themselves on the course of action to be taken there and their ultimate objective. The period from April 1968 to August 1968 revealed many swift changes of policies and attitudes which could only have been due to these factors. First of all, they were late in apprehending the nature of forces which had brought Dubcek to power and which set the tone and pace of his policy. Having perceived rather late that it would militate against Soviet interests, they did not seem to know how to tackle the situation and mishandled it from beginning to end. No really serious attempt seems to have been made to put pressure upon Dubcek from behind the scenes. Instead, a rising crescendo of public polemics in doubtful taste merely turned the world public opinion against the Soviet objectives. The Czech leaders, too, ignored the warnings conveyed through Bucharest of the Soviet intentions to intervene in Czechoslovakia failing a change of policy there. The Soviet misgivings persisted even after the intervention and Moscow appeared to be very poorly informed about the conditions in Prague. The consequence was that Dubcek had to be put back in power, even if it was only for a temporary period. The only saving grace of this whole sorry business was that there was not much bloodshed, largely due to Czech self-control, but also due to restraint on the Soviet side.

Damaging as the Czech affair was to the Soviet image abroad, its effects at home were far more serious and deleterious. It altered the entire political perspective of the regime. Till Czechoslovakia, it had been possible to foresee an evolution in the liberal direction despite the Sinyavsky and Daniel affair. After Czechoslovakia, liberalism was at a discount.

A noticeable feature of trends after Czechoslovakia was the waning emphasis on reform at home. The ideas of economic reform in Czechoslovakia had come under fierce attack in the Soviet press and, as if by association, the advocacy of reform became muted on the home front too. In any case, the intelligentsia had been thoroughly shaken by what had happened and had little fight left in it. A small number of people voiced their opposition in public but the majority remained ashamed, silent and rather worried about the future. Those in official positions supported the regime. The masses remained indifferent to the fate of Czechoslovakia.

Another element in this deteriorating situation was China. After relative quiet on both sides, the Chinese resumed criticizing the Soviet leaders from the middle of 1965. When the 'Cultural Revolution' started in China in early 1966, the Chinese Red Guards harassed the Soviet Embassy in Peking, Chinese students passing through Moscow staged violent demonstrations in Red Square, there were mutual recriminations on both sides and accusations of border violations. The Chinese also refused to co-operate with the Soviet Union in helping Vietnam jointly against the American attacks. In 1967 the relations became even more strained after violent attacks on the Soviet Embassy in Peking and the mutual expulsion of each other's diplomats. Tension increased sharply in the middle of 1967 when a Soviet merchant ship, *Svirsk*, was detained in the port of Tailien (Dairen), its captain arrested, paraded through the streets and the ship damaged by a mob. It was allowed to sail only after a severe warning by Kosygin to the Chinese Prime Minister Chou En-lai that such 'arbitrary and lawless acts' were going to have serious consequences. But this was followed by another assault on the Soviet Embassy in Peking when its furniture and documents were destroyed.

1968 was a relatively quiet year in bilateral relations between Peking and Moscow, though the Chinese continued to make strong attacks on the Soviet Union and bitterly abused the latter over Czechoslovakia. Minor pinpricks on both sides occurred and there were unofficial reports of clashes on the border. The quietness of that year proved to be the prelude to a real storm in the next.

In 1969 a number of serious border clashes took place between China and the Soviet Union which increased tension to fever pitch and to many people it appeared that fighting on a large scale was only a question of time. The first clashes occurred on 2 March at Damansky Island on the River Ussuri, which forms the border between the two countries for a long stretch in the Far East. On the Russian side thirty-one people were killed, including an officer, and fourteen were injured. Both sides gave contrary versions of the incident but it is significant that the Chinese never gave their casualty figures. On 15 March a bigger clash took place in which the casualties were even larger but no exact figures were made available. The Soviet reaction was one of anguish and anger and tremendous anti-Chinese feeling was unleashed in the country. Officially, the Russians sent a long note on 29 March, which was moderately worded and asked the Chinese to refrain from further violent action and invited them to resume border talks which were broken off in 1964 by Peking.

Another serious clash took place in the Sinkiang region on 13 August and circumstantial evidence suggests that the Chinese lost a large number of their troops in the fighting. Apparently the Russians used a provocation by the Chinese to teach them a sound military lesson. Meanwhile, both the Soviet and Chinese governments had continued exchanging notes, protests and statements about their dispute. The Chinese elaborated upon their border claims in a long and compre-hensive statement on 24 May. The Soviet reply came in a statement on 13 June, which refuted all the Chinese claims and renewed the offer of talks. The Russians, however, were now exasperated and worried. The Soviet Foreign Minister Gromyko in a speech to the Supreme Soviet on 10 July 1969, was moved to say that 'even our worst enemies have never resorted to such unseemly methods and on such a scale as the Chinese leaders are doing.'[4]

A surprising halt in these border incidents came when Kosygin, on his way back from Hanoi after attending the funeral of Ho Chi Minh, made a detour to Peking and had a meeting with the Chinese Prime Minister Chou En-lai at the airport. For some time after the meeting all polemics from the Soviet side stopped. It was not at all clear what had actually gone on during this meeting. The only visible evidence of any change was the opening of border talks between the two countries in Peking. The Russians deputed one of their ablest negotiators, the former Ambassador to Peking and Deputy Foreign Minister, Vasily Kuznetsov, as head of the delegation. Eight months later he was replaced but still no progress was made towards a settlement. Polemical battles between the two countries had resumed but there were no border shootings.

The Soviet and Chinese positions on the border remain poles apart in principle but not in reality. The Chinese know that the Russians are not going to give up any territory, but they want an admission that these territories were acquired by 'unequal treaties'. The Russians cannot afford to admit this even in theory. It would be giving hostages to fortune, as any future Chinese government could use these arguments to demand territory again from the Soviet Union. Therefore, while prepared for minor adjustments of the border, the Russians are determined not to give up any sizeable chunk of their territory. The Soviet view of the Chinese territorial claims was summed up by Mikhail Suslov, a top-ranking member of the Party Praesidium, in a report to the Central Committee Plenum held on 14 February 1964. He declared, 'we proceed from the fact that no territorial disputes exist between the USSR and the CPR, that the Soviet-Chinese border evolved historically and that there can be a question only of a certain clarification of the border where this may be necessary.'[5] The Soviet view remained unchanged in subsequent years. But the Russians also recognized that the border problem could be settled by Peking provided it was willing to co-exist on the political and ideological level with Moscow. The Soviet efforts after the Kosygin-Chou meeting were directed to finding some ground for political understanding and these efforts were buttressed by the hope that Mao was getting old and might soon lose control of the country. Mao's successors, whoever they may be, are unlikely to continue his policies for long.

Troubles do not always come singly. Since the June 1967 war between the Arabs and the Israelis, the Soviet Union has had a succession of mishaps. There was Czechoslovakia in 1968, the fighting on the border with China in 1969, the continued burden of arming the North Vietnamese and the Arabs and, to top it all, extremely bad weather throughout 1969 which affected agriculture and industry adversely. The cumulative effect of all these drawbacks was a growing sense of frustration which surfaced towards the end of 1969 and continued into the next year. A strong undercurrent in favour of doing away with the post-Stalin gains of liberal political attitudes took particular hold among a section of the party rank and file. Favourable references to Stalin in every conceivable context became frequent; criticisms were frowned upon and vanished.

The archetype of these sentiments was a singularly bad novel, which had an immediate *succès de scandale*. *What's it you want?* written by the conservative Kochetov, appeared in the autumn of 1969. It was a long tirade against any kind of liberalism and a stern call to Stalinist values, with particular emphasis on disciplining youth. The novel was serialized in the monthly *Oktyabr* on the eve of Stalin's ninetieth birthday on 22 December. But contrary to widespread apprehensions that Stalin would be officially rehabilitated on the occasion, *Pravda* reiterated the unfavourable evaluation of Stalin made by the Twentieth Party Congress. But a bust of Stalin was quietly placed on his grave in Red Square, in June 1970.

Meanwhile, to ease some of the external strains and the heavy financial burden of the arms race the Soviet Union went ahead with a disarmament dialogue with the United States. Already, Soviet-American co-operation had made it possible for a nuclear non-proliferation treaty to be signed by most countries, with the notable exception of China and France among the nuclear powers and India and Brazil among the non-nuclear states. In September 1969 bilateral talks between the Soviet Union and the United States commenced on Strategic Arms Limitation in the important and expensive field of missiles, with a view to abandoning the race for even more sophisticated and destructive rockets. At the end of the year a dialogue also began between Moscow and Bonn to sign a non-aggression agreement between the Soviet Union and the Federal German Republic and to solve the problem of East Germany's recognition. This was part of the drive for a European Security Conference which the Russians wanted to call to settle some of the problems of Europe. Their dual purpose was to ease the remnants of the Cold War tensions in Europe and to be able to devote more attention to China which was displaying an aggressive mood.

Though Stalin was not rehabilitated, hardening of ideological line and tendency towards greater conformism prevailed. Alexander Solzhenitsyn, whose works after *One Day in the Life of Ivan Denisovich* could not be published in the Soviet Union – *The First Circle* and *The Cancer Ward* were published abroad to great acclaim – was expelled from the Writers' Union in November 1969. In February 1970 Alexander Tvardovsky, editor of *Novy Mir* and a staunch defender of liberal and experimental writers and artists, was removed from his post. Almost no worthwhile works of younger writers were printed in journals or brought out in book form. But they circulated in typescripts clandestinely, by a unique system of *samizdat* (self-publication). The authorities frowned upon it, but by and large were either helpless or unwilling to crack down upon it completely.

More serious rumblings were heard on the economic front. There was a scarcity of meat and other necessities and consumer goods. The awareness was generally strong that something had gone wrong somewhere and the leaders themselves admitted it. At a Central Committee Plenum held in December 1969, Brezhnev made a long report about the conditions in agriculture and industry. Although the report was never published, it was no secret that it took an extremely gloomy view of the situation and made it clear that the weather was not to be blamed solely. Evidently, the economic reforms had been only a limited success and since there was an unwillingness to experiment further with even more radical methods, there were frequent calls to return to the model of command economy as practised by Stalin, or near enough to it. The liberal riposte was that the reforms had not had enough time to work, that more reforms, and not fewer, were needed.

Though the reasons for all these troubles were not very clear, and they were not altogether due to faulty policies since an element of bad luck was also present, it was evident that some drastic steps would have to be taken to remedy the situation. The crisis, despite the critics, was not so acute that it could not be overcome. Whenever faced with difficulties, the Soviet economy has shown an astonishing capacity at best to overcome, at worst to muddle through it, and survive. But it was in a somewhat sombre mood that the people celebrated the one hundredth anniversary of the birth of Vladimir Lenin on 22 April 1970.

15 Two of the great achievements of the First Five-Year Plan, launched in 1928, were the hydro-electric power stations of Magnitogorsk and Kuznetsk, linked by the Turkestan–Siberia railway ('Turksib'). Here the workers are manually laying the tracks.

16 In agriculture the pace of collectivization was speeded up by the Five-Year Plan, but did not pass unopposed by the peasants, who were starved into submission. Here they queue up for work on the first collective farms in the 1930s.

17–19 The Dnieper Dam, built during the period of rapid industrialization, is the source of vast quantities of hydro-electric energy, feeding many plants and power stations. In 1939 World War Two broke out and with the invasion of the Germans in 1941, the Great Patriotic War began for the Russians. The photographs below show the destruction of the factory district of Stalingrad, at that time a new industrial town, which suffered extensive devastation; and the new Stalingrad, now renamed Volgograd – a modern city with new schools, theatres, factories, research institutes and houses.

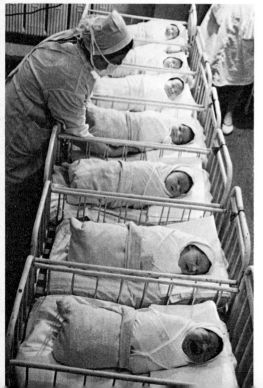

20 Cultivation of maize in the Krasnodar region, near the Black Sea. The flat, fertile 'black earth' belt, granary of the USSR, stretches nearly 3,000 miles, from Kiev to the Altai Mountains. 21 The first citizens of 1966 in a maternity home in Naro-fominsk, near Moscow.

22, 23 Opposite above: an appalling monument to the architectural taste of the Stalin era, the Lomonosov State University, Moscow. In the foreground is the Sternberg Institute of Astronomy. Opposite: a view of the modern Kalinin Prospekt, a busy shopping street in Moscow.

24–26 Opposite top: N. Khrushchev and
L. Brezhnev congratulating the astronauts
Nikolayev and Popovich on their successful
space-flight. Opposite: Chairman of the
Council of Ministers A. Kosygin, with the
President of Pakistan, Mohammed Ayub Khan,
and the Prime Minister of India, Lal Bahadur
Shastri, during the Tashkent conference.
Opposite below: from the White House,
America reaches out to encircle the USSR in
Korea, Iran, Turkey, Formosa and Vietnam –
a cold-war cartoon from *Krokodil*.

27–29 Russia has long been famous for its
ballet. Above: Irina Kolpakova and Vladilen
Semyonov in Tchaikovsky's *Sleeping Beauty*.
Right: Innokenti Smoktunovsky as Hamlet in
the film directed by Gregory Kozintsev. Below:
Bella Akhmadulina autographs a book of her
poems for Bulgarian authoress Lada Galina.

30 Chess is an integral part of the Russian way of life. Big matches are
followed with the absorbed interest other countries give to football. Here
a group of citizens and Red Army men follow a Petrosyan v. Spassky
game, arguing moves and variations like the aficionados they are.

8   The economy

UNLIKE WESTERN MARKET ECONOMIES the Soviet economy and those of the other socialist states are centrally planned. This means that the state regulates every aspect of economic life, from its simplest level, the private plot of the peasant, to the most complex of giant industrial enterprises.

The planning of the economy began almost as soon as the Bolsheviks gained power in the Revolution. In December 1917 the Supreme Council of National Economy (VSNKh) was set up. In the early stages, of course, private enterprise did not altogether disappear and it was the task of VSNKh to provide an operational guide line for the nationalized sector of the economy. The VSNKh underwent many structural changes as the state control over the economy became tighter. It was completely abolished in January 1932.

Its functions were taken over by two other institutions. Firstly, in 1932, three industrial People's Commissariats (later Ministries) were set up for heavy, light and timber industries. Their number gradually expanded to the present number of some thirty or more ministries. As a rule each ministry is divided into a number of departments (*glavki*) which are responsible for functional considerations such as supplies, investment etc., and for parts of the sector which the ministry controls. For example, one department in the Petroleum Industry Ministry may be responsible only for oilfields in a specific area. Enterprises are under the direct control of one such department in a ministry. In many cases the Union Ministries in Moscow have their republican counterparts or republican departments.

Secondly, and even more crucial for the economic development of the USSR, was the development of the planning agencies. The most important of these is Gosplan, or the State Planning Commission. It was originally formed in 1921 as a department of the Council

137

of Labour and Defence with the purpose of formulating long-term abstract plans. Practical planning, until the end of the twenties, was done by the planning department of the VSNKh. Gosplan, however, earned the wrath of Stalin when its members opposed the crash industrialization programme in 1928 and many of its leading members, mostly Mensheviks and able economists, disappeared. Gosplan was subsequently reorganized and it assumed the role of a co-ordinating body within the government. The chief of Gosplan since then has usually been a Deputy Prime Minister.

Gosplan has undergone many transformations, its functions curtailed or expanded according to the outlook of the current leaders. The last major reform in the economic administrative system was implemented in 1965, about a year after the fall of Khrushchev. The reason for this reform was explained by Prime Minister Kosygin in a long speech delivered at a Central Committee Plenum on 27 September of that year. As a result of these reforms, planning functions were concentrated in Gosplan, but a State Committee on Material-Technical Supplies (Gossnab) was established to take charge of all supplies to enterprises. In effect this means that planning of production and supplies are under separate organizations. Nevertheless, their functions overlap since Gosplan carries out the task of allocating supplies on the basis of planned production. It specially looks after the supply of raw materials, fuel, plant and equipment, timber, and building materials.

There are also Gosplans at the Republic level, their plans generally dovetailed with Union plans. The operational plans are for a period of five to seven years but these are more of a general guide to development targets. The enterprises are mainly concerned with the annual plan in their day-to-day operations. This is because long-term plans can never be very precisely drawn up and changes have to be made to them in the light of actual developments in the economy. Of course, the annual plans are related to the long-term plan as they are formulated with a view to the over-all economic policy which the long-term plans envisage.

Planning is a complex process, in which availability of resources has to be matched to the economic and social goals. Serious alterations have to be made when imbalances become evident and great effort is required to see to it that the complicated links in the process are not broken, disrupting a wider area of economic activity. For instance, if a factory or railway line is not completed according to schedule, it can affect production in other industries. Therefore, a number of key projects are accorded priority, in an attempt to ensure their completion in time. All factories and farms are given quantitative targets to fulfil.

Despite these measures, the course of economic development is rarely smooth and methods of planning and their improvement is always a controversial subject among the Soviet economists and leaders. So is the important question of priority within the framework of planning. Even with her vast resources the Soviet Union cannot achieve everything all at once. Therefore, in theory at least, greater investment has to be made in those sectors which are most necessary or need urgent development and there are often differences of opinion, sometimes voiced in public, on this very vexed question.

The complex network of planning bodies, ministries and enterprises makes it essential that some check and control over their activities should be exercised and means found to persuade them to operate on prescribed lines. The chief instrument for such checking and inspection is the People's Control Committee, an all-union organization with subordinate committees at republican and local levels. It has a large team of inspectors at every level who have powers to delve into records and documents and to interrogate. Its work is mostly concerned with breaches of rules and instructions, and one frequently reads of erring officials and managers being criticized by the Committee.

Another important role in this respect is played by the Ministry of Finance, whose local officials must audit the accounts of enterprises. The Ministry also determines the number of managerial and economic personnel in each enterprise through its Establishments Commission. Besides, the Finance Ministry controls the investment banks, which keep a close eye on all investment expenditure by the enterprises. Moreover, the State Bank automatically exercises an inspecting and checking role because the enterprises have to maintain an account with it and all payments made are scrutinized by the bank to see that they conform to regulations. The State Arbitration Committee is another body which decides disputes between enterprises, and various ministries also have their arbitration tribunals to deal with disputes between organizations under their jurisdiction.

The most powerful control is exercised, however, by the Communist Party, since in the last analysis, it must approve everything

NORTH SEA

ARCTIC

Arctic Circle

BALTIC SEA

FINNO-KARELIAN S.S.R.

Murmansk

Riga

Niemen

Bug

Dvina

Pripet

1

3

2

Brest-Litovsk

Lvov

Chernovtsy

Ternopol

Vinnitsa

Zhitomir

Dnepropetrovsk

Kirovograd

Cherkassky

Nikolaev

Kherson

Zaporozhye

Odessa

Belgorod

Batum

Minsk

4

Dnieper

Chernigov

Kiev

Desna

5

Kharkov

Sumy

Belgorod

Kursk

Donetsk

Lugansk

Don

Rostov

Pskov

Novgorod

Komarovo

LENINGRAD

Archangel

Vologda

MOSCOW

RUSSIAN

Gorky

Kirov

Lipetsk

Voronezh

Kazan

Simbirsk

Penza

Saratov

Ulyanovsk

Volga

Kuibyshev

Volgograd (Stalingrad)

Orenburg

Astrakhan

Perm

URAL MOUNTAINS

SOVIET

Sverdlovsk

Tyumen

Chelyabinsk

Kurgan

Magnitogorsk

Ob

Irtysh

Toms

Novosibirsk

BLACK SEA

CAUCASUS

Krasnodar

Stavropol

Tiflis

7

8

9

Baku

CASPIAN SEA

KAZAKH S.S.R.

ARAL SEA

Lake Balkhash

TURKMEN S.S.R.

Ashkhabad

UZBEK S.S.R.

Bukhara

Tashkent

TADZHIK S.S.R.

KIRGHIZ S.S.R.

Danube

1 Estonian S.S.R.
2 Latvian S.S.R.
3 Lithuanian S.S.R.
4 Byelorussian S.S.R.
5 Ukrainian S.S.R.
6 Moldavian S.S.R.
7 Georgian S.S.R.
8 Armenian S.S.R.
9 Azerbaijan S.S.R.

0   MILES   500   1000

0   KM   500   1000

EDGAR HOLLOWAY

O C E A N

KAMCHATKA

Magadan

F E D E R A L   S O C I A L I S T   R E P U B L I C

Yakutsk

Lena

SAKHALIN

Lake
Baikal

Chita

Amur

Khabarovsk

Irkutsk

Ussuri

MONGOLIA

Ulan Bator

Vladivostok

TAINS

C H I N A

Pekin

———— U.S.S.R. after Second World War
- - - - Soviet Socialist Republics

Map of the Soviet Union today

that is decided. The Party thus plays a vital role in the economic life of the country in all its aspects.

The wages of all categories of workers in the Soviet Union are fixed by the State Committee on Labour and Wages, in close consultation with Gosplan and the Ministry of Finance. In recent years two predominant trends in the wage policy can be noted. Generally wages are rising and minimum wages are being fixed at a higher level. In many cases where there were no guaranteed minimum wages, a minimum wage has been made obligatory. The second noteworthy aspect is that differentials in wage scales are being reduced. Whereas a decade ago there were sharp differences between wages of various categories of workers, the ratio of these differences has now been reduced. One special category of people who have particularly benefited from wage reforms are the members of collective farms, who now have a minimum wage guarantee and are also being given pensions, which they did not have before.

Equally important, in the context of Soviet economy, is the pricing system. No prices can be altered without the approval of the Union Government, except in some special cases. The whole question of prices in the Soviet Union is a complex and difficult one. Some order is now being brought about by the State Committee on Prices, which is attached to the Council of Ministers. The main categories of prices are factory wholesale prices – the prices at which enterprises sell their goods to wholesalers – and industrial wholesale prices, the prices at which goods are transferred to users. These include a turnover tax. There is also a special category of agricultural prices for goods supplied to farms and for agricultural use, as well as special prices for agricultural raw materials for industry. In the beginning, the agricultural prices were used to drain income from the countryside, but lately, more equitable prices are being paid as the necessity for regeneration of agriculture has forced itself upon the Party and the government.

The retail price policy of the Soviet Government follows a simple rationale. Prices are so fixed that the supply meets the demand, except where, for social reasons, some goods are sold dear or cheap, such as drinks, particularly vodka which is expensive, and children's clothes, which are priced cheaply. Prices vary in different geographic zones and between cities and villages, largely because the distribution costs in villages are higher. The prices of key items of daily necessity rarely change and this change can only be made if authorized by the Council of Ministers and Gosplan.

The organization of enterprises in the Soviet Union can be divided into four main categories. These are: state enterprises in industry and agriculture; non-agricultural co-operative enterprises; collective farms; and the small private sector, which includes agricultural holdings of collective farmers and state employees and the private craftsmen, individual peasants and professional services. It must be noted, however, that it is illegal in the Soviet Union for any private individual to employ labour for the production of goods for sale. Thus a private watch repairer, for instance, cannot hire an assistant to help him. The only exceptions are domestic help and secretaries. It is also illegal to resell anything for profit. If a man produces small toys in his spare time, he can sell them but he cannot buy toys from another person and sell them for profit. State enterprises actually account for 99 per cent of the gross industrial output. In the agricultural sector, however, the bulk of production is contributed by the collective farmers, although in recent years state farms have increased their share. Private plots, however, contribute a significant share of meat, vegetable and dairy produce.

Another feature of Soviet planning is that the country is divided into eighteen large economic zones, in which industrial development is planned according to their economic character. They are not self-contained units but they complement each other in developing the most suitable lines of production, thus helping to achieve economy of effort for the country as a whole. (See appendix, pp. 212–15.)

Thus it can easily be seen that in the formation of economic policy, the Soviet planners have to take account of very complex factors of geography and natural resources. They have to ensure in their long range plans that all areas develop evenly although disparities still continue. This is not to forget that a conscious effort is made to allocate development projects to those areas which still lag behind. The upsurge in the economy of Central Asia, for example, would not have been possible but for the attention given to its development.

By any reasonable standard the Soviet economic achievement is an impressive one although there are serious shortcomings in the way the economy is run. There are several reasons for the particular way the Soviet economy has developed, some practical, some theoretical and some ideological.

The salient feature of the system is that it is dedicated to economic development, notably a rapid and massive development of industry. As such, it can be judged by the criteria applied to developing economies; but since the effort was on such a gigantic scale, it can be simultaneously judged as a 'war economy'. One of the most frequent criticisms of the Soviet economic system is that it has not led to balanced development. This is true but also beside the point. To effect change in stagnant and backward economies politico-social factors have to be taken into account and people 'mobilized'. A balanced advance in all sectors thus becomes an impossible and irrelevant task. What is needed is continuous assaults on one or more bottlenecks to break out from interlocking and vicious circles of stagnation.

Basically, this was the strategy adopted in the Soviet case. The frequent campaigns undertaken in the course of the Five Year Plans were usually concentrated on a few industrial or agricultural sectors. When it was found that these campaigns had been overdone, they were switched over to another field. The excesses of some of these campaigns caused much waste and suffering. The usual criteria of investment and other economic values could not apply in these cases because it was largely uncharted territory, in which the Russians became pioneers. The Soviet economic model thus became an example of what some western economists – not in any unfavourable sense – term 'unbalanced growth'. These economists believe that not only should there be conscious organization of the development effort but that it should be on a long-term basis and that adoption of a gradualist approach will be self-defeating if the economy is to be lifted out of the rut.

This was not, of course, the ideological basis of the Soviet approach. But it is necessary to realize that because the Soviet economy was driven by a specific, Marxist ideology, it was not, therefore, inherently wicked or wrong-headed. It had sound logic behind it and the over-all economic success achieved confirms this analysis. Moreover, it would be equally unjust to claim that the Soviet planners consciously go about planning bottlenecks. It is simply that the fast tempo of growth they adopt inevitably leads to shortages and strains and this leads to further stimulation of economic efforts to overcome them. There is, therefore, a method in this strategy.

It follows that such an economy can only be a centralized command economy in which vital decisions about allocation of resources, priorities, and other relevant decisions are made at the top and enforced by a hierarchy of political and administrative bureaucracy. A Polish economist, Oscar Lange, claimed that such an economy, 'essentially, can be described as a *sui generis* war economy'.

It does not follow that similar methods are either efficient or rewarding for an economy which has overcome its backwardness. For one thing, the question of priorities becomes an artificial one to the extent that it does not have to choose one sector for development at the expense of another. Its resources have grown, so that more or less equal priorities can be given to several sectors, without holding up one and damaging another sector.

To some extent, therefore, the debate in the post-Stalin period about priorities was an artificial one, a hangover from the past. By the end of the Khrushchev period the Soviet economy had grown until it could afford to invest in agriculture and industry simultaneously without feeling undue strain and still look after the expensive demands of a modern defence force for the country. The resources, of course, were not infinite and a certain balancing had to be done so as not to overstrain them in any particular direction. In this respect decisions about priorities were important. But the debate had nothing like the fierceness of the industrialization debate of the twenties.

The Soviet economy, however, has to face new and tougher problems which have not been satisfactorily solved up till now. Besides, as the economy grows in complexity ever new problems face the planners. But it is important to know what reforms have been carried out and for what purpose, and what appears to be the future direction of the changes in the economy of the Soviet Union.

The reforms carried out so far aim in one particular direction. They seek to reorganize industry on a more rational and efficient basis and to provide greater autonomy to the enterprises. Thus, they have sought to alleviate the problems created by over-centralization, waste and duplication. It is not an easy task, when long-ingrained habits require that the enterprises should be utterly dependent upon one or another of the central organs, that their production targets should be set by Gosplan and their wages and other funds should be distributed along pre-determined lines.

For judging efficiency, the criterion of profit has to be used. The term 'profit', however, is used in a special sense: enterprises are encouraged to seek high revenue from their sales and then allowed to retain part of this revenue, after deducting material and labour costs, as incentives for greater production. It was believed that this would encourage managements to produce those goods which they could really sell to consumers and not simply to fulfil their targets by manufacturing a large quantity of goods not required by anybody, or unsaleable because of poor quality. Efforts were also made to ease the supply of raw materials by better liaison between producers and consumers. Lastly, factories were encouraged to plan on a long-term basis themselves, keeping in view the national plan as a whole.

The reforms were carefully planned and preceded by experiments in some factories. Of course, not all factories switched over to new methods overnight. In essence the reforms were not introducing any radical change in the economic system but only altering it somewhat. Even so the results were encouraging at first. But in a few years it was discovered that the reforms were not stimulating economic growth as they should. The reforms began towards the end of 1965, and by the end of 1969, their substance and retention had become a matter of fierce debate among Soviet planners and economists as we have seen (p. 126).

Behind this debate about the efficacy of the reforms was the question of how far the Party was prepared to go to satisfy consumer needs and whether it felt that economic decentralization would result in a diminution of its authority over the country. The main argument of the critics of the reforms was that when factory managers were given some degree of independent responsibility, wages and costs went up but productivity did not show a corresponding rise. At the beginning of 1970 the issue was still unresolved.

The fact that the Soviet economy was in a critical stage towards the end of the sixties did not mean that it was threatened by a breakdown. Simply, it had reached a point where serious choices of ideology as well as method had to be made. Yet there was no indication that they were about to be made and from past experience it could be surmised that any serious decisions would be postponed for at least some time. Or if taken, they would be in the nature of a compromise. At worst, therefore, a slowdown in the growth rate of the economy was implied, not a halt in economic growth as such.

9   Political institutions

THE SOVIET UNION differs from all non-communist states in that the Communist Party exercises supreme power. The Supreme Soviet, in constitutional terms roughly equivalent to the British Parliament, is 'wholly subordinate' to the Party. Since the Revolution the political institutions have undergone many transformations, but the bedrock on which the structure of the state rests is the cardinal principle of Party supremacy. This frequently creates complications since unavoidably the functions of the Party and Government sometimes overlap and create parallelism in work. The Party workers have to be constantly reminded not to overstep this uncertain demarcation line. In practice, however, this line is often inevitably violated. But since the authority of the Party always prevails in the end, it does not lead to any constitutional crisis.

There have been three major constitutional changes since the Revolution of 1917. In the immediate aftermath of the Revolution the constitution of 1918 was promulgated, but this was largely a codification of the existing institutions. The guiding principle in the formulation of this and subsequent Constitutions was Lenin's thesis that in revolutionary Russia parliamentarism should be abolished and the administrative and legislative organs merged.

At the end of 1922 it was decided to form the present Union of Soviet Socialist Republics and a new Constitution was approved in January 1924. In the next ten years a great transformation took place in the social and political structure of the USSR. Stalin felt that a new Constitution should reflect and embody these changes. On 5 December 1936 the new Constitution was approved by the Extraordinary Eighth All-Union Congress of Soviets.

The Constitution of 1936 was highly democratic in principle and Stalin went so far as to claim that it was the only thoroughly democratic

Constitution in the world. In reality, Stalin did not observe the Constitution himself but followed his own fancy, a fact which has been freely admitted in the post-Stalin period. Although there have been many amendments to the 1936 Constitution, it has not been replaced. Some years ago a Commission was set up to prepare a new Constitution but so far there has been no sign of any concrete progress in this direction.

The Communist Party organization, however, still accords with the ideas of Lenin, who envisaged it as a revolutionary vanguard of dedicated workers, tightly disciplined and closing ranks against outsiders. Lenin's theory on the role of the Party, which in 1903 split the Russian Social Democratic Workers' Party to which he belonged, was formulated in a pamphlet called *What is To Be Done?* published in 1902.

After the split, Lenin's followers came to be known as the Bolsheviks (majority) of the Russian Social Democratic Workers' Party. In 1918 the name was changed to 'All-Russian Communist Party (Bolsheviks)' and in 1925 to 'All-Union Communist Party (Bolsheviks)'. In 1952 the suffix (Bolsheviks) was dropped and the ruling party came to be known as the Communist Party of the Soviet Union (CPSU).

In the years after the Revolution there was a strong bias in favour of admitting working-class members to the Party. But gradually the Party has become more broadly based. It is usual nowadays to refer to it as the 'vanguard of the Soviet people' which also indicates that probably only a minority of the members of the Party are now working class. In 1969 the total membership of the Party was 14 million. This figure includes candidate or probationer members. The CPSU does not allow any other political party to function in the Soviet Union and thus remains unchallenged in its exercise of power within the country.

The base of the Party is formed by the primary organizations, consisting of members chosen according to their professional activity and not exclusively on geographical areas. From this basic unit the structure rises pyramidally to *raion* (district), *okrug* (circuit), *oblast* (region), *krai* (area), Union republics, and lastly the Central Committee of the CPSU. The *gorod* (town) unit is in a special category. Although lower in rank than *oblast*, some of the town party units are much more powerful because of the size and importance of their towns. Moscow and Leningrad are obvious examples of this kind. At the apex of the pyramid is the Politburo of the Central Committee headed by the General Secretary.

The organizational structure of the Party is based on the principle of 'democratic centralism'. According to Article 19 of Party Statutes, this involves (a) the election of all leading Party bodies from the lowest to the highest; (b) periodical reports of Party bodies to their Party organizations and to higher bodies; (c) strict Party discipline and the subordination of the minority to the majority; (d) the decisions of higher bodies strictly binding on lower bodies. The last two conditions ensure that centralism in fact triumphs over democracy since in practice dissent, even within closed Party meetings, on any point of substance may be subjected to disciplinary measures. Besides, the elections are always on the basis of a single-list system. Therefore, in reality, those elected to many posts in the Party are the product of a mixture of procedures of free election, election from below and approval from above.

It is also remarkable that, although procedures are laid down explicitly for elections from the level of primary organization to that of Republic Central Committee, the procedure for the election of the Central Committee of the CPSU is not very clear from documents. Since the Central Committee is the most powerful organ of the Party, this is somewhat surprising.

According to the rules, membership of the CPSU is 'open to any citizen of the Soviet Union who accepts the Party's Programme and Statutes, actively participates in the construction of Communism, works in one of the organizations of the Party, fulfils Party decisions and pays membership dues.' In reality recruitment is more selective and those preferred are the more active and politically conscious. There is a probationary period of one year for new members, and during this period they are known as 'candidates'. Their application to join the Party must be supported by three Party members who have been in the Party for at least five years and who have known the applicant for at least one year at work. After the application is approved by the primary Party organization with a two-thirds majority, it has to be endorsed by the next highest Party organ. The candidate member has a right to take part in the meetings of his primary organization but has no voting rights. The procedure is repeated when after a year a candidate applies to become a full member.

The lowest age limit for joining the Party is 18 years and those below the age of 23 may only belong to its youth branch, Komsomol, the Young Communist League. The monthly membership fee ranges from 10 kopecks to 3 per cent of a monthly salary. An entrance fee of 2 per cent of the monthly salary is paid on admission as a candidate member.

The organizational structure of the Party is rather complex. There is the primary organization and its general Party meeting which decides upon all activities. The general Party meeting must be held monthly, but the frequency of these meetings diminishes as the organization goes up in scale. Thus a district and regional Party conference is only obligatory once every six months. At the Republic level Party Congresses must be held every four years. This also applies to the All-Union Congress of the CPSU. The last such gathering, the Twenty-third Party Congress, was held during March and April of 1966. The next one was announced for March 1971.

From the district level upwards there is an 'executive organ' which directs the general work of the organization. This is known as the Party Committee up to the area level and as a Central Committee at the Republic and Union levels. The greatest authority, however, is exercised by the bureaux and secretariats of these organizations, who conduct the day-to-day business and are permanently in session.

Of the higher bodies, the Party Congress is theoretically the 'supreme organ' of the CPSU, which lays down policies, decides upon ideology and all such matters of importance for the Party and the country. An Extraordinary Congress can be convened by the Central Committee or at the request of one-third of the members of the last Congress. The ratio of representation at the Congress is decided upon by the Central Committee. For the Twenty-third Party Congress there was one delegate for every 2,500 members with full voting powers and one delegate for every 2,500 candidate members with 'consultative' voting power only.

The Party Congress also elects the Central Organs which cannot be changed except by another Congress. (By Central Organs is meant the all-powerful Central Committee and the less powerful Central Revision Commission.) The Central Revision Commission is mainly concerned with supervising the working of the Central Committee and auditing the accounts of the Treasury. Its chairman reports to the next Congress on the interim period.

The election of the Central Committee by a Congress is a far more serious affair. This also consists of full and candidate members. The candidate members take part in its deliberations but do not have voting rights. This is what is meant by a 'consultative' vote. In between the Congresses no one can be co-opted to the Central Committee and in case of a vacancy occurring a candidate member is called upon to fill the place. But on very rare occasions this rule seems to have been relaxed. A member or candidate member can be expelled only by a two-thirds majority vote at a plenum or meeting of the Central Committee. The Twenty-third Party Congress elected a Central Committee of 195 full members and 165 candidates: The Central Committee, according to the Party rules, must meet at least every six months. These meetings can of course be held more frequently.

Just as the Central Committee directs the work of the Party in the interval between the Congresses, the work between the plenums is directed by the Politburo elected by the Central Committee. Supreme political authority in the Soviet Union resides in the Politburo. The General Secretary of the Central Committee, who heads the Politburo, is the leader of the Party and the country. It is a position of great authority which Stalin occupied all his life after being elected – and which he abused. The proceedings of the Politburo are never published. At present it consists of 11 full members and 10 candidates, but their number is variable. For some years after the Nineteenth Party Congress in 1952 the nomenclature of Politburo was changed to the Party Praesidium. After the death of Stalin the title of General Secretary was changed to First Secretary. Both titles reverted to their original form at the Twenty-third Congress.

Very little in fact is known about the procedure for the election of the Politburo or how it functions, but it was once revealed by Khrushchev that the Praesidium, as it was then, met at least once a week and that decisions, when not unanimous, were by a simple majority vote. This probably still remains the practice. The word of the Politburo on any question affecting the Soviet Union is final: there is no higher authority.

During the Stalin era, of course, even the Politburo did not matter. It is, however, a moot question whether its power can be circumscribed by the Central Committee. It must be considered that the members of the Central Committee are likely to be elected only on the recommendation of the General Secretary or the Politburo. It is inconceivable that even the Congress delegates would dare to elect anyone as a member of the Central Committee who was disapproved of by the leaders. Besides, most of the members of the Central Committee are people who hold responsible posts in the Party.

It does appear, however, that a working system is emerging in which the authority of the General Secretary remains unchallenged, so long as he can carry the majority of the Politburo with him, but in case of sharp differences within the Politburo, the Central Committee's decision becomes the binding one. It will be recalled that when faced with the challenge of Malenkov and Molotov, Khrushchev saved himself by rallying the Central Committee, but he was also ousted when he could no longer carry the Central Committee with him. This is undoubtedly an arrangement which is both rational and plausible. The Central Committee cannot carry out day-to-day decision-making and this must be entrusted to the Politburo. But the final control seems to be reverting to the Central Committee in the sense that its voice is decisive in appointing new leaders. No doubt the Central Committee is still dominated by the Politburo in the last analysis, but it is no longer an utterly passive or rubber-stamping body as in the days of Stalin. In time it might acquire even greater authority and control over affairs.

In discussing the functions of the Central Committee the important role of its permanent secretariat should not be overlooked. This is the executive organ carrying out the decisions of the Central Committee and the Politburo. It is almost a duplication of the normal government machinery, with several departments under secretaries from among the members of the Central Committee. This permanent staff wields tremendous influence, not only in executing the Party policies but in formulating them, in shifting information and carrying out other important tasks. In every case the authority of a Secretary of the Central Committee is greater and wider-ranging than that of the ministers in the Government.

In many cases members and candidate members of the Politburo hold a Government portfolio directly. The Prime Minister, of course, is invariably a member. Other important jobs in the Government are also entrusted to the Politburo members; the most notable of these is the Chairmanship of the State Committee for Security (the KGB). This department is responsible for the most sensitive functions connected with the security of the state, including intelligence work, domestic and foreign, and counter-intelligence. The enormous powers enjoyed by its predecessor in the Stalin days have been whittled down but it still remains a formidable apparatus, not to be trifled with. It is usually the KGB which deals with any kind of political opposition or dissent. Because of the past misuse of this apparatus, when it slipped out of Party control, it is now invariably headed by a member or candidate of the Politburo, so as to keep it under complete Party control and scrutiny.

Similarly, the important task of political control of the powerful Soviet Army is also within the purview of the Central Committee. At every level in the Red Army there are political officers whose job is to propagate the Party line and to keep out any ideological disaffection. Despite some recent wild speculations to the contrary, if there is one country where the army is completely subordinated to the political authority, it is the USSR. In this respect the relationship between the army and the CPSU is more akin to the relationship between the British Army and the Government, than between the White House and the Pentagon, since the Pentagon operates a powerful political lobby which questions and even obstructs the White House occasionally.

THE NATIONALITIES PROBLEM
The Soviet Union is a federation and this is well reflected in the administrative structure of the country. Demographic factors, however, account for certain specific features for the population is very unevenly divided among the fifteen republics. In January 1970 the total population was 241·7 million. Over half the population, some 130 million, lives in the Russian Soviet Federal Soviet Republic (RSFSR), which is ethnically overwhelmingly Slav. The other two Republics with Slav predominance are the Ukraine, with over 47 million people, and Byelorussia with more than 9 million. Thus, these three republics account for nearly three-quarters of the population. Only two other republics have more than 10 million of a population, Uzbekistan and Kazakhstan, but they have mixed ethnic composition. In fact, officially there are 110 separate nationalities inhabiting the Soviet Union, each with their own language, though the predominant language is Russian. The largest non-Slav group is the Uzbeks, who number more than 6 million.

Because of its diverse ethnic composition, the problems of nationalities is a serious and constant one for the Soviet Union. Lenin gave considerable attention to the problem so that none of the minorities would feel discriminated against. It is always a sensitive question and much Soviet effort is devoted to ensuring that every nationality in the USSR is equal and treated fairly. At the same time, any manifestation of nationalism in the republics, whether it be Ukraine or Lithuania, Georgia or Uzbekistan, arouses official anger, anxiety and denial that such nationalism exists.

The sensitivity of the Soviet authorities can be easily explained. Though the Russians form the majority of the population, the Soviet Union is in fact a vast conglomeration of different peoples, different in their ethnic background, different in their historical experience and different in their linguistic loyalties. To concede any legitimacy to feelings of nationalism, therefore, is to open Pandora's box and risk the disintegration of the Soviet Union in its present form. Of course, there is no such danger of disintegration in sight, whatever the critics may say. The anger is there because even to discuss such a prospect is assumed to be wishing for the dismemberment of the Soviet Union. The official explanation, therefore, is always that the nationalities problem has been solved in the Soviet Union. The undoubted economic progress of Central Asia and other republics is presented as a model to resolve this kind of ethnic and linguistic problem elsewhere where it exists in an acute form.

Nevertheless, it is not unnatural that, here and there among ethnic groups, desire for greater assertion of their own identity does exist. These are more of a nuisance than a political challenge to the authority of Moscow. In the long run, however, as the minorities advance culturally and materially, a readjustment in relations between Moscow and the Republics will take place. Indeed, the process is already going on and in many spheres, economic, cultural and educational, the Republics are enjoying greater power and control than they did even a decade ago. The process, however, will stop short of threatening the disintegration of the Soviet Union.

The Jewish problem is part of the bigger problem of relations between different nationalities within the USSR and their relations with the Russian majority in particular. But the Jewish problem has some special features. The Jews are not concentrated in a specific geographic region and their grievances, sometimes legitimate, constantly receive world-wide publicity. Another difficulty is that there has been a Russian and Slav tradition of anti-Semitism which cannot be denied and is hard to eradicate completely. Then there is also the widespread distrust of the Jews at official and party levels. They are not trusted because they are considered to be cosmopolitans and to have emotional and physical contacts with the Jews of the Diaspora and of Israel. The vulgar anti-Semitism of the people, although it has become very weak, and the more sophisticated distrust react upon each other to a certain extent and produce some discrimination on occasions.

This is sad because the Jewish community had made a tremendous contribution to the Russian and Soviet culture and continues to do so. But to claim that such discrimination amounts to persecution is an exaggeration and is misleading, and certainly no service is done to the Soviet Jews by a perpetual campaign against the Soviet Union on this score.

This is not to deny that there has been a qualitative decline in the easy acceptance of the Jews since the early days of the revolution, more particularly since the Second World War. Karl Radek, a Jew and one of the brilliant early Bolshevik leaders exterminated by Stalin, has recorded that Dzerzhinski, another Bolshevik leader and head of the Cheka (security service) after the revolution, 'studied socialism through Polish and Russian works, and for the sake of his work among the Jewish workers he studied Yiddish. Later it was a great joke to us that at the headquarters of Polish Social Democracy, which contained quite a number of Jews, Dzerzhinski, former gentleman of Poland, and a Catholic, could read Yiddish.'[1] Such warm feelings towards the Jews, devoid of any bias, unfortunately no longer exist at many levels.

The real test of the transition from the inequity of the Tsarist empire to a socialist state is not whether the empire has been dismembered or not but whether all nationalities have equally gained from the Revolution or not. In the complex situation of Russia after the Revolution perhaps the minorities did not reap an immediate reward. Some of them also started from a very backward stage in their development. But it can be safely contended that since the Revolution they have gained more and more, even where there is some unevenness in their development. Soon enough, they will have little to complain about on this score.

Like all large nations which have evolved through a mixture of races and cultures, the Soviet Union is a tapestry woven with great effort. But it cannot be taken apart piecemeal without being destroyed completely. For this reason no one and nothing will be allowed to take it apart.

GOVERNMENT STRUCTURE

The supreme organ of state power in the Soviet Union is the bicameral Supreme Soviet. It consists of the Council of the Union, to which deputies are elected in the ratio of one per 300,000 inhabitants, and the Council of Nationalities in which representation is on a territorial basis, each Union Republic, Autonomous Republic, Autonomous Region and National Circuit being allowed 25, 11, 5 and 1 deputies respectively.

Elections to the Supreme Soviet take place every four years. It is obligatory for it to meet every six months and both chambers meet concurrently. A joint session is also usually held. The sessions normally last only a few days, most often only two to three days. There is provision, too, for extraordinary sessions of the Supreme Soviet to be held. The main purpose of the Supreme Soviet is to pass laws, approve the annual budget of the state and carry out the other usual functions of parliamentary bodies, but most of its activity is only formal since a controversial debate never takes place and voting is usually unanimous. Most of the work of the Supreme Soviet is done in between the sessions in various committees of the deputies.

The elections are for one candidate only in each constituency. Although non-Party candidates are included, the lists are prepared by the Communist Party. It might therefore be asked, what is the purpose of the elections? It is mainly for educational and propaganda purposes in which the political and other relevant issues are brought before the public in a concentrated way. They also help to demonstrate the continued hold of the Party over the people. Lastly they serve as a safety valve to test public opinion and feelings on questions which are agitating the people. For weeks before the elections, millions of Party workers are engaged in contacting the voters and in ensuring that they vote on election day, which is usually a Sunday from early morning till midnight.

A deputy is required to be at least 23 years of age, but no other qualifications are laid down. When elected, he has the right to draw his salary from his place of work and expenses for transport and other emoluments. Although visibly the deputies may not have such an important role, in fact they devote considerable time to listening to their constituents' complaints and grievances, in many cases interceding with the higher authorities on their behalf, and carry out functions very similar to those of members of parliament in other countries. The private and not so visible activities of the deputies are, therefore, of greater value in the Soviet political system than is usually realized.

The main burden of work falls on the Praesidium of the Supreme Soviet, which is composed of a Chairman and 15 Deputy Chairmen, a secretary and 16 members. The fifteen Deputy Chairmen are the fifteen Presidents of the Supreme Soviets of the Union Republics. Among the 16 members of the Praesidium are high Party officials and leaders, including the General Secretary of the Central Committee of the CPSU.

The USSR Council of Ministers is the 'highest executive and administrative organ of the State power of the USSR' and in fact the Federal Government of the Soviet Union. It is responsible to the Supreme Soviet, and when the Supreme Soviet is not in session, to the Praesidium. The Council of Ministers is enjoined to operate within the laws enacted by the Supreme Soviet, but it also has the right to take legislative initiative. Its decrees and ordinances are binding throughout the territory of the USSR.

The Council of Ministers is formed at the first session of a newly elected Supreme Soviet. First, a Chairman of the Council of Ministers is approved. He then submits his Government to the joint session of the two chambers for approval. Between sessions, individual ministers can be appointed or released at the recommendation of the Chairman by the Praesidium of the Supreme Soviet. It is not necessary for members of the Government to be members of the Supreme Soviet.

Apart from the Chairman, equivalent to the Prime Minister in the British parliamentary system, the Council of Ministers consists of two First Deputies and Deputy Chairmen, Heads of All-Union and Union-Republican Ministries, Chairmen of State Committees, the Head of the Central Statistical Administration, the Chairman of the State Bank and other equally important heads of departments. The special duties of the Council of Ministers are to co-ordinate and supervise the Armed Forces and national defence and to exercise over-all control over the country's foreign policy and foreign trade. In the most important internal affairs the Council of Ministers and the Central

Committee of the Party often announce joint decisions. This is a reflection of the notion, which is fundamental to the Soviet view of a government, that the Party should rule, the government simply administer. In any case many of the leading members of the Council of Ministers, including its Chairman, are members of the Politburo and at all levels the government and Party machine is intertwined. A sharp conflict between the Party and the government is thus impossible, though occasionally differences of opinion may arise because of the way the government outlook is affected by the practical problems of administration.

Ministries in the USSR are of three kinds: All-Union, Union-Republican and Republican. The All-Union ministries directly exercise their control over the whole territory of the USSR. The Union-Republican ministries share the responsibility with ministries in the Republics where they exist, since all Republics may not have equivalent ministries. In some cases there are ministries in Republics concerned with purely local problems and their counterparts do not exist at the Union level.

A minister is personally responsible for the affairs of his department and is helped by a collegium of senior advisers. In case of any difference of opinion between the two, the minister takes his own decisions after communicating the substance of difference to the Council of Ministers.

The collegium, however, also has a right of appeal to the Council of Ministers. A minister is empowered to issue instructions (*instruktsii*) and orders (*prikazy*) within the limits of his ministry's sphere of activity, and within the confines of existing laws and regulations and policy directives by the Council of Ministers. Instructions are rules of a general character. Orders concern concrete implementation of the existing rules.

Each of the 15 Union Republics has its own Council of Ministers. The only difference between the Republican and All-Union Council of Ministers is that the former's powers are confined to the territory of the Republic. One rung down are the Councils of Ministers of the Autonomous Republics, which must operate within the limits laid down by Union-Republic ministries. One noticeable feature in recent years has been the gradual expansion of the rights of the Republican ministries, particularly in the industrial sphere, where they now control most of the enterprises within their territory.

In the Soviet political system a great deal is made of the local Soviets, the organs of state power which exist at various levels below the Republic level. This is not surprising since one of the potent slogans of the Revolution in its early days was 'All power to the Soviets'. Officially they are considered to be the mainstay of political life in the USSR.

The local Soviets are elected on the basis of adult franchise and within them are Communist Party groups composed of all the deputies who are Party members. They have a secretary in close touch with and subordinate to the local Party Committee. The Soviets elect an Executive Committee, which carries out all the administrative tasks and is simultaneously responsible to its Soviet and to the next higher Executive Committee in the hierarchy. The Executive Committees form departments and administrations for services within the local community and for industry and agriculture. The emphasis of the work of the Soviet Executive Committees is invariably on economic questions.

The trouble, however, is that the local Soviets have become rather powerless bodies while the real authority is enjoyed by the Executive Committees. Although constitutionally the local Soviets are required to meet several times in a year, very often the Soviets are not called into session at all for long periods. It is a matter of frequent complaint in the press that the local Soviets are treated in cavalier fashion and that their functions are usurped by the Executive Committees. Much of the work of the local Soviets is also carried out by the permanent Commissions elected by the Soviets. Much confusion prevails at the level of local government, and the Executive Committees exercise far more power in reality than is given to them by the constitution.

Efficient functioning of the local Soviets thus remains an open and live issue in theory but in practice it really makes little difference since the local Party Committee exercises the vital powers necessary to run the administration smoothly and to direct the Executive Committees in their work.

The principle of the separation of the judiciary from the executive does not exist in the Soviet Union since it is considered that the courts are participants in the constitution of communism, and, therefore, active and effective executors of state policy. The present court system in the Soviet Union has a three-tiered structure. At the base are the People's Courts, followed by the Regional Courts and the Supreme Courts.

People's Courts are courts of first instance which serve the rural districts and towns. Regional Courts exist on a circuit, region and area basis. They have appellate jurisdiction and are courts of first and second instance. Lastly, the Supreme Courts are at the Republic level, Autonomous as well as Union Republics, and above all stands the Supreme Court of the USSR. While the People's Courts have no functional subdivisions, all other courts have one collegium for civil and another for criminal cases. In the armed forces a separate system of military tribunals exists, topped by the Military Collegium of the USSR Supreme Court. All regional courts and Supreme Courts, with a few exceptions, have a Praesidium.

Judges are elected and all of them serve a five-year term. The judges of People's Courts are elected by a general election in their districts, those of regional Courts by their regional Soviets, and Supreme Court judges by the corresponding Supreme Soviets. The judges are not required to have legal training or qualifications but generally about 80 per cent of those elected have been found to have received legal education. There is some debate as to whether possession of legal knowledge should not be made compulsory for those seeking election as judges. The overwhelming majority of the judges and other members of the judiciary are, of course, members of the CPSU.

The Soviet political system is highly complex, its complexity increased because of the extensive and effective control exercised by the Party in every walk of life. It must be said too that the whole system has become progressively more and more bureaucratic. This is a matter of some concern to the Party leaders but they can only alleviate it from time to time, not cure it of the bureaucratic spirit. Any reform directed against bureaucratic practices often only produces more bureaucracy.

Another problem caused by the system results from the Party control of the state. Dissent is neither tolerated nor understood. It can be argued that there is enough scope for the people to air their grievances through the Party itself, through the Soviets at all levels and through the judicial and administrative system. It is fair to say that the effectiveness of these legitimate ways of seeking redress is far greater than is normally assumed. However, since all this takes place behind the scenes, in a hidden, almost surreptitious manner, it is difficult for any foreigner, used to the open societies of the west, to assess it. There is no reason, of course, why more open procedures cannot be introduced without impairing either the authority or the image of the Party and the State.

Another factor which creates misgivings is the long record of Stalin's gigantic abuse of the system and the fact that the Soviet authorities have not revealed the whole truth about these abuses. Therefore suspicion about the system persists and is transferred to its present operation. The harsh treatment meted out to some political and literary dissenters in recent years has reinforced this suspicion.

The system, however, despite all its faults and virtues, is not on the verge of collapse. Any system that has survived the misuse by Stalin must be given some credit for resilience and adaptability and though the adaptability of the Soviet system is low and the impulse for radical reform weak and diffused, it is capable of survival and re-invigoration. To expect perfection from any political system is utopian and the great weakness of the Soviet propagandists is that they claim perfection for their system as it has existed, as it exists and as it will exist. This is a tall claim and cannot be entertained by any reasonable and un-biased person.

Nevertheless, one obvious lesson from the history of the Russian Revolution is that the system established by it will successfully muddle through and survive in the face of great odds.

10 External relations

THE EMERGENCE OF RUSSIA as a socialist state has brought about an upheaval in international relations. For more than half a century the rest of the world has been concerned about the Soviet Union and the Soviet Union's relations with other countries. It is widely held that ideology takes precedence over other interests, but a cool look at the course of Soviet foreign policy since its inception proves that this is an exaggeration. Soviet policies in general have specific qualities of their own but these can be explained to a large extent as the results of the interplay of geographical factors and power politics. Ideology, independent of these factors, has played a smaller role.

The most fundamental element in Soviet foreign policy is a continuous search for security, a security which geography and history have denied Russia since the beginnings of her history. This preoccupation persists, though manifested in different ways because Russia has clearly emerged as one of the two super-powers. This vastly improved the security of the state but could not banish the feeling of insecurity history has bequeathed to the Soviet people.

It is true that ideologically Lenin and his comrades were committed to a world revolution, but even they saw it as a process taking place independently, a spontaneous culmination of the capitalist phase of history, rather than a task to be carried out by the Soviet state on others' behalf. Their hopes of such a world-wide revolution never materialized. Even in Germany, which they considered to be ripe for revolution, their hopes met an early setback, Besides, they were thinking much more of how revolutions abroad would help the new, weak socialist state of the Soviet Union than the other way round. They certainly made appeals for peace couched in revolutionary forms, over the heads of governments, to the peoples of the world. But this revolutionary rhetoric made little difference to their actual behaviour in diplomacy.

The first task of the new government was to survive. Its first major diplomatic test was the Brest-Litovsk peace treaty with Germany, signed in 1918 on terms which were not at all favourable to the Soviet Union. It was done upon Lenin's insistence against strong opposition from the Central Committee of the Bolshevik Party and from the Left Socialist Revolutionaries. That the Brest-Litovsk treaty itself became a dead letter because of other developments in Europe and Germany is another matter; it does not invalidate the basic assumption behind its acceptance – survival of the Soviet Revolution at the time.

But security was not the only motivation. The new regime was in no sense a continuation of the old. Both for ideological reasons and as a result of circumstances it had no alternative but to play a different role in the world from that of Tsarist Russia. Unlike the Tsarist regime, it could not pursue the will o' the wisp of an empire, nor identify itself with the powerful capitalist states of the west – which in any case were hostile to it. Nor can it be overlooked that the new leaders of Russia were sincere in their fiery vision of a new world to come. Therefore the new foreign policy of Russia was different not only in form but in substance.

Everything about the Soviet Union attracts myth. The foreign policy of the country has been shrouded in the myth of revolutionary expansionism. It is held, for instance, that the Soviet leaders' support of the national liberation movements in Asia and elsewhere was but a continuation of the Tsarist policy of seeking an empire there. It is also held that the Soviet rulers were insincere in their support of the revolutionary movements because they did not physically intervene in their favour. Similarly, the profession of peaceful coexistence, put forward by leaders of the Soviet Union from Lenin onwards, has been seen as a ruse to lull the suspicions of the outside world. In other words, whatever the Soviet Union did was from ulterior motives and wrong.

The reality is different. Soviet foreign policy is much more limited by what is conceived to be possible than by the rigid criteria of an active revolutionary ideology. Like any other power the Soviet Union has made grave mistakes, sometimes misbehaving in an outrageous manner. As a rule, however, Soviet policies have been cautious, correct and shaped with an eye to the national self-interest.

Of course, the early Soviet leaders had a distinct attitude of their own towards the outside world, by which their assessment of events was influenced. They perceived the powerful western states to be inimical to the new Russia, and this was confirmed by the intervention – half-hearted and inept though it was – by America, Britain, France, Japan and others. As for the rest of the world, it was not yet born; it was either colonized by the European powers or controlled by them. For the Soviet state this posed a security problem of infinite importance. The country was surrounded by states which could be used for hostile intrigue against her, and so, naturally, wherever there was a breach in this solid phalanx the Russians tried to use it in their favour.

Out of this tactical necessity were born the friendly relations with Afghanistan, which brought some relief from the constant tension on the border with Iran, and the threat from the colonial British Indian Empire, as they perceived it in Moscow, on the other side of Afghanistan. Even if the Soviet leaders had not been revolutionary, they would have been stupid not to sympathize with anti-British movements in India. With Turkey, too, the new regime was able to establish friendly relations when Kemal Ataturk came to power in 1924. The Russians even provided some economic help to Afghanistan and Turkey.

Asia, however, was still slumbering and Africa was remote and distant from the more pressing Soviet problems nearer home. Till the end of the Second World War, therefore, the history of Soviet foreign policy is by and large a history of her relations with the Western countries, specially Britain, France and Germany. Europe was a promise, and a threat. As the promise of proper Marxist revolution in the highly industrialized countries faded, the threat loomed larger and larger. The policy of Lenin, and of Stalin too, was progressively influenced by the need for postponing the catastrophe of another war as long as possible. Since they could do little to influence the governments of the time, they fell back upon the only means available to them of trying to influence public opinion and of using communist parties in these countries to take up opposition to whatever was considered to be against the interests of the Soviet Union.

There was also a positive element in this negative approach. Soon after the death of Lenin, the Soviet Union embarked on a gigantic programme of economic development, and the ruthlessness with which Stalin implemented it created havoc within the country. In this unsettled state, the Russians could do very little to oppose effectively

Western schemes against them, except to try to play the game in their own way. While there were constant efforts by Western powers to form a grouping against the Soviet Union, Moscow's diplomatic endeavour was constantly to break it up through bilateral manoeuvres.

Trade played a considerable role in the limited success the Soviet efforts had in this direction. The very countries which took the lead in treating the Russians as political pariahs were eager to have a share of the Soviet market. When the slump came, the compulsion to sell goods increased even more and from time to time Moscow was able to negotiate loans and credits to finance its purchase of goods from them. The mutual distrust remained.

This state of affairs also enhanced the feeling of insecurity and its concomitant, the siege mentality. Stalin is often blamed for creating it, but he merely exploited it to impose cohesion upon the country, to demand sacrifices on a heroic scale and to spur the people to a greater endeavour. This must not be forgotten in the face of so much verbal aggressiveness in Soviet pronouncements of the period. Moreover, this verbose militancy was accompanied by practical diplomacy to keep the growing crisis defused.

There was another factor. It is all too easy to judge Soviet actions after the Revolution and up to the Second World War as if she were already the super-power she appears today. But Russia had been weakened greatly by war and revolution, and the defeat at the hands of the Japanese in 1905 was still very much alive when the threat from Germany began anew. Ever present in Soviet minds was the fear that Germany and Japan would combine to launch a simultaneous invasion from east and west, and this trap had to be avoided at all costs.

The superhuman effort which Stalin made to keep on good terms with Germany was not simply because of any sentimental importance which Moscow attached to ties with Germany. It was an effort to keep Germany detached from the rest of Europe and thus prevent the formation of a joint front. The redeeming feature of the whole situation for the Soviet Union was that the continental powers were themselves as much afraid of Germany as they were nervous about the revolutionary stance of Soviet policy.

In the colonial world it was not the practical efforts of the Soviet Union which troubled the imperialist powers. Such activity was on a minuscule scale and mostly consisted of helping ineffective revolutionaries or backing newly established communist parties. But the very

165

existence of the Soviet Union, outside the imperialist power system, served as an inspiration, a model to be emulated, a source of moral support and sometimes guidance. In the evolution of the nationalist movements of Asia and Africa the importance of the Soviet example cannot be exaggerated. One perceptible result was that the nationalist movements acquired an economic content in their outlook and propaganda. They no longer talked simply of political freedom but linked it with economic welfare as well. They did not necessarily subscribe to the economic philosophy of communism as such; indeed, quite often nationalist movements were at loggerheads with communists in their own countries. But the fact that they could no longer ignore economic questions was a tribute to the constructive element in the Russian Revolution and an even greater tribute to the success of the Five Year Plans in the Soviet Union. Nevertheless, many nationalist parties and leaders felt alienated from the Soviet government because of the fierce attacks made upon their integrity during some of Stalin's foreign policy manoeuvres. It perplexed them greatly, and even after some of these countries had won freedom, relations between them and Moscow were at best cool till Stalin's death.

There was a dualism in Soviet policy: the aim was to retain for Moscow a very special position as a revolutionary regime and yet to carry out the normal functions of diplomacy and be accepted by other governments on terms of equality. This duality has persisted, sometimes giving rise to complicated situations and creating an impression that there is more behind the Soviet moves than there is in reality. Soviet propaganda has been able to claim that the policy pursued by Moscow is justifiable on special grounds, not purely in terms of conventional diplomacy. The results have not always been happy and others have either resented it or tried to claim similar liberty for themselves.

Whatever the successes or failures of Soviet diplomacy in the Stalin period, the new position which the Soviet Union acquired after the Second World War and the change in the world power structure presented Soviet diplomacy with new dangers and challenges. To a certain extent it was a paradoxical situation. The Soviet Union was now accepted as a super-power yet remained relatively weak, at any rate for the first few years after the war. It had assumed responsibility for the new communist states in Eastern Europe which were established after the war, and to a lesser extent for China as well after the success of the communist revolution there, but these states could be protected only by conventional diplomacy and by general acceptance of the post-war status quo.

Looking at Soviet relations with the outside world after the Second World War, one is struck by the extreme conservatism of Stalin's actions, his total refusal to provide any covert aid to the left-wing movements in Europe at the time. It was not a question of a change in objective. The main Soviet objective undoubtedly remained to eliminate the overwhelming presence of America on her periphery in Europe and also in Asia. But in order to attain this objective, the Russians were at no time willing to start a military conflict. Perhaps the extreme hostility between the two super-powers during the Cold War period also had a restraining influence. Even without the Cold War, it is difficult to imagine Stalin undertaking a military adventure to conquer other nations for communism. Stalin did take risks where direct Soviet interests were involved but not to the point of jumping over the brink into an abyss.

Stalin's foreign policy had run into a dead end in the last years of his life. In Europe, the situation had been stabilized by a tacitly recognized and accepted division of the Continent into two blocs. Since Soviet attention at the time was almost exclusively focused on Europe and the American presence there, there was not such great awareness of the new Asia which was knocking on the door waiting to be recognized. The appearance of Communist China, the Korean War which followed, and the new tensions which these events gave rise to brought Asia back into the focus of Soviet policy but its full significance was still obscured.

The historiography of Soviet foreign policy has so long been concerned with her relations with the West, written mostly by westerners for westerners, that the Asian dimensions of her policy tend to be neglected. For most writers it has been of peripheral interest and if in recent years there has been greater recognition of the importance of Asia to Moscow, it has been mostly in terms of the Sino-Soviet schism. Important though this is, it is not the only factor. The element of competition with America is equally important, since it is the American influence in Asia which the Russians have to contend with. Besides, the Soviet Union needs good bilateral relations with these countries in her own interests.

As a world power, Soviet interests are in theory of a global nature and ideology reinforces this. In practice, however, such interests remain dependent upon Soviet capacity to assert this power effectively and to be seen to be doing so. The Cuban crisis in 1962 demonstrated vividly the limitation of physical Soviet power. It is in this context that the crash programme for building the Soviet navy as well as her merchant fleet assumes great importance. And though Soviet expansion in both these fields has been very rapid, and within a decade she will perhaps overtake the United States, the alarm created by it in Nato circles is somewhat overdone. The size of a navy is not always an accurate guide to its striking power and almost all outside observers are agreed that Soviet naval expansion is remarkably defensive and limited in character. For Soviet policy even such a limited kind of expansion has the advantage of making her presence credible. This appears to be the primary aim – not a threat to challenge other countries or to enforce her own policy.

Much has also been made of the view that the expansion of the Soviet navy is designed to fill the vacuum in the Indian Ocean and the Mediterranean regions. This may be so, but even on this score the alarm is exaggerated. The welcome given to the Soviet navy by the ex-colonial countries, vitally affected by the security of these oceans, indicates that they are far from averse to such a presence. For historical reasons, and for too long, the Western powers have treated the oceans of the world as a vast lake in which they hold sway, and politically and commercially they could hold the smaller countries to ransom. Now that the Russians are breaking this monopoly they resent it. However, there is little they can do but accept it.

In every region of the world the Soviet Union has different kinds of problems to deal with and equally different goals, but the over-all aim of Soviet foreign policy can be described as peace, security, stability, and enhancement of super-power status.

America, naturally, is the biggest challenge for Soviet foreign policy. On both sides there have been changes of tactics and attitude. The two countries no longer confront each other with unrelieved hostility, but have steadily moved towards seeking accommodation with each other on political as well as on the more difficult and complex military problems. They both remain wary of each other but recognize that the nature of nuclear power makes a conflict of war dimensions between them extremely dangerous as well as unlikely. Throughout the post-war period, particularly since the death of

Stalin and the end of Truman's presidency in the United States, they have shown an anxiety to avoid a direct confrontation. The Cuban episode in 1962 was the sole exception and it was the consequence of a combination of extraordinary circumstances. There is also recognition by the Soviet policy-makers that in many vital matters American power is still superior, though the Russians are closing the gap in some respects. The convergence of their interests, therefore, lies in the necessity to avoid a direct military clash.

There is no convergence of interests otherwise. They still compete with each other, sometimes fiercely. The Russians have not given up their aim of reducing the American presence everywhere to manageable proportions and to supplant it with their own if they can. The Americans still want to restrict the Soviet influence as much as they can, to treat it as a challenge and even a moral issue, since the Soviet Union is, after all, a communist state.

Where direct bilateral interests are concerned, the two countries have gone a long way towards finding ways and means of avoiding conflict and sometimes even competition. On questions of disarmament and control of nuclear energy for military purposes they have begun to co-operate. Step by step they have sought to establish an equilibrium in the esoteric, astronomically expensive and destructive field of missiles. A treaty, which included Britain as a sponsor, was signed in August 1963 banning all nuclear tests except those underground. In July 1968 the nuclear non-proliferation treaty was signed, banning the spread of nuclear weapons to non-nuclear countries. In November 1969 formal bilateral talks began between the Soviet Union and the United States in Helsinki in an attempt to work out an agreement to control offensive and defensive missile systems. These talks came to be known as SALT (Strategic Arms Limitation Talks). All these developments are the fruits of recognition on both sides that in a war neither of them will be victorious and both will be ruined.

In bringing the two super-powers closer in this fashion, an important if indirect role has been played by other nations. The smaller countries as well as nations like China and India have made it impossible for the two powers to be able to rely on controlling them in any way where big-power interests conflict with their own interests. This also compels Washington and Moscow to find a modus vivendi lest they become embroiled in a war through other conflicts in which they may be backing opposite sides.

That there are many issues on which their interests clash, there can be little doubt. The Vietnam war is a good example of how both sides, while backing two different parties to the hilt, have tacitly agreed not to come to blows themselves. There the Soviet weapons have played a tremendous role in increasing and sustaining the fighting capacity of the North Vietnamese against the American combat troops in South Vietnam. Yet the Americans have to pretend that they are fighting simply the North Vietnamese and have to allow uninterrupted delivery of Soviet arms to Hanoi. In the Middle East, the Russians back the Arabs and the Americans the Israelis, both supplying a huge quantity of arms and ammunition to their friends. But both sides not only refuse to be drawn into a direct conflict but also try to find a political solution on their own by means of bilateral meetings or conferences with the British and French, who also have stakes in the region. Neither the Americans nor the Russians have been willing to sacrifice their own interests for the sake of compromise although both want to prevent the persistent local antagonisms from boiling over.

Another source of future conflict between the two super-powers may be China. The Russians have noted with considerable anxiety that the Sino-Soviet schism has gradually shifted American sympathies towards China. This tendency has become even more pronounced since the violent border conflicts between the two communist states in 1969. Moscow cannot sit idly by while Peking and Washington move towards a rapprochement. For this reason, too, the Russians would like to maintain a degree of cordial bilateral relations with the United States and at the same time to keep on trying to improve relations with Peking as well. It is a game which can go on for a long time to come. The prospects, therefore, are of correct but on the whole cool relations between Moscow and Washington.

Soviet-American relations are important because they are between super-powers. The Soviet relations with China are of much more intimate concern to Moscow, and much more of a permanent headache. China is a rival for leadership of the communist movement, a great danger to the security of the Soviet state and potentially a world power antagonistic to the Soviet Union; she therefore threatens a wide range of Soviet interests.

Equally important is the way Chinese behaviour affects and complicates almost every aspect of Soviet relations with the outside world. China cannot but exercise a baneful influence on the internal policies of the Soviet Union so long as the dispute remains bitter and violent, since it creates internal tensions which demand stricter control in every sphere of life, and diverts much-needed funds to extra military expenditure on the borders with China.

The main consequence of the ideological dispute is not that Peking has replaced Moscow as leader of the movement, but that Moscow now has to pay greater heed to the other parties and at the same time make sure that the Chinese are kept away from making greater mischief in Eastern Europe. To some extent Moscow has been helped by the excesses of the Cultural Revolution, which is acceptable to very few communist parties with the exception of some extremist splinter groups. The dispute does make it possible for some of them to be neutral but on the whole the Russians have regained the position they lost under Khrushchev though not to the extent of the undisputed mastery over the world communist movement which they enjoyed in Stalin's time. Nevertheless, Moscow will have constantly to adjust its policies so as not to be outflanked by Peking.

The danger to the Soviet security is an obvious one. The Soviet Union has a long land frontier with China, running to 4,150 miles. This frontier is intersected by Mongolia about halfway along and Mongolia has a 2,700-mile-long border with China. Since, for all practical purposes, the Russians are responsible for the security of Mongolia and cannot allow it to be endangered, they have to look after the whole length of 6,850 miles of the northern Chinese border. Any insecurity on this stretch poses a tremendous problem for Moscow. Though Soviet firepower is greater and more effective than that of China, the Chinese have greater manpower and any struggle could be very bloody as well as prolonged. This is what worries Moscow. Even if the Russians are able to deal with the immediate threat to their security it will continue to grow in proportion to the growth of Chinese power. Therefore, unless there is a measure of understanding between the two countries, a Chinese sword of Damocles will always hang over the Soviet Union. The Chinese know this and exploit it to the maximum.

The Chinese threat to Soviet power is not purely local. Peking, too, aspires to a big-power role in the world, especially in Asia. The Russians, who have just broken through the *cordon sanitaire* of Western empires in Asia, are not simply going to sit back and see it replaced by a new one controlled by Peking. China undoubtedly has certain advantages. In South-East Asia geography favours the Chinese. In the rest of Asia they can project a crude image of Asian solidarity and revolutionary mystique. They have not hesitated to inject an element of racialism into their propaganda against the Soviet Union, and to counter all this, Soviet diplomacy will be constantly on its toes in Asia. This competition with China is one element in the great interest shown by Moscow in South Asian affairs.

Of course, the present state of tension between the two countries need not be a permanent one. A change of regime in Peking or some other factor may bring about an easing of relations. In the winter of 1969–70 there were faint signs of such a thaw, although it remained uncertain whether relations would improve to any significant degree; but even if quarrels give way to peaceful co-existence, the Soviet Union will have to remain wary of China for a long time to come.

China aside, the Soviet Union has cultivated the Asian countries in no uncertain manner. To some of the countries, like India, Indonesia, Iran and lately Pakistan, it has provided aid on a spectacular scale and Soviet bilateral trade with these countries has grown at a phenomenal rate. Practically every Asian country, big or small, now has dealings of some kind or another with the Soviet Union and Soviet views on matters concerning Asia can no longer be ignored as they were in the past. This is a staggering achievement for the diplomacy of a country which was virtually sealed off from Asia until twenty years ago and has since made headway there against great opposition from America and the West.

One reason why Soviet interest in Asia grew so rapidly was the stalemate in Europe, which brought about a stability in Soviet relations with that continent and negated hopes of further revolutions in European countries. Asia was unstable and ripe for revolution and the communist take-over in China added impetus to this view. But Stalin failed to understand the intense nationalism of Asia, and when the communist parties in some of the Asian countries tried to stage revolutions, largely at the behest of Peking rather than Moscow, they failed miserably. Into the bargain, the nationalist leaders of these countries became suspicious of Soviet motives and many of them proceeded to join Western-sponsored military blocs. The Russians, however, recovered rapidly from this setback.

The next phase in Soviet policy was to back the non-aligned countries in Asia. These were the countries which had avoided joining anti-communist military blocs and generally had more socially conscious political leadership. India was obviously the archetype of such countries and during the Khrushchev phase Soviet involvement with India grew to such an extent that China began to object. In the Sino-Indian border conflict, the Chinese attack upon India in October 1962 was designed not only to diminish the stature of India but also to sabotage Soviet success there. After a little hesitation, Khrushchev supported India against China and publicly deplored Chinese tactics. This had important repercussions on Sino-Soviet relations and the Chinese made much of the fact that for the first time a socialist country was supporting a non-socialist country in a dispute with another socialist country.

The fact remains that the Soviet Union found it convenient to encourage non-alignment, which in effect meant undercutting the role of the West in these countries and establishing Soviet influence. It was also hoped that it would block expansion of Chinese influence as well.

Arms supplies were other means by which Moscow could and did court some of the non-aligned countries and even lent diplomatic support in their disputes with other, aligned Asian states. Thus the Soviet Union provided valuable backing to India in the United Nations against Pakistan's claims on Kashmir, which were backed by the Western countries. Similarly support was extended to Indonesia in her dispute with Malaysia although the relationship was complicated there because of the pro-Peking shift in Indonesian policies during the last years of Sukarno.

But arms and diplomacy were not the only means. Where the Russians really scored was in fully appreciating the strong urge towards industrialization which existed in all the newly independent countries. They were short of capital and industrial skills and the Western countries, enthusiastic about supplying them with arms or providing some help with light industries, were, on the whole, reluctant to help with heavy industry. They were more apt to lecture them about improving agriculture and leaving such complex things as heavy industry to the West for the foreseeable future. This enhanced the Soviet image by comparison, since the Russians were only too willing to come forward to help in such projects. They argued that by providing the basic industries they were accelerating the process of social change, and this was indisputably true. Thus the Soviet Union

173

appeared as agents for desirable change and the West as upholders of the colonial status quo.

A new phase in Soviet policy began about the time of Khrushchev's fall. Instead of selecting a few countries for intensive attention, Moscow sought a wider base for its influence. In the process it muted its all-out support for the non-aligned countries and turned to the aligned ones as well, in order to wean them somehow from the military pacts and to ensure that they did not jump to the Chinese side of the fence. The example of Pakistan, which aligned with China once the rift between Peking and Delhi had taken shape, served as a warning. With the Cold War gradually fading out and ceasing to be profitable, the aligned Asian states were also interested in a rapprochement with the Soviet Union, Without making a fuss about their formal ties with the West, the Russians began to pour in aid and reassure them diplomatically.

It is an ironical comment upon the much-vaunted military pacts promoted by America that their members had to turn to the Soviet Union to realize ambitious industrial projects, for some of which they had pleaded in vain with their Western partners for years. Countries like Iran and Turkey, though still suspicious of the Russians, responded eagerly to these overtures and soon became cautious about offending Soviet interests. Iran, for example, signed an undertaking not to allow foreign bases on her soil. Turkey was in a more difficult position as a member of Nato but nevertheless managed to tone down its strident anti-Russianism in return for economic aid and Soviet expressions of regret about some aspects of conduct in the past. The success of Soviet-Asian policy so far is thus the result, not of some fluke but of cold calculation.

Even in South-East Asia, an area where American presence and fear of China are predominant factors, the Russians have slowly gained despite setbacks. While Indonesia was lost first to China and then to a pro-Western alignment after the fall of Sukarno, Soviet relations with Burma and Malaysia improved and even solidly pro-western countries like Thailand and the Philippines showed increasing desire to have better relations with Moscow. The Vietnam war complicated the situation in this region, but in the post-Khrushchev period the Soviet leaders made a determined bid to regain the goodwill of Hanoi, which had shifted to a pro-Peking position earlier. Similar approaches were made in the Far East, where the communist regime of

North Korea was again cultivated, and to some extent drawn away from China. Economic and political ties with Japan also improved though the Japanese remained too strongly allied to the United States and wary of China to respond very ardently towards the Soviet Union.

The most remarkable transformation of the Soviet position in Asia has taken place in the Middle East. It is established in the region as a major power. In some countries of the Middle East, Western influence has been virtually wiped out and the Soviet Union is well on the way to becoming the dominant external power in the region as a whole. Initially, the opening for Soviet diplomacy was provided by the hostile reaction of some Arab countries to the Western attempts to dragoon them into an anti-Soviet military pact, the notorious Baghdad Pact, set up in 1955. The Soviet position was further strengthened by the Suez crisis in 1956, when Soviet arms began to flow freely to Egypt and Moscow undertook the construction of the vast Aswan dam. In their antagonism to and fear of Israel, the Arabs found that among the big powers only the Soviet Union was willing to help them and provide arms without having to balance supplies to Israel. And although relations between the Arabs and the Russians have not always been smooth, Moscow has increasingly come to rely upon President Nasser of Egypt as a statesman interested in radical change in the Arab world as a whole.

But if Moscow is willing to provide arms and aid, it is not willing to intervene directly against Israel, which would involve a sharp conflict with America. The June 1967 war between the Arabs and Israelis accentuated Arab dependence upon the Soviet Union. Soviet influence as well as her military presence became more and more pronounced. Besides, although the Soviet Union generally supports the Arabs its position is not absolutely identical with theirs. Soviet pronouncements make a point of recognizing Israel's right to exist as a state, while the Arab politicians dare not express such a sentiment for fear that it will undermine their position with the people in their own countries.

Africa is another region where the Soviet Union has displayed greater interest in recent years. On the whole, however, Soviet policies there have not been so successful as in Asia. There are a variety of reasons for this. African politics are more unstable than Asian, and the Soviet Union has found it rather difficult to find elements on which it can rely. Western influence in Africa is still very strong, with economic stakes of a highly profitable nature. This means there is more determined opposition to Soviet attempts to befriend the African states. In general, too, Soviet expertise about Africa is uncertain and rather superficial and the Russians made a number of serious mistakes in their approach to the dark continent. While Moscow has the capacity and knowledge to recover even from grave mistakes in Asia and to regain its position, it does not seem to have a similar capacity in relation to Africa. Therefore, Soviet dealings with Africa have become cautious, except for the Arab states of the north like Algeria where Soviet influence has become great. Nevertheless, Soviet interest in Africa is growing and given a certain degree of stability in African politics as well as a deepening of the level of Soviet expertise about African affairs, the Soviet position need not always remain weak. The Soviet handling of the Nigerian civil war, with its backing of the Federal side, suggests that lessons have been learnt from past mistakes.

Latin America is a region remote from the Soviet Union. Soviet involvement with Cuba, however, has encouraged her interest there. Since the Cuban crisis the Russians have sought to make a more comprehensive bid for influence in Latin America, primarily by means of trade. Although the Russians have succeeded in establishing sounder diplomatic and economic relations with many of the Latin American countries, they concede that American influence is still likely to predominate there for a long time to come. The only satisfaction which Moscow can derive in its dealing with that part of the world is that revolutionary-reformist movements are still very much alive there, as is the anti-American sentiment of the people. Potentially, therefore, Latin America as a region of Soviet influence is not altogether unpromising. But while the level of Soviet diplomatic activity is high in Latin America, the area is of too peripheral interest for the Russians to get closely involved. The main Soviet preoccupation in that region will remain protection of Cuba from a counter-revolution, in other words, an American take-over.

An important role in the expansion of Soviet relations with all the developing countries is trade. The Soviet Union is in a position to supply them with capital goods and machinery and in return offers a potentially big market for a variety of raw materials, consumer goods and light engineering goods. The market of course is a Soviet state monopoly and carefully regulated to maintain a balanced foreign trade. But as over-all Soviet foreign trade expands, the Russians are buying more and more from developing countries. For these countries an additional attractive factor in such trade is that many of their products cannot be sold in the Western market, where the tariff walls are high, quality control is more rigorous and quotas are allocated. Since for most of them export of these goods is even more important for development than simply aid, they look upon the Soviet Union with great favour and expectations. Another point of interest is that though the Soviet intake of goods is strictly controlled, the market inside is almost insatiable and the level of Soviet purchases can go on rising for many years to come. The attraction of trade with the Soviet Union is thus a positive factor for Moscow to make use of in its approach to these countries.

Peaceful co-existence with Asian and other developing countries, despite occasional setbacks, is good politics and good business for Moscow, and even more so for the developing countries. They will not necessarily line up with Moscow, as some naïve critics of Soviet foreign policy might maintain, but will have greater interest in becoming neutral in the race between Moscow and Washington or for that matter between Peking and Moscow. In their bilateral relations with the developing countries, two kinds of complications cause most trouble to the Russians: first, the competition from Peking and Washington; and second, the mutual antagonisms of the developing countries themselves, which can be very destructive. Nearly two decades of close involvement with Asian affairs, and the stature which the Soviet Union has acquired there, have now focused the attention of Moscow on finding some way to reduce the nuisance value of both these factors and further enhance the Soviet standing and power in Asia. The suggestion for an Asian security system, initiated by Mr Brezhnev at the World Communist Conference in July 1969, was a step in this direction. Though the idea may be a long time maturing and finding general acceptance, and no concrete proposals about it appear to have been made, it must be considered more in the nature of a multi-lateral political and anti-war treaty than a military pact. The usual fate of military pacts in Asia will hardly tempt the Soviet policy-makers to attempt such a task, nor is there any evidence that they want to get involved in promoting such an enterprise. But a broad institutional framework in which Moscow enjoys some influence is a much more practical proposition. It also has the advantage that it leaves room for other powers to join if they care to. In the coming years more will be heard of this matter.

It is nearer home, in Eastern Europe, that the Soviet Union faces a continuous challenge. The Communist states of the region act like a protective girdle on the western frontiers of the Soviet Union. Here ideology and national self-interest are completely intertwined and Moscow regards any weakening of the communist ideology in these states as a danger to its security and to the cohesion of the communist bloc as a whole. Twice in fourteen years, in Hungary in 1956 and in Czechoslovakia in 1968, there has been military intervention by the Soviet Union because it was considered that such a threat had developed. Clearly the Russians will not allow any change in the status quo in Eastern Europe which they consider to be against their interests.

Yet they have to deal with the problem of evolving a system in which the smaller members of the socialist community will not feel utterly dominated by Moscow. Unless they do, resentment against the Soviet Union will continue to deepen, even if the governments in power are unable to express it and unable to allow public feelings to be expressed on the subject. There seem to be only two possibilities. Firstly, that after a long and perhaps painful process Moscow will find a means of adjusting the relationship in such a way that the Soviet presence becomes more discreet and Eastern European countries are more or less free to do anything they like so long as they do not break away from the socialist camp. Secondly, that changes will take place in the Soviet Union itself which will make greater liberalism ideologically acceptable all round. But for the time being the parameters of East European reformism and nationalism will continue to be determined by the ideological views of Moscow and its feelings of insecurity *vis-à-vis* the West. It is also possible that if West Germany and Moscow can resolve their differences and arrive at a genuine détente in Central Europe, the Russians will be less worried about the loyalty of the East European countries.

It is a remarkable fact that following the Czechoslovak affair in 1968, and after passions had cooled, the Russians, with some energy, set about achieving a détente in Europe and organizing a European security conference. The dangerous situation created by the intervention in Czechoslovakia has thus not been entirely ignored. The emergence of the Social Democrat–Free Democrat coalition in West Germany has also speeded up the search for a long-term détente in

Europe, though it may still take time and very hard bargaining. The olive branch extended by Moscow to Willy Brandt is in its own way a historic event since the antagonism between the Communists and the German Social Democrats long antedates the Cold War. By burying this particular hatchet a significant new chapter has been opened.

Soviet foreign policy is thus determined by shrewd national self-interest. Ideology is not unimportant but it takes second place. For this reason, Soviet foreign policy is geared towards preserving peace and not towards heading for a war, either with the United States or with anybody else. This is matched by the very intense longing for peace which is so characteristic of the public mind in the Soviet Union. There can be no doubt that this is a product of historical experience since each war, even if it brings ultimate victory, has caused too much suffering for the Russian people. The corollary to this is an equally strong sense of insecurity, which accounts in part for over-sensitive tactical manoeuvres at the diplomatic level. China, however, is in a special category, and causes much more intense feelings in the Soviet Union than any other question. Serious trouble may arise on this score.

11   The arts, sciences and intelligentsia

AMONG THE ART FORMS, literature has always been the chief glory of
Russia and it has remained so. It is one of the most enduring gifts of
enlightenment which Peter the Great brought to Russia at the beginning of the eighteenth century. The mixture was awkward at first and
a nineteenth-century poet, Griboyedov, has described the result of
this intermingling of cultures as '. . . a mixture of tongues, the language of France with that of Nizhnii Novgorod'. Although he was
making fun of upper-class mannerisms, at a deeper level it was
true of almost all of Russian culture throughout the eighteenth
and nineteenth centuries. The Petrine revolution continued its
work through the eighteenth century by a process of assimilation.
The secular ideas of Western Europe at the time thus found new
roots in the hostile climate and legacy of the orthodox Muscovite
tradition.

Undoubtedly, the Russian literary tradition goes back to the Kievan age and even to an earlier period if popular, oral traditions are to
be included. But modern Russian literature began only after Peter the
Great. One consequence was that Russian literature gradually acquired
a dominant note of protest, of social criticism, since in the conditions
of Russia the writers had to battle against officialdom on the one side
and the illiterate orthodoxy of the masses on the other. At the beginning of the eighteenth century the note of protest was indirect, mainly
through translations of French radical writing, but by the time of
Catherine the Great it had produced the first masterpiece of Russian
literature, full of sharp criticism, Radishchev's *Journey from Petersburg
to Moscow* in 1790. Throughout the eighteenth century, the transformation of the Russian language continued and the modern
literary style was established. (The first effective Russian grammar,
by Lomonossov, was published in 1755.) The beginnings of the

Russian classical verse forms also appeared during this period, preparing the way for the Golden Age of Russian literature which was to follow in the nineteenth century.

The summit of creativity in literature spans the period from 1820 to 1880, beginning with Pushkin and ending with Dostoevsky and Chekhov. The period opened with Alexander Griboyedov's *Woe from Wit,* a comedy in verse which pungently satirized the upper class and earned the disapproval of the authorities. Though completed in 1823, it was not staged till 1831 and the full text was not published till the 1860's. Griboyedov was murdered in Teheran in a popular rebellion against the Russian Imperial Government, which he represented there. He was only thirty-four. Alexander Pushkin's genius also began to flower about the same time and by 1825 he had published a number of mature works and early portions of his masterpiece *Eugene Onegin.* Pushkin has remained an unsurpassed master of the Russian language, excelling in every form of literature. He died tragically in a duel at the early age of thirty-eight. The great significance of Pushkin for Russian literature lies in the fact that he encompassed and rose above all the contemporary literary trends like neo-classicism, sentimentalism and romanticism and thus within a brief span of time made the transition to realism possible.

A contemporary of Pushkin, Mikhail Lermontov, an utter romantic, is perhaps the second greatest poet of the Russian language. The portent of the social criticism which was to be interwoven in Russian literature from this point onwards was best expressed by Nikolai Gogol's *Dead Souls,* an unusually amusing picture of the searingly painful reality of the existence of the serfs and rural Russia. These were, of course, the most remarkable authors which the first phase of Russia's literary flowering produced, but there were many others, less remarkable but highly gifted writers whose work lives on.

Realism was to dominate the great literature of the period after Pushkin. The foundations were laid by Ivan Krylov, a fable writer, whose creations are masterpieces of popular language, vivid, precise and full of homely wisdom. He died in 1844, a few years after Pushkin.

This literary upheaval was closely related to the new philosophical and ideological trends which were sweeping through Russia at the time, mainly influenced by romantic and idealistic German philosophers like Schelling and Hegel. The widespread interest in German philosophy had its sequel in unexpected ways. It produced, first of all, lines of demarcation between different ideologies, ranging from the reactionary Official Nationality group to the Slavophiles and numerous groups of Westernizers.

At the core of the Slavophiles' philosophy was the belief in the superior nature and destiny of Russia. In this sense, the Slavophiles were puritan nationalists. Their concept was one of integrating all the subjects of the Empire into one whole culture which was predominantly Russian. This integration accomplished, Russia would not only overcome the degenerative influences of the West but even set an example to it. The Slavophiles, though reactionary in their outlook and social philosophy, were by no means on good terms with the Imperial government, which looked upon them with suspicion since they also believed in freedom of conscience, speech and publication.

The Westernizers, too, took their cue from the German idealistic philosophers. Though they differed among themselves, they were one in asserting that Russia could progress only in co-operation with Western civilization and were far more critical of Russian institutions and conditions. The leading Westernizers of the nineteenth century were Vissarion Belinsky, Alexander Herzen and Mikhail Bakunin. Belinsky, who died in 1848 at the early age of thirty-seven, made a lasting contribution in the realm of literary criticism, where he established that political and social criteria were the main basis for judgment on works of literature. His philosophy of literary criticism became the predominant one in Russia, and heightened the sense of social commitment in subsequent creative works.

Alexander Herzen travelled a long way from an idealistic philosopher to a radical critic of the Russian system. In 1848, at the age of thirty-five, he left Russia and died in exile twenty-two years later, busy to the last in opposing the Tsarist regime. In Herzen the long-lost social conscience of Russia found a militant voice, albeit a most civilized and liberal one. His memoirs, *My Past and Thoughts,* are essential reading for an understanding of the period, and great literature too. Bakunin, a revolutionary anarchist, also died in exile, but his influence went far beyond Russia; his message of total destruction in order to achieve total freedom had a powerful appeal for the European intelligentsia, and this played a part in the Paris revolution of 1848.

The radical, revolutionary ideologies thus acted as leavening in the bread of literary and artistic creativity. The unsatisfactory nature of

182

the emancipation of the serfs, and the reforms which followed, also served to intensify radicalism. Consequently, denial of all authority became a fashion among the intelligentsia, and nihilism their philosophy. As Pisarev, an extreme rationalist and a young and eminent literary critic, remarked: 'What can be broken, should be broken.' Out of such extreme rationalism grew nihilism, populism and terrorism. Underlying these trends was a strong feeling of anarchism which had widespread appeal in nineteenth-century Russia and which found such diverse advocates as Count Tolstoy and Prince Kropotkin.

The counterpart to these nihilist tendencies were positivist and utilitarian ideologies which laid the foundation for the socialist and Marxist ideologies to come. Nikolai Chernyshevsky (1828–1889) was an early and influential figure in providing this direction, although he spent 22 years of his later life in exile in Siberia. His novel *What Is To Be Done?* became a popular socialist-realist tract. With greater reservation than some of the other contemporary idealists, Chernyshevsky believed in the salvation of Russia through peasant communes. This line of approach, with a strong moral overlay, was further advanced by Nikolai Mikhailovsky (1842–1904), an influential figure in the populist movement.

The literary counterpart of growing populism was the novel, above all the novels of Ivan Turgenev (1818–1883), also a rationalist. It was one of Turgenev's characters, Bazarov, who was the archetype of a nihilist and started the vogue for the term. He depicted the evolution of the educated Russian society in a series of novels, of which *Fathers and Sons* is the best-known. Above all he conveyed the atmosphere of Russia in his time.

Fedor Dostoevsky (1821–1881) was a contemporary of Turgenev but no two writers could be more different. Dostoevsky, a greater novelist, some would maintain perhaps the greatest the world has ever produced, was a realist. But his realism consisted of deep psychological investigations of human character and motives. Dostoevsky was also ostentatiously Slavophile and wholly Russian but in his case this meant to be a universal man. It was this profoundly universalist base of Dostoevsky's creations which assured him of a continued appeal though he must be recognized as one of the greatest anti-rationalists of the nineteenth century, if not of all time, and the harbinger of the modern psychological novel in Western literature.

The third star in this firmament was Count Leo Tolstoy (1828–1910). He is undoubtedly the most famous of all Russian writers and *War and Peace* and *Anna Karenina,* his two masterworks, are household words in the Soviet Union. The canvas of Tolstoy's novels was utterly realistic on a moral and psychological plane. In particular *War and Peace* is a near-perfect work of art which revolutionized the scope of the novel everywhere. In his later works the moralist in Tolstoy became too pronounced, but his best works, which also include *Resurrection* and *The Kreutzer Sonata,* remain the summit of the Russian novel in the nineteenth century.

There were other remarkable writers who were a little overshadowed by the three giants, but Ivan Goncharov's *Oblomov,* a masterpiece of an obituary on the old Russia of serfdom, must be mentioned.

From the beginning of the 1890's a new style and greater realism began to pervade Russian literature. The one undisputedly great writer of this new era was Anton Chekhov (1860–1904), who gained popularity with his short stories, published in 1880. Chekhov's short stories, at least the best of them, are like tone-poems which convey intensely a particular mood or atmosphere with superb economy of words. The feeling he conveyed best was the unsurpassable isolation of human beings from each other and their failure to break through this barrier.

Chekhov began as a short-story writer and continued to write in this form till the end, but he made an important, inimitable contribution to the Russian theatre with a number of plays, which include *The Seagull, The Three Sisters* and *The Cherry Orchard.* Chekhov's characters, whether in his stories or in his plays, are always the same; boring and utterly bored, ordinary and doing nothing but indulging endlessly in futile talk, really in monologues since nobody listens to anybody. They are only redeemed by Chekhov's gentle but devastating humour. They are like some very finely and sharply etched miniatures by a master, without any identity of their own but reflecting the provincial life of the middle class and the intelligentsia in Russia towards the end of the nineteenth century. The influence of his style was strongly felt by the writers who followed him, though those who simply tried to imitate him failed disastrously.

Chekhov's emergence as a playwright coincided with the emergence of a new and original style in the Russian theatre. Although the beginnings of the theatre in Russia can be traced to Peter the Great's efforts to westernize Russian culture, the theatre really began to develop only in the eighteenth century. By the end of the century many public and private theatres were established in towns throughout Russia and many of them later became remarkable for their originality and experimentation, despite censorship of plays. In the late nineteenth century the Moscow Art Theatre was directed by Constantine Stanislavsky, who founded the psychological realist school of acting and who produced Chekhov's plays. In particular, *The Seagull* became a triumph of production.

Allied to the theatre, ballet and opera also began to flourish by the end of the nineteenth century, although ballet was already established in the eighteenth century to which a French choreographer, Marius Petipa, made a great contribution. Russian ballet won its spurs with Tchaikovsky's masterpieces *Swan Lake* and *The Sleeping Beauty,* and the new modernist masterpieces of Igor Stravinsky, *The Fire Bird, Petroushka* and *The Rite of Spring*, added to the glory. Some magnificent operas were also produced during this period, among them Mussorgsky's *Boris Godunov* and Borodin's *Prince Igor*. Decorative art was particularly brilliant and contributed to the success of the stage and opera.

Much of this artistic renaissance took place in a brief span of some 20–30 years before the Revolution. It was a period of great experiment and turmoil in Russian life. This revolution in creativity, which reflected the political and ideological ferment, preceded the epoch-making changes in government and society and was launched by a periodical *The World of Art (Mir Isskustva)*, brought out in 1898 by Serge Diaghilev and Alexander Benois, both closely connected with theatre and ballet.

The four outstanding painters of this period were Marc Chagall, Vassily Kandinsky, Kasimir Malevich and El Lissitsky. They all played an important role in revolutionizing Western art through their example and even more by their theories. They all went into exile some years after the Revolution. Among the sculptors of this period the most outstanding were Vladimir Tatlin, Naum Gabo and Antoine Pevsner. While Tatlin was influenced by Picasso and was a pioneer of abstract art, Gabo and Pevsner were constructivists. Gabo and Pevsner left Russia in the 1920's, when experimentation became impossible and socialist realism the dogma.

The 'Jack of Diamonds' group, founded by Mikhail Larionov and including Natalia Goncharova, Robert Falk and other talented painters, played an important role in the arts at this time. The group as a whole favoured non-figurative painting and was greatly influenced by the French impressionists, especially, in the case of Falk, by Cézanne. Larionov and Goncharova settled in Paris before the Revolution.

Finally the end of the nineteenth century saw a brilliant revival in Russian poetry, really the heart of Russian literature. Among the experimental prose writers the name of Andrei Bely is best known but he was even more important as a poet. Moreover, it is in poetry that the still unborn new Russia cast its shadow over the arts. The poets belonged to many different schools but they were numerous and splendid. Alexander Blok, a symbolist, was the most outstanding of them, undoubtedly one of the best in Russian literature. But there were other symbolists like Innokenty Annensky, Bely, Valery Brissov and Constantine Balmont. There were Academists like Nikolai Gumilev, Anna Akhmatova and Osip Mandelshtam – the latter considered by many to be the greatest poet of all in nearly a century. There were Futurists like Velemir Khlebnikov and Vladimir Mayakovsky. The careers of many of these, and some unclassified poets and writers like Sergei Yesenin, Boris Pasternak and Marina Tsvetayeva, spanned the great divide of the Revolution and they had tragic lives.

Both in literature and the other arts the four decades to the Revolution, starting from the first publication of Chekhov, were a period of tumultuous, contradictory, confusing and high creativity. These were the decades when the creative genius of the Russian people burst out in all directions, experimenting and creating exuberant forms, sounds and colours. Ripples of this creative wave reached other European countries as well and transformed the arts there.

This exuberance of creation continued for a few years after the Revolution, but, tragically enough, a puritan, mechanical philosophy of artistic concepts triumphed over the liberation promised by the Revolution; its consequences were disastrous and disheartening for the Soviet arts and artists. Many could not survive the strain and committed suicide; others perished in Stalin's purges; still others went into exile. Soviet art became dull, drab and almost worthless, though it showed signs of a revival after Stalin and some great poets and writers survived all the changing official attitudes to the arts.

What went wrong? There was, of course, no inherent reason why the Revolution could not live in peace with the arts. Indeed, it promised them even greater freedom and offered material facilities for the creative intelligentsia to carry on its work without deprivation. This honeymoon, however, was short-lived. The struggle between the arts and authority became one of concepts and since one concept had power to enforce itself, it smothered others. For literature, the really appalling consequence of the Revolution was that realism, which had contributed so much in so many ways to its achievement and success, became the death sentence for the arts. Under the steam-roller of realism, any deviation, any experiment, any genuine creation of independent spirit was crushed either to extinction or conformity. A factor of importance may have been the annihilation of large numbers of the liberal intelligentsia during the war and the civil war.

The conflict between the successful Revolution and the arts, which became so fierce, arose partly out of circumstances. The great wave of symbolism and other exotic-mystic philosophies which had found favour with writers and artists was to a large extent due to the depression which followed the failure of the 1905 revolution. A dejected intelligentsia sought to escape from the realities of life, and therefore from artistic realism itself. When the October Revolution came some 12 years later, this wave of non-material philosophic thinking was still at its height, encouraged by the anarchism and chaos of the decade between the two revolutions. The Revolution itself initially gave a boost to these trends as it struggled to survive, and left the arts more or less alone, except to try to enlist the creative talent on its own side.

Another cause of mutual disillusionment between the political leaders and the writers and artists was that many of the latter were unsympathetic to the Bolshevik Revolution, some even hostile, because it did not meet with their ideal of a revolution, which was more romantic and utopian. Even some of those writers who later opted in favour of the new regime and were extravagantly lauded for this reason, held themselves aloof for a time. This did not improve relations between the new regime and the creative intelligentsia. A number of highly talented writers and artists went into voluntary or forced exile. Some of them later returned but many never came back, continuing to work in exile. Those who left at the time included

187

Ivan Bunin – who later won a Nobel Prize for literature, the first Russian writer to do so – Balmont, Remizov, Khodassevich, Tsvetayeva, Vyacheslav Ivanov and many others.

Some of them remained behind despite their disagreement and had a precarious existence. These included Boris Pasternak, who also won a Nobel Prize to the great displeasure of the authorities, and Anna Akhmatova, perhaps the last of the great poets in the Russian language to have survived the Stalin era.

From the very beginning of the Bolshevik regime the Party and government leaders paid special attention to creating a proletarian literature, and the rift between them and the writers followed from this. But even so, till 1929 the writers were allowed relative ideological freedom. In 1929 two organizations existed for them, one for the militant Marxists called the Association of Proletarian Writers, better known as RAPP, and the other the All-Russian Union of Writers, to which most of the outstanding writers belonged. Characteristically, Stalin used the RAPP to break up the other union in 1929 and then proceeded to break up the RAPP a few years later.

Acceptance of socialist realism as the ideology of a writer became compulsory for admission to the new Union of Writers when its First Union Congress was held in 1934. Central to this concept was the ideal of *partiinost* (Party-mindedness). Unless he displayed it in his writings, a writer was considered to be deviating from socialist realism and had to pay a heavy price for such deviation. In other words, realism, which was used by the nineteenth-century Russian writers to criticize the shortcomings of society, was now to be compulsorily used for lauding uncritically, humourlessly, the existing society in the name of socialism, no matter how bad or harmful the actual conditions might be. Thus socialist realism became an obligatory filter on the intellectual lens, through which all that was unpleasant or vital or disapproved of by the Party was eliminated. Woe betide anyone who failed to use the filter.

The toll was heavy. Among some very talented writers and satirists was Yevgeny Zamyatin, who took the courageous step of writing to Stalin and was allowed to emigrate. Boris Pilnyak, also a biting satirist, had a sadder fate, disappearing in the great purges of 1936–38. Isaac Babel, a short-story writer of genius, and Osip Mandelshtam, a great poet, also perished. Mikhail Zoshchenko, a humorous writer of considerable stature, whose talent was destroyed by sheer persecution though he outlived the Stalin era and resumed writing towards the end, summed it all up when he wrote in the thirties, 'Oh, my esteemed reader! It is hard to be a Russian writer!' He might have added, it was even harder to be a Soviet writer.

A mysterious role in all this was played by Maxim Gorky (1868–1936), whose major works were written before the Revolution. He won fame as a realistic short-story writer and with his play *The Lower Depths*. His later writings were imbued with Marxism, although he had an ambivalent relationship with the Bolsheviks. Although he supported them till the 1905 revolution, he later opposed them and became an émigré in Italy from 1906 to 1913. He opposed the Bolsheviks when they took power but co-operated with the regime from 1919 and did his best to help intellectuals who got into difficulties with the new government. But he again went into exile from 1921 to 1928 and even denounced the Communist government, but, reconciling himself to it, returned to become the first Chairman of the Writers' Union in 1932. He ended as an apologist for Stalin and Stalinism, and even his natural death was exploited by Stalin for his own ends.

The names of countless writers could be added to the list of those who suffered or perished. Many fell silent and did not resume writing till Stalin was safely buried. The war brought some relief and writers were allowed a little more freedom since everybody was united in a common endeavour and there was little need for dissension. In 1946, however, Zhdanov launched a brutal campaign against all talented writers who did not toe the line, and the atmosphere in the arts became sickening with mutual denunciations and destruction of trust among the intellectuals. The period from Stalin's ascendancy to his death, therefore, is a sterile period in the Soviet arts. And if, despite the difficulties, some creative work was done, it was before 1946. Afterwards, nothing happened. Some good writers survived, and continued to work, because their work did not cause undue ideological problems. Among these Konstantin Paustovsky is an important name. In terms of realism the only worthwhile name is that of Mikhail Sholokhov, specially for his *And Quiet Flows the Don*.

The years from Stalin's death to the present day have been years of a creative breakthrough on a smaller scale, almost a minor renaissance, although at present the signs point in some measure to a setback for the liberals and a renewed demand by the Party for ideologically orthodox and safe literature. The history of the post-Stalin period in Soviet literature is highly complicated, and full of ups and downs. But several significant trends, some of them contradictory, have to be noted which have a bearing on the future growth of Soviet arts.

First and foremost there has been a revival in poetry. It is as if the contemporary Soviet Union has found its voice through the terse, telegraphic, concentrated language of poetry rather than prose. It is the poets who get most of the adulation today, and poets like Yevgeny Yevtushenko, Andrei Voznessensky and Bella Akhmadulina have become as well known abroad as at home. There are many other gifted and articulate poets of this generation, among them a Kazakh poet, Oljhas Suleimanov, who writes in Russian and deserves to be far better known than he in fact is. His fame, however, is beginning to spread.

Although younger writers may face unusual difficulties in publishing their experimental work, they have a wide audience and somehow or other do manage to be published. Ideological conformity, though demanded, is not enforced so harshly as before, and writers are developing sophisticated techniques to find ways round it. Thus, in spite of the obstacles, much good work can be and is being done. Some of this may not yet be officially published but the important thing is that the Russian literary tradition has revived vigorously.

Moreover, new genres of writing are developing rapidly. Science fiction is becoming popular, pioneered by the distinguished palaeontologist Ivan Yefremov, whose *Andromeda* is a classic. Among the new writers in this genre the brothers Arkady and Boris Strugatsky deserve special attention. Their highly sophisticated work raises serious philosophical questions about the future of society. Science-fiction writers seem to have fewer ideological inhibitions imposed upon them. Others are experimenting with language and form to bring it nearer to the ordinary language of the people. Short-story writers like Vasily Aksyonov, Yuri Kazakov and Yuri Nagibin are doing some very useful and notable work in this field.

A most significant aspect of the current artistic scene is the conscious or unconscious attempt to forge links with the recent past. The twenties and early thirties of this century are seen through a golden haze in which Russian art was leading the world with new ideas. One of the most touching and rewarding developments is the personal ties which have developed between the younger generation

190

of writers and some of the older generation who have survived the Stalin era with their spark of creativity still alive. For instance the links between Pasternak and some of the younger poets, specially Andrei Voznessensky, and the links between Valentin Kataev and prose writers like Aksyonov, are important. Through these links – not only personal – Soviet writers are rediscovering and reinterpreting the whole past of their literature. A unique role in this process was played by Ehrenburg's memoirs, published in the early sixties, which revived the memories and personalities of those writers rehabilitated after Stalin and those still awaiting rehabilitation. Some of these dead writers, like the poets Tsvetayeva and Mandelshtam and the novelist-dramatist Bulgakov, have come as a revelation to the younger generation. Beyond that, there is a strong tendency towards reinterpreting the nineteenth-century classical writers and an attempt to rescue them from jargon-ridden official adulation, and to make them appear fresh, vital and still relevant to the modern age.

Undoubtedly the most outstanding prose writer of the post-Stalin period in Russian literature, some would say of the twentieth century, is Alexander Solzhenitsyn. The importance of Solzhenitsyn's work is not merely stylistic: he has gone back to the classical nineteenth-century realism of Russian literature, and imbued it with the pain and anguish of society, which he himself experienced as a prisoner in Stalin's camps. More than that, Solzhenitsyn is the first Soviet writer for a long time to raise fundamental questions, and to realize that questions are more important than answers. He has revived the search for truth. But the shabby treatment he has received at the hands of the authorities is not the best encouragement for the integrity of the artist in the Soviet system.

A positive outcome of the Soviet period has been the emergence of non-Russian writers from Asian and other republics who are making a great contribution to Soviet literature, some in their own language and others in Russian. Suleimanov has already been mentioned. Chingiz Aitmatov, Fazil Iskander and Rasul Gamzatov are other examples which can be cited. From Latvia and Lithuania, Vatsietas and Bielshevitse bring a new sensibility to Russian literature and it is likely that their contribution will be even greater in the future.

In spite of everything, there is an easier atmosphere in the arts. Although no really outstanding painters have emerged in the post-Stalin period, many younger artists are doing daringly experimental work which, though officially disapproved of, is relatively widely known. They have broken from the tradition of sterile Soviet academism. Foremost among them is Ernst Neizvestny, a quite original sculptor in many ways. Among the painters, Boris Zhutovsky, Anatoly Kabakov, Vladimir Yankilevsky and Vladimir Yakovlev are the leading experimentalists; Anatoly Kaplan is in a category of his own, confining himself to Jewish themes. Altogether, therefore, the progressive writers and artists enjoy a high degree of patronage, if not from the Party and the government then from the wide circle of intelligentsia which takes an interest in their work, follows developments in the arts closely and encourages and supports those who are in trouble.

This relative easing off has its other side too. In order to survive, socialist realism has turned towards sensationalism and scandalmongering, having lost hope of attracting the intelligentsia on its own merits, and turned to a sort of scatological revival of Stalin and Stalinism. Vsevolod Kochetov, the doyen of conservative writers, and Ivan Shevtsov, a more inarticulate muck-raker with a strong tinge of anti-semitism, are not only published, but published in extraordinarily large editions. Scurrilous philistinism has thus usurped the place of socialist realism.

It cannot be said, however, that such writers have no audience or appeal. Unfortunately, they have a vast, relatively unsophisticated public which not only takes their vulgarized Marxism seriously but believes in it and defends it. They are the Soviet equivalent of the silent majority everywhere else. The work of such writers fulfils another function. Since no pornography is encouraged or allowed to be published, novels like Kochetov's *What's It You Want?*, Shevtsov's *In The Name of The Father and The Son* or *Love and Hate* become ideal substitutes. For want of a better term these works can best be described as political pornography since usually they attack some political or intellectual figure on ideological grounds and emphasize the villain's moral depravity. The difference between Kochetov and Shevtsov is that while Kochetov acts as the spokesman for the silent majority, Shevtsov simply arouses its baser instincts.

Yet another trend which is gaining some ground is a watered-down version of the old Slavophilism. The Slavophile writers scorn any western-inspired innovation and are therefore reserved about the modern Soviet writers. But they also do not accept the straitjacket of socialist realism in its entirety, and tend to dwell on the specific Russianness of characters and institutions. Vladimir Sholoukhin is a good example in this genre. But for tactical reasons the Slavophile writers, who are few in number, find it more convenient to ally themselves with the establishment writers, despite the hostility they encounter from them, rather than with the progressive writers.

The difficulties of Soviet writers and artists have been compounded by censorship and the Writers' Union, two millstones grinding the soul of creativity. Censorship performs the function of an ideological and political watchdog: nothing can be legally published without the imprimatur of the censorship (*Glavlit*, as it is widely known). Though the Writers' Union is ostensibly there to look after the material welfare of creative writers, it does the exact opposite. For all that is bad, reactionary and Stalinist in present-day Soviet literature, the Writers' Union is directly responsible. It is controlled by a group of aged and faded writers whose creativity has long since dried up, and acts as a benevolent relief society for the third-raters and conservatives. Yet since it has wide patronage at its disposal and can deprive a writer of his livelihood by excluding him from membership, as it did with Akhmatova, Pasternak, Solzhenitsyn and many others, it can blight the career of any writer. It exercises dangerous and destructive powers over creative writing and there are many – including Sholokhov, who is intensely hated by all progressive writers – who hold that only a great transformation or, better still, the abolition of the Writers' Union can make great Soviet literature possible again.

As in literature, so in the theatre and the cinema there has been a revival. Stalin destroyed Meyerhold, the great name in Soviet theatre in the twenties and the thirties. After this, official approval was given only to the realistic theatre of Stanislavsky, a tradition preserved rather than enriched by the Moscow Art Theatre. In the post-Stalin period, however, many interesting and daring directors came up who quickly restored the vigour of the Soviet theatre. Foremost among these are Lyubimov at the Taganka Theatre, Yefremov at the Sovremennik and Efros who has worked in different theatres.

Some of the plays staged by them have not been permitted to continue in the repertory. What has offended the authorities most in the case of Efros is his bold reinterpretation of established classics like Chekhov's *Three Sisters*, which had to be taken off after only a few performances. This has indeed become one of the most significant trends of the current art scene. The old classics are being searched to find contemporary relevance and in the theatre such relevance is pointed out in such a way as to leave no doubt that the comment of the character on the stage is a criticism of the present. This annoys the authorities but is popular with the more intellectual audiences.

All good Russian literature, however, has a tremendous resonance, and this is a very important aspect of it: yesterday, today and tomorrow. The resonance of Soviet literature is like a whisper in a big empty hall. The whisper carries and echoes back from all corners. The work of a Soviet writer similarly echoes back from all corners, except that he is not addressing an empty hall but a vast and eager readership which is familiar with every nuance of his writing. This resonance is the greatest strength of the Soviet writer, even when he is in difficulties. It helps Soviet literature to survive.

In the twenties and thirties, the Soviet cinema was respected for its technique as well as its ideas, but it suffered a decline under Stalin, only reviving after his death. The names of Sergei Eisenstein, Vladimir Pudovkin, Alexei Dovzhenko, Mark Donskoi have an honoured place in the history of the cinema. Today the tradition is upheld by directors like Sergei Gerasimov and Sergei Bondarchuk, and Chukrai, Tarkovsky, Kozintsev, Romm and many other directors are doing experimental work of great value. It is somewhat ironical, however, that one of the best works of the post-war Soviet cinema, *Andrei Rublev*, directed by Tarkovsky, has been shown to only a limited audience at home but is proudly exhibited abroad.

The arts have undergone every conceivable vicissitude since the Revolution and although the sciences have not escaped entirely, on the whole the great tradition of the nineteenth century in scientific research has been maintained and improved upon. Many scientists and some branches of science were victimized by Stalin, but scientists and technologists were also essential for the industrial transformation of the Soviet Union upon which he had embarked. For this reason, though restricted, they were given material privileges to compensate for it and their work was encouraged.

One of the primary objectives of early Soviet policy on science was to ensure control by the Party of scientific and academic organizations. This took some time. But the rapid spread of universal education and an upsurge in scientific industrial activity also tended to favour central, political control of science and scientists. Besides, many of the most influential figures in the science establishment are members of the Central Committee and many scientists are members of the Party. Thus the Party can influence the course of science in many indirect ways. Directly, it exercises authority through the Department of Science and Establishments of Higher Education, which is attached to the Secretariat of the Central Committee. The greatest role in the actual development of science and education, however, is played by the USSR Academy of Sciences, an autonomous body with responsibility for all scientific research. Naturally, the leading members of the Academy of Sciences are Party members. But an important channel of communicating the Party decisions and advice is the Chief Academic Secretary of the Secretariat, who is believed to be the official representative of the central apparatus of the Party.

Although Soviet science came under a cloud in Stalin's time and there were few outstanding achievements, the post-war Soviet success in matching the Americans and manufacturing a nuclear bomb, and the post-Stalin lead in space achievements made it clear that, given opportunity and resources, the Soviet scientists were equal to any task. The unusually large number of people with higher education in the USSR compared even with America caused the West to fear that Soviet scientific achievements would become unsurpassable. Yet Soviet science has still not fully recovered from the blight of Stalinism which particularly retarded developments in genetics and cybernetics.

The glamour of Soviet science in the post-Stalin period, however, concealed some serious deficiencies, which became obvious in the very field which the Russians had made their own – space research – as the Americans overtook the Soviet Union and successfully landed the first men on the moon. The Soviet contention that their priorities in the space programme had changed and manned landing on the moon was no longer considered a priority objective, had a large element of apology about it.

In essence the story was the same as with the economy: comparative failure of co-ordination, and lack of proper organization. This may seem paradoxical since the sciences are centrally controlled and planned and even, compared with other countries, over-organized. This is because some obvious deficiencies have not been overcome. Though the Soviet Union spends vast sums on scientific research, not enough resources are put into development. Another factor is the relatively unsophisticated tools of research in most branches, apart from the priority ones. Yet another problem is that of finding a proper balance between fundamental and applied research. At the moment the resources given to fundamental research are disproportionately high. It will need a reorganization of scientific education and research as well as greater emphasis on the application of research to production, for a real breakthrough to be made.

The problem exists on two levels. One is mostly organizational – to inject a spirit of competition into a highly organized field. Decentralization by itself is no solution unless there is constant and keen competition among the scientists and research organizations to better each other's performance. At another level the malaise has ideological-political roots. Since even the scientists are supposed to accept the philosophical dogmas of the Party, many of them play safe by avoiding controversial propositions and innovations. This stultifies creativity. As Academician Kapitsa has maintained, 'an atmosphere of free discussion, polemics and airing of ideas, even if some of them are radically wrong' is essential for a high level of creativity. The insistence of the authorities on 'correct' ideas, therefore, inhibits daring experimentation and the formulation of new theories. It also inhibits the ruthless discarding of established theories which have proved wanting.

This is not a problem which can be solved overnight. Therefore, while sincerely desiring scientific progress and theoretically committed to a rational, scientific way of life, the Party finds itself in the curious position that though it has made use of science to change society, it is unable to lose its own suspicions that the scientists may run away with their freedom, may lose sight of the socialist ideal of society, the essence of Soviet philosophy.

In its own way the Party has gone a long way to satisfy the scientists. As a group they are possibly the most privileged in Soviet society, except for high-ranking Party workers, entertainers and sportsmen. Even their intellectual interests are catered for by making available for them greater information about developments in the outside world than for any comparable group. The scientists for their part are not slow to exploit this preferential treatment. The nature of their jobs make them relatively immune from the kind of pressures which can be exerted upon, let us say, historians, since scientists cannot become such political risks. Even when their offence is great, their punishment is relatively light. This may be one reason why the prevalence and expression of dissent is more common among Soviet scientists than among other academic professions.

Yet it would be a mistake to make too much of it. For one thing, scientists are relatively non-political. What they are most interested in is less interference with their own work, and this may come by degrees. Moreover, the majority of the scientific intelligentsia, the engineers and technologists, have an even narrower outlook and are seeking enlargement of their own freedom to manoeuvre. Therefore, to glamourize dissident scientists or to entertain any illusion of the scientific intelligentsia leading a political revolution, as some Western observers tend to do, is to misread the situation in the Soviet Union.

It is all the more essential to keep a proper perspective on the whole question of dissent in the Soviet Union. It is understandable that in the outside world there is indiscriminate excitement at any expression of dissent by any Soviet citizen, and a strong urge to make a hero of any intellectual defector. This is of very dubious value to anybody and even harmful to the genuine intellectuals who try to move the Soviet Union forward on the path of modernity. Articulate dissent, moreover, is confined to a very small number of people and it is significant that the same names keep cropping up whenever dissent in the Soviet Union is spoken of. Even as a group, the dissenters represent only a fraction of the intelligentsia. Their political objectives are limited, their philosophy is incoherent and their outlook on the world is simplistic. These dissenters are isolated from the people almost completely, and if they tried to influence the masses their reception would be even more hostile than the reception given to the Populists by the nineteenth-century Russian peasantry. It is a measure of their failure that their names are better-known abroad than in their own country, their manifestos find a more ready audience outside Russia than within. They do not act so much as catalysts of change in Soviet society as excuses for the orthodox to be even more rigid and unyielding in their attitude to change. Some of them are genuinely courageous but not very discriminating or wise in their behaviour. Approbation abroad, therefore, is no indication of their effectiveness at home.

It is also important to be aware that despite all the restrictive features of Soviet intellectual life, it still possesses tremendous vitality. Therefore, one cannot be altogether pessimistic about the future of

Soviet arts. One of the great heretics of Soviet literature in the thirties, Yevgeny Zamyatin, wrote: 'I am afraid that the only future possible to Russian literature is its past.' The upsurge of Soviet intellectual and literary life in the post-Stalin period has, if nothing else, proved how wrong and rash such judgments can be about the Soviet arts or even about Soviet life.

12   Conclusions and speculations

MORE THAN HALF A CENTURY after the Revolution the Soviet Union remains a challenge to which no one can be indifferent. The passions aroused by the mere words Soviet Union is a sign that Soviet society is neither sick nor doomed to failure as its critics would have us believe. If a tally is made of all the pessimistic forecasts about the course of the Revolution, by now the Soviet Union would have vanished from the maps of the world: that this has not happened is proof of the vitality of Soviet society.

It can be all too easily overlooked that since the Revolution a genuine, far-reaching transformation has taken place in the social and economic structure. There is no reason to believe that the people would want to be uprooted from the new structure of society, even though it can be shown to have certain limitations. The real problem is whether or not these limitations can be overcome and, equally important, in what way.

It is futile to deny the legitimacy of the Russian Revolution, by speculating whether it could have been avoided had some parties to the drama acted differently. 'Men acted as they did because they could not act otherwise.' The Revolution did not take place in a vacuum and its course was influenced by the social environment which produced it in the first place and the political material it found ready to hand in that environment. Lenin was aware of it when he declared, 'We are building a new order out of the bricks the old order has left us.' There can be no doubt that a revolution had to take place to bring Russia out of the quagmire of corruption and stagnation, and the misery of a social order which had still not recovered from the effects of serfdom and feudalism. What complicated the progress of the Revolution was that, like all previous attempts in Russia, it had no revolutionary class behind it. Even so, decades of revolutionary endeavour and propaganda, and Lenin's brilliant synthesis of the proletariat and peasants, succeeded in giving this Revolution the character of a mass intervention in a historical event; this synthesis began to collapse even in his lifetime and Stalin's brutal repression of the peasantry was the price paid for this breakdown.

Half a century later the Bolshevik regime was still there, despite all the travails it had had to pass through, and this was unforgivable for many, since throughout history revolutionary regimes had proved to be transitory. The difference was that the heirs to the revolutionary regime of October 1917 found themselves rulers of a mighty power and a stable society.

Of course, the Revolution was not concerned with making Russia a big power, but with social equality, a vision of a communist society where the workers ruled. Whatever the shortcomings in the fulfilment of this revolutionary utopia, one major achievement in terms of socialist ideals has been the elimination of private property other than that for personal use. This is why so much of the talk about capitalism regaining ground in the Soviet Union because of economic reforms is not only beside the point but absurd. The basic approach of the managers of Soviet industry and the managers of industry in a capitalist society is quite different. The manager of a Soviet factory works for the community and is paid by the community, whereas the manager of a factory in a non-socialist system works for his personal profit. This crucial difference in their approach has drawbacks for Soviet economy. In the Soviet system it has become difficult to make the managers and workers sensitive to cost and profit and this is one of the problems which reforms are meant to deal with.

The success of the Revolution cannot only be judged in terms of abstract principles. It has to be assessed with a view to the welfare of the masses whose interests the Revolution purported to serve. By this criterion, the Revolution has succeeded in transforming the living standard, the scope of public welfare and the level of education among a relatively backward people, nearly to the level of highly developed countries. This is not an achievement which can be shrugged off, and if qualitatively it still falls behind the most advanced of the developed nations, there is a good possibility that the difference in some spheres can be made up in the coming years.

The greatest economic significance of the Revolution was that it overcame the all-round inertia of Russia which had prevented any significant development before. Revolutions, even those revolutions which survive, usually rely upon a class of vested interests to sustain them. In the case of the Russian Revolution, which was theoretically made possible and sustained by the working class allied with the peasantry, it can be said that its vested interests included the whole people. Despite its shortcomings, of which the Soviet intelligentsia itself can be highly critical, no support can be found anywhere in the Soviet Union, contrary to Western speculations, for undoing the Revolution. There can be no restoration in the Soviet Union as there was in England after the Cromwellian Commonwealth.

The Revolution has also industrialized the Soviet Union at a faster pace than would have been possible under any other circumstances. But despite all these manifold achievements, it is the problems and failures of the Soviet system which usually loom larger: failures always appear dramatic. It is also true, however, that the great pace of transformation in Soviet society, and some of the means used to bring it about, have created their own problems which must be solved for a healthy future growth.

Economic problems are naturally to the fore because they determine the outcome of almost every other problem in the Soviet Union. At the beginning of the nineteen-seventies the leadership of the Soviet Union was torn between a desire and need to evolve new forms and modernize industry and agriculture, and a desire to return to old forms. There is a fear of new forms and new methods because they are unknown, and the orthodox hold that they would lead to the emasculation of socialism in the Soviet Union. It is also tempting for them to think that because great feats of construction and industrialization were carried out under the old system, as the people, despite everything, worked with a will and dedication, it is sufficient to go back to the old methods.

This is a fallacy. Though traditionalist sentiments have a strong appeal within the Party and the government apparatus, there is also a growing realization that adoption of new forms does not necessarily mean the abandonment of ideology, but is a recognition that the economy has simply outgrown the old system. The crux of the economic problem, therefore, lies in effective harmonization of political ideology and scientific ways of running the economy. This amounts to another revolution and therefore any clear-cut, permanent solution is unlikely. It is much more likely that economic reforms will proceed in a zig-zag way, their pace now slackening, now quickening according to the prevailing political climate. Basically, the ideological status quo will be maintained for a long time to come.

The main accent of the reforms will be on material incentives, for very good reasons. The real problem of contemporary Soviet economy is not a question of priorities, though it is important to bear in mind that the highly expensive technology of modern warfare has strained the Soviet economy in recent years and this is a fact acknowledged by the Soviet leaders. But broadly speaking the national resources are vast enough to meet consumer as well as military and industrial needs. The essential problem is the relatively low productivity of Soviet industry and agriculture as compared with other advanced economies. Much more serious is the ever-widening gap in technology between the USSR and the USA. This, allied with a strong urge for a better life, makes it imperative that every possible means be used to improve productivity on a national scale.

Even under the conditions of Stalin's command economy it was recognized that the means for greater productivity were better wages and living conditions. In contemporary conditions, direct incentives to labour must be combined with greater social expenditure on welfare and greater availability of consumer goods, which will add to the comfort and pleasure of the population as a whole. Therefore it is likely that in the near future more emphasis will be placed upon provision for improved welfare, better-quality consumer durables and other goods in greater quantities and varieties, which will in turn necessitate a reform in the cumbersome distribution process and the structure of prices. This process, combined with reforms of the managerial system throughout industry, is intended not only to make enterprises more productive but to make them profitable in economic terms, so that wastage of resources is reduced to a minimum. Whether this will be sufficient by itself remains to be seen.

In this context, renewed efforts will also be made for better liaison between science and industry. Although the Soviet Union expends a vast amount of resources on scientific research, its benefits to industry are not always either evident or commensurate with the expense involved. Therefore, in technology Soviet industry tends to trail behind the latest advances and this adversely affects any increase in productivity. How to solve this problem has long been a subject of debate but there have been tentative signs that many research institutions are associating with industrial enterprise to facilitate application of research to industry directly. The expectation was that a better balance between fundamental and applied research might be thus established.

The incontrovertible lesson of all these controversies and of the painful but exhilarating experience through which the Soviet Union has passed is simple enough. The Soviet Union now has alternatives to choose from, whereas it can be argued that in the early years of the Revolution and before the forties, there were no other choices open to her because of scarcity of economic resources. Hence the triumph of Stalin and his totalitarian, crude and inefficient economic methods.

Many social problems have also accumulated as a consequence of the economic revolution. The most important is perhaps the rapid urbanization of the country in the last half-century. The rate of urbanization would have been higher still but for restrictions imposed on settling in towns and the extremely slow modernization of agriculture which continued to hold up population in the villages. The twin effects were enormous pressure on housing in the cities and a widening gulf in living standards between the city and the village population. This was a deliberate policy and its effects were accentuated by the neglect of agriculture. Theoretically, the Party has always been committed to the ideal of equalizing the rural and urban population, but it is only during the last decade that concrete steps in this direction have been taken and it is not a coincidence that these measures followed a conscious effort to modernize agriculture. The difference in living standards and social facilities between the countryside and the cities is still tremendous in the Soviet Union despite the efforts so far made to eliminate them. But the compelling necessity of providing a better life for the peasants and the village community must gradually tend to reduce the gap.

The pressures from the rural community for a better life join with the urge of the urban community for a higher standard of living, for more consumer durables, for better facilities for entertainment and above all, for more spacious and private living accommodation. At the top of the list of priorities for most families in the Soviet Union is the demand for their own flats, since a majority still live in communal flats, sometimes three or four people in a room, sharing the bathroom and the kitchen with other families in the flat. Even the fast rate of construction of prefabricated houses has not yet created conditions in which one flat for one family can be assured. This overcrowding has an inhibiting effect on social life in many ways, most particularly on the birth rate which has become alarmingly low in the Russian federation itself, the most urbanized of all the republics, the increase being eleven per cent in eleven years. Many other social problems are connected with housing conditions although there is a fair prospect that, within the next ten to fifteen years, the Soviet population will be marginally better housed than populations of most other countries and paying extremely low, even nominal rents.

The pressures of these social problems will increase even more as the purchasing power of the wage earners rises either through direct wage increases, as has happened in the case of the collective farmers, or through bonuses, in the case of the industrial workers. Even though some of these gains might be nullified by inflationary pressures, better economic conditions will exert a powerful influence on social aspirations which in turn will lead to further changes in policy in order to satisfy the new demands created by them. The pressures will be felt less perceptibly than in non-communist societies perhaps. They will not perhaps lead to any violent upheaval, but they will nevertheless be acute.

This inevitably touches upon fundamental questions of ideology. Stalin achieved the monolithic unity of the Party and its total supremacy in the political arena by terror. The terror is gone but the emphasis on monolithic unity and supremacy remains. A constant element in official Soviet thinking about ideology is the fear that maybe the supremacy of the Party will be challenged either by the masses or by the intelligentsia, or that its unity will be destroyed by dissension from within. This fear has a baneful effect upon the trends towards adaptation to new conditions which have emerged since the death of Stalin. Yet in ideological matters the Party cannot stand still. The tension resulting from this elemental clash between the pressures for change and resistance to them for fear of losing authority, explains much about the change of ideological gears in the post-Stalin era. If Khrushchev's de-Stalinization campaign was a response to the need felt for change, his half-way abandonment of it was due to a fear of the consequences.

After Khrushchev, the de-Stalinization process was purposely put into reverse, though it stopped short of any re-Stalinization. This was again due to a fear in the higher ranks of the Party that the uproar about de-Stalinization had adversely affected its authority and if continued further would undermine it even more thoroughly. Stalin thus became a problem from which the Party found it difficult to disentagle itself. Even the promotion of Lenin as the ultimate authority and sanction behind the Party's policy did not help matters much because it begged a whole number of pertinent questions. Above all, it left little room for flexibility in ideological matters.

It is difficult to see how any ideological concessions can be made by the Party so long as it feels itself threatened with possible loss of authority. Its dilemma is that it is aware of the need for innovation; but innovations cannot be introduced so long as the old dogmas are considered sacrosanct. Pessimists even argue that, faced with such an unpleasant choice, the Party will revert to conditions of Stalinism. This is an extremist viewpoint and there is little warrant for it in the situation actually prevailing in the Soviet Union.

A more likely evolution may be that very slowly the Party will find a modus vivendi which will allow it to tolerate dissension within its ranks within a broad framework, without any serious danger of losing its grip on the country and the government. This will necessitate a high degree of adaptability of political outlook to creative scientific methods of administering the economy and responding to the social demands. The process will not be easy or straightforward, but given the dynamics of a one-party state, the legacies of Stalinism and the ideological nature of the Soviet Communist Party, no other possible alternative exists, unless it be chaos or petrification. Neither is likely to be permitted either by the Party or by the people.

External factors will also have a role to play in the future evolution of the Soviet Union, even in ideological matters. China is obviously a problem which requires constant and utmost attention from Moscow. It is also a unique case in which clash of ideology and national interests inseparably intertwine, investing the dispute with a degree of bitterness which has rarely been surpassed in international affairs. Despite recent signs on both sides that a search for détente between them is on, at best such a détente can only be fragile and temporary.

Ever since the communist revolution in China, relations between Moscow and Peking have been of an ambiguous nature. Stalin and Mao reached an accord because the Chinese wanted protection against America and the Russians wanted to prevent the Chinese from joining the ranks of Communist rebels like Tito. After Stalin, the

Russians made an even greater effort to conciliate China, but there was a fundamental contradiction involved in their respective positions and this grew rather than diminished in subsequent years. The Russians were seeking national security within the international status quo, the Chinese seeking similar security by aiming to sabotage it. The Chinese revolt against the status quo was partly a response to the American domination of the Pacific region. Ironically, now that the American preponderance in the region is lessening, the Chinese are seeking accommodation with Washington, in order to secure themselves against any possible Soviet threat, and to this the Americans are responding cautiously. This aggravates the incompatibility of the viewpoints of Moscow and Peking even more.

In dealing with China, therefore, Moscow will have to take into consideration the position of America. It will also have to strive to prevent any consolidation of a Sino-American alliance, offering Washington inducements in the broader field of mutual relations. This interplay of China and America will, therefore, have a great bearing on the whole spectrum of Soviet foreign policy, particularly in Europe and Asia, the two continents contiguous to Soviet borders. The primary factor in the evolution of any new Soviet policy will remain consideration of national security above all and the secondary factor will be the need to contain the influence of China and America.

It must also be assumed that the logic of power politics makes a Sino-American rapprochement more likely than a Soviet-American one, however preposterous the idea may sound.

As to the question most frequently raised these days, whether a war between China and the Soviet Union is inevitable, a considered answer can only be in the negative. Barring some sudden and unforeseen development which compels one side or the other to embark upon a major conflict, the pattern seems likely to be frequent acts of brinkmanship by China followed by tough but strictly limited retaliatory measures by the Soviet Union. The Soviet Union is too cautious and wary in its policies to take the enormous risk of being bogged down in an unending war with China.

But Soviet relations with the outside world cannot be perceived in terms of foreign policy alone. Few countries have such an intense interest in the outside world as the Soviet Union has, irrespective of political relations with any country at a given time. This is of prime significance in the shaping of the Soviet mind and its world outlook.

206

It is also a complex process which is difficult to analyse thoroughly. Like so much else in Soviet attitudes it is also an inheritance of past thought-patterns, which have changed more in form than in substance.

No visitor to the Soviet Union can fail to notice the great curiosity about the outside world which exists hand-in-hand with some apprehension. These emotions date far back. Alexander Herzen, in his autobiographical *My Past and Thoughts,* has portrayed this feeling with ironical accuracy and deep feeling. Recalling the visit of Humboldt, the renowned German scientist, to Moscow, he wrote:

> Humboldt, on his return from the Urals, was greeted in Moscow at a solemn session of the Society of Natural Scientists at the university, the members of which were various senators and governors – people, on the whole, who took no interest in the sciences, natural or unnatural. . . . To this day we look upon Europeans and upon Europe in the same way as provincials look upon those who live in the capital, with deference and a feeling of our own inferiority, knuckling under and imitating them, taking everything in which we are different for a defect, blushing for our peculiarities and concealing them. The fact is that we were intimidated, and had not recovered. . . . They talk in Western Europe of our duplicity and wily cunning; they mistake the desire to show off and swagger a bit for the desire to deceive . . . and this with no ulterior motive, simply from politeness and a desire to please; the bump *de l'appro-bativité* is strongly developed on our skulls.[1]

Herzen also recalled the reception accorded to Franz Liszt, the musician, a few years later:

> Things were not much better among us in the non-official world: ten years later Liszt was received in Moscow society in much the same way. Enough silly things were done in his honour in Germany, but here his reception was of quite a different quality. . . . No one listened to anybody but Liszt, no one spoke to anybody else, nor answered anybody else. I remember that at one evening party Khomyakov, blushing for the honourable company, said to me,
>   'Please let us argue about something, that Liszt may see that there are people in the room not exclusively preoccupied with him.'[2]

This deference to the outside world is still characteristic of Soviet life. Though the feeling of inferiority is no longer so deep-rooted, it is still there even if laid over with a patriotic feeling of Soviet achievements since the Revolution. Of course, there is no doubt that the Soviet Union still seeks affinity with the western mind, with one difference. Now the predominant object of its attraction, admiration and envy is no longer France or Germany as in the nineteenth century but America, and for a good reason. In power terms, the Russians consider themselves equal only to the Americans and superior to everybody else. Only an American can expect to receive the kind of red-carpet treatment in the Soviet Union today which a Humboldt or a Liszt received in the old Russia.

This is not surprising. The Russians believe that they have mastered modern technology to a degree comparable only to America. Therefore, America excites their admiration, notwithstanding any reservations they might have about its policies. This admiration is not confined to any particular section of society but includes the highest and the lowest. In particular, the intelligentsia at all levels, dissident or otherwise, has an attitude towards America which falls little short of worship. The defection of Svetlana Stalin to America can be thus symbolically interpreted as a dream fulfilment, the realization of the American fantasy in the Soviet mind. In the presence of the Americans, the Russians feel and behave as if they have achieved a perfect understanding with them – sometimes with embarrassing results, since this feeling is only rarely reciprocated by the other side. A little of the naïveté in this attitude comes out when, in private, the Russians are not averse to advocating an alliance of western races against the alien, Asiatic Chinese. True, this is done somewhat discreetly and partly in response to the racial tones of anti-Soviet propaganda by China, but is is somewhat symptomatic of the constant Russian efforts to establish an affinity with western civilization, which is almost synonymous with American civilization in their eyes.

Of course, other foreigners are also treated with a degree of deference not usually displayed by the Russians among themselves. To this extent all foreigners are unusually privileged, only the Americans more so. The paradoxical situation, therefore, exists in which any foreigner is put on a little pedestal of privilege but isolated from the Soviet people nevertheless. The privilege accorded him is an acknowledgment that he is used and entitled to a different standard of life and behaviour. His isolation is a sign that his unhealthy example is considered to be dangerously contagious. A large part of the Soviet Union is screened from the prying eyes of foreigners anyway, since they are seldom allowed beyond certain well-defined areas.

It would be unfair, though, to regard the privilege accorded to foreigners as a simple matter of calculation. On the contrary, it is also based on an innate warm-heartedness and friendliness which is characteristic of all the Soviet people. It accords with their great sense of hospitality, the conviction that a guest in their country is entitled to the best they have to offer, be it accommodation, food or entertainment. That the tourists in general and those in possession of convertible currencies in particular are so much better catered for is, alas, an aspect of modern commercial needs rather than a reflection upon the people's innate sense of hospitality. It has little to do with ideology, except that the official attitude conveyed through the mass media is one of great distrust of all foreigners, be they tourists or not, be they from capitalist countries or communist.

This influx of tourists and visitors, combined with the widespread habit of listening to foreign broadcasts for news, does in the end have a discernible influence on the Soviet outlook. The effect is like opening a window in a room which has been closed for a long time, only it is not a window which can easily be closed again, simply because the Soviet Union as a big power has to maintain a wide range of contacts with the outside world and foreign visitors cannot be kept out entirely, even if their numbers can be restricted. The compulsions of foreign policy and ideology also operate against any renewal of the kind of isolation which Stalin imposed during his heyday. The result is a constant process of mutual revaluation of the Soviet view of the outside world and the world's view of the Soviet Union.

Thus a slow but perceptible change in the Soviet outlook is taking place all the time. But ultimately, of course, what matters is not so much its view of the world beyond the frontiers, but the nature of transformation which takes place within the country. It is certainly a question of economic development, but it is even more a question of ideology which shapes the policies of the Soviet Communist Party and the state and which in the last analysis determines economic policy.

The basic problem is: though the Soviet Union has arrived in the modern world, it is not yet completely a part of it. Essentially, this is so because what is in theory a dynamic ideology has been reduced in practice to a static set of rules, rigid in conception, restrictive in practice and holding up progress to a great extent. When all the causes are explained and excuses made, it emerges that it is the inability of the present system to disassociate itself from the blight of Stalinist degeneration of communism which is the root cause of most of the troubles in the Soviet Union. Consciously or unconsciously, it pervades life. The most unfortunate and absurd part of it is that ideological disassociation from Stalinism has come to be regarded as disassociation from communism itself.

It explains why, despite all her achievements, by and large the Soviet version of communism has ceased to make a revolutionary appeal to the intelligentsia of the world, the prime carriers of any moral, ideological or political gospel. The Soviet authorities have reached a stage where they seem determined not to understand that to question the present ideological stance of the Soviet Union is not to side with the really hostile enemies of the Soviet Union but to share anxiety about its future.

The problem, in all its profundity, has been best posed by Isaac Deutscher, Drawing up a balance sheet of the Soviet Union on the fiftieth anniversary of the October Revolution, he wrote:

In the Soviet Union the moral crisis of the post-Stalin years consists of a profound disturbance of the nation's historical and political consciousness. Since the Twentieth Congress, people have been aware how much of what they once believed was made up of forgeries and myths. They want to learn the truth but are denied access to it. Their rulers have told them that virtually the whole record of the Revolution has been falsified; but they have not thrown open the true record. To give again only a few instances: the last great scandal of the Stalin era, the so-called Doctors' plot, has been officially denounced on the ground that the plot was a concoction. But whose concoction was it? Was Stalin alone responsible for it? And what purpose was it to serve? These questions are still unanswered. Khrushchev had suggested that the Soviet Union might not have suffered the huge losses inflicted on it in the last war had it not been for Stalin's errors and miscalculations. Yet those 'errors' have not become the subject of an open debate. The Nazi-Soviet Pact of 1939 is, officially, still taboo. The people have been told about the horrors of the concentration camps and about the frame-ups and forced confessions by means of which the Great

Purges had been staged. But the victims of the Purges, apart from the few exceptions, have not been rehabilitated. No one knows just how many people were deported to the camps; how many died; how many were massacred; and how many survived. A similar conspiracy of silence surrounds the circumstances of the forcible collectivization. Every one of these questions has been raised; none answered. Even in this jubilee year most of the leaders of 1917 remain 'unpersons'; the names of most members of the Central Committee who directed the October rising are still unmentionable. People are asked to celebrate the great anniversary, but they cannot read a single trustworthy account of the events they are celebrating. (Nor can they get hold of any history of the Civil War.) The ideological edifice of Stalinism has been exploded; but, with its foundations shattered, its roof blown off, and its walls charred and threatening to come down with a crash, the structure still stands; and the people are required to live in it.

In despair, he added, 'Sheltered by continuity, the irrational aspects of the revolution survive and endure together with the rational ones. Can they be separated from one another? It is clearly in the Soviet Union's vital interest that it should overcome the irrationalities and release its creative powers from their grip. The present incongruous combination breeds intense disillusionment; and because of this the miseries of the revolution may, in the eyes of the people, come to overshadow its grandeur.'[3]

Perhaps the most depressing aspect of the Soviet Union as it moved into the seventies was that mythology in history writing increased, if anything. The revised version of the *History of the Communist Party of the Soviet Union* which came out in October 1969 in limited circulation considerably glossed over criticisms of Stalin made during the Khrushchevian revision. It was revised yet again within a few months with the list of Stalin's misdeeds further reduced and remaining criticisms softened.

Equally glaring was the studied omission of all of Lenin's comrades from any mention, except in an oblique, critical and increasingly contemptuous way, when tributes were paid to Lenin on the hundredth anniversary of his birth on 22 April 1970. The main document prepared for the occasion, read by Mr Brezhnev, had this to say about a greatly troubled and momentous epoch in Soviet history:

Not everyone understood and accepted Lenin's idea that it was possible to build socialism in an economically backward, predominantly peasant country in a capitalist encirclement. The Right and the 'Left' oppositionists strove to impose either capitulationist or adventurist ideas, and to get the country off the Leninist path. The political struggle, which became especially acute after Lenin's death, was protracted and intense. But Lenin's ideas triumphed.[4]

The gaps in this statement are colossal. The demand for a truthful history of the Revolution and after is not an academic question. In essence it is a call for the resurrection of the clean ethos of the Revolution. The old and the young are vitally interested in it, the old to rehabilitate their past, the young to face the future with a clean slate. Among the very young, who grew up after the de-Stalinization debate, the attitude is significantly still more radical. They do not want, and are not interested in, excuses for Stalinism at any price. This vividly comes out in reports of a secret discussion about a six-volume party history which leaked out to the western press a few years ago. One old Bolshevik at the meeting exploded: 'Young people often ask me, "How could Lenin find himself surrounded with "enemies" and "traitors"? Who supported him and why?" '[5]

Another, a woman called Sedugina, pointed out:

Look what is written in the draft – that at the Sixth Congress a Central Committee was elected – a general staff to lead the insurrection. It is said that it was a militant and united general staff. Now look through the minutes of the Congress, see who were the members of this general staff. In Stalin's time almost all of them were numbered among spies and traitors. How did these spies and traitors manage to lead the Great October Socialist Revolution? How could they lead a country which stood up to the whole capitalist world? To write of seventeen people as spies and traitors means defaming the Communist Party.

These are explosive questions, not so much for the outside world which knows more of the truth, but for the Russians, and no answer can be provided by those in a position to give them because they have become prisoners of the Stalinist web of lies. To be sure, they are not comfortable with the situation, and are perhaps embarrassed, but their inability to come clean inflicts a wound on the present and future development of the Soviet system because it encourages cynicism and even utter disbelief. The interest for the Russians lies not in who was right or wrong but that the facts are not being given them to decide for themselves.

The situation is all the more gloomy because any radical change of direction in the Soviet Union must come from the Communist Party leaders. There is no opposition party which can provide a corrective and, in the foreseeable future, none is likely to be allowed to emerge. As for the small section of dissenting intelligentsia which is vocal, it too has a limited perspective. Even the most distinguished among them, for instance the great scientist Sakharov, have mostly utopian, somewhat naïve views when it comes to practical matters of state-craft. Other less distinguished dissidents as a whole often create the impression that they are content to repeat whatever criticisms of the Soviet Union are heard from abroad and do little original thinking of their own. To give a specific example, when in their writings the dissidents discuss the problems of Soviet foreign policy, they seem oblivious to the power basis of foreign policy. What they advocate may be music to western ears because it reads like an unconscious parody of what western critics of Soviet Union say day in and day out, but it can hardly be considered a meaningful contribution to any genuine discussion of Soviet foreign policy.

That even the intelligentsia as yet lack the capacity to do their own thinking is a consequence of the rigid, ideologically disciplinarian system which has prevailed so far. In this respect, it has only margin-ally improved upon the system evolved by Stalin. Above all, the inertia overcome by the Revolution has been replaced by another sort of inertia which was fostered by Stalin's methods. This inertia has to be overcome for any substantial progress to be made but those in authority know that this may unleash another revolution and there-fore are reluctant to risk the necessary effort. The greatest irony of all is that the heirs to a revolution which changed the course of history are now afraid of their own history. The past has become a shackle, not a lesson. Unless there is a radical change, the past cannot be cleaned up, and unless the past is cleaned up, the spiritual future of the Soviet Union will remain uncertain, despite all the material progress.

zone	area (km^2)	pop. (approx.)	territory covered
Central	485,200	over 30 m.	centres round Moscow
Volga-Vyatka	263,200	over 8 m.	Gorky and Kirov regions; Mari, Chuvash and Mordvinian Autonomous Republics (AR's)
Central Black-Earth	167,700	over 8 m.	Belgorod, Voronezh, Kursk, Lipetsk and Tamov regions
North-West	1,662,800	over 12 m.	European part of RSFSR: Leningrad, Pskov, Novgorod, Vologda, Murmansk and Archangel regions, Karelian and Komi AR's
Volga	680,000	over 17 m.	Ulyanovsk, Panza, Kuibyshev, Saratov, Volgograd and Astrakhan regions, Tataria, Kalmyk and Bashkiria AR's
North Caucasus	335,000	over 13 m.	Krasnodar and Staropol territories, Rostov region, Daghestan, Kabardino-Balkar, North Ossetian and Chechen-Ingush AR's
Urals	2,115,700	over 16 m.	Perm, Sverdlovsk, Chelyabinsk, Orenburg, Kurgan and Tyumen regions, Udmurt AR
West Siberian	999,000	over 10 m.	Altai territory, Novosibirsk, Tomsk and Kemerovo regions

industry	agriculture
...gineering, chemicals, textiles, fuel, power, metallurgical; ...achine tools and instruments; cars, diesel locomotives, ...il coaches, river craft	grain and vegetables, especially potatoes
...bour intensive engineering and metal-working, ...utomobiles, river craft, milling machines; timber, ...oodworking; chemicals, textiles, leather, footwear, fur, ...atches	wheat, rye, oats, barley, buckwheat; fibre flax; animal husbandry; dairy produce
...on-ore, non-ferrous metals, coal; metallurgical, ...gineering, steel; equipment for chemical, food, mining ...d building industries and farms; sugar refineries, distilling, ...ilk processing, grain-milling	animal husbandry; winter wheat, barley, maize, sugar beet, sunflower seeds
...ipbuilding, machinery for power and electrical industries, ...gineering, machine-tool building, instrument-making, ...el and metallurgical; turbines, generators; timber, paper, ...ulp; local and deep sea fishing (herring, sea perch, cod and ...addock)	animal husbandry; butter and preserved milk
...ower engineering, machine-building, instrument-making; ...l, gas, chemicals; fishing, foodstuffs, especially flour ...illing; hydro-electric power	spring wheat, rye, millet, hemp, potatoes, sugar beet, sunflower, mustard, tobacco; animal husbandry
...nemical, based on oil, gas and coal resources	winter wheat, millet, rice, sunflower seeds, sugar beet; fruits, fine-fleece sheep breeding
...netallurgical plants, non-ferrous metals, iron, steel, copper, ...nc, nickel, aluminium, magnesium; engineering, mining, ...etallurgical and transport equipment, power and electrical ...gineering, railway carriage wagon plants; timber, paper, ...ulp	spring wheat, winter rye, oats, barley, maize; vegetables
...al, petroleum products, iron, steel, rolled metals, ferrous ...loys, aluminium, zinc; engineering, chemical	spring wheat, oats, rye, sunflower, sugar beet, hemp; animal husbandry, (meat, wool, eggs, honey and dairy products in the future)

zone	area (km^2)	pop. (approx.)	territory covered
East Siberian	4,000,000	over 8 m.	Krasnoyarsk territory, Tuva and Buryat AR's, Irkutsk and Chita regions
Far East	6,200,000	over 6 m.	Amur, Sakahalin, Kamchatka, Magadan regions, Khabarovsk and Maritime territories, Yakut AR
Donets–Dnieper	221,000	18 m.	Dnepropetrovsk, Donetsk, Zaporozhye, Lugansk, Kirovograd, Poltava, Sumy and Kharkov regions
South-West	269,000	over 20 m.	Vinnitsa, Volyn, Zhitomir, Trans-carpathian, Ivano-Frankovsk, Kiev, Lvov, Rovno, Ternopol, Khmelnitsky, Cherkasky, Chernigov, Chernovtsy, regions of the Ukrainian Union Republic
Southern	269,000	6 m.	Crimean, Nikolayev, Odessa and Kherson regions
Byelorussian	207,600	over 9 m.	
Kazakhstan	2,715,000	over 12 m.	
Baltic	174,000	over 7 m.	Estonia, Latvia, and Lithuania Union Republics
Transcaucasian	186,000	over 12 m.	Azerbaidjan, Armenian and Georgian Union Republics
Central Asian	1,279,000	20 m.	Uzbekistan, Kirghizia, Tadjikistan and Turkmen Union Republics

industry	agriculture
ydro-electric power; gold, tin, nickel, mica, graphite, ırospar; timber, furs, coal, chemical	animal husbandry
mber; gold, shipbuilding; fishing (especially crab and lmon), whaling, furs (sable, squirrel, ermine, marten, coon and fox)	soya beans
ɔal, iron, steel, chemical, oil, gas, rock salt, phosphorites, itrogen and nitrogenous fertilizers; machine building, ɔwer generating equipment	maize, winter wheat, sunflower seeds, sugar beet; animal husbandry
ıgineering, metal-cutting machine tools, electrical ɔparatus, radio, optical devices, automation appliances, ımeras, medical equipment, agricultural machinery, sugar ⁏fineries, chemicals, natural and oil gas, sulphur	winter wheat, sugar beet, maize, sunflower, flax; animal husbandry, especially pig and sheep breeding
ıgineering, ship-building, farming machinery; fish and uit canning, wine production, flour milling, edible oil xtraction, food industry, especially wheat and milk	winter wheat, sunflower
ıachine tools, motor vehicles, tractors, farming machinery ⁏specially heavy duty lorries); chemicals (in next decade)	rye, wheat, buckwheat, barley, flax, sugar beet, potatoes
rrous and non-ferrous metals, copper, zinc, lead, iron, ɔal; oil, meat processing	spring wheat, millet; sheep, cattle and horse breeding
⁏ectrical engineering, radio and instrument making, railway ɔaches, buses, fishing boats; textiles, leather, paper, ırniture; fishing, meat and dairy products; computers and ⁏ectronic products	dairy farming; stock breeding for meat and pig, poultry farming
il, gas, machine building, metallurgical, power, machine ɔols, ball bearings, electric locomotives, lorries, drilling ɋuipment, agricultural machinery; synthetic chemicals	subtropical plants, tea, cotton, tobacco; sunflower, sugar beet, winter wheat, barley, maize; fruit and vegetables
xtiles, cotton and textile machinery; vegetable oil, dried ıd canned fruit and wine, fishing; hydro-electrical power, ıatural gas	crops only under irrigation: cotton, vegetables, fruit; oil crops, rice, wheat, maize; sheep breeding

Notes on the text

I THE BEGINNINGS

1 Quoted in Lionel Kochan, *The Making of Modern Russia*, p. 15.
2 Quoted in Bernard Pares, *A History of Russia*, p. 70.
3 Referred to in Bernard Pares, *A History of Russia*, p. 82.
4 George Vernadsky, *The Mongols and Russia*, p. 390.
5 Robert J. Kerner, *The Urge to the Sea*, p. 35.

2 THE TSARDOM – HIGH NOON AND SUNSET

1 Bernard Pares, *A History of Russia*, p. 258.
2 Quoted in Bernard Pares, *A History of Russia*, p. 323.
3 Quoted in Ronald Hingley, *The Tsars*, p. 244.
4 Quoted in Michael T. Florinsky, *Russia: A History and an Interpretation*, p. 111.
5 Jawaharlal Nehru, *An Autobiography*, p. 16.

3 THE REVOLUTION

1 Konstantin Paustovsky, *In That Dawn: Story of a Life*, p. 7. Translated by Manya Harari and Michael Duncan.
2 Leon Trotsky, *The History of the Russian Revolution*, pp. 318–19. Translated by Max Eastman.
3 Quoted in Louis Fischer, *The Life of Lenin*, p. 673.

4 THE STALIN ASCENDENCY

1 Quoted in Alec Nove, *An Economic History of Russia*, p. 174. The passage is from Mikhail Sholokhov's *Virgin Soil Upturned*.
2 Alexander Solzhenitsyn, *One Day in the Life of Ivan Denisovich*, p. 190. Translated by Ralph Parker.
3 Andrei D. Sakharov, *Progress, Coexistence and Intellectual Freedom*, p. 52. Translated by the *New York Times*.
4 Quoted in B. Ponomaryov, A. Gromyko and V. Khvostov (Editors), *History of Soviet Foreign Policy 1917–1945*, p. 305. Translated by David Skvirsky.

5 THE PATRIOTIC WAR – AND AFTER

1 Quoted in Alexander Werth, *Russia at War*, p. 324. The passage is from Dimitri V. Pavlov's *Leningrad 1941: the Blockade*.

6 THE KHRUSHCHEV PHASE

1 Guiseppe Boffa, *Inside the Khrushchev Era*, p. 37.
2 *The Dethronement of Stalin* (full text of the Khrushchev speech), p. 31.
3 *Ibid.*, p. 17.
4 Alec Nove, *An Economic History of the USSR*, p. 331.
5 *Istoriya kommunisticheskoi partii sovietskovo soyuza*, p. 609.

7 THE POST-KHRUSHCHEV PERIOD

1 *Istoriya kommunisticheskoi partii sovietskovo soyuza*, p. 628.
2 The *Daily Worker*, 15 February 1966.
3 Quoted in Michel Tatu, *Power in the Kremlin*, p. 487.
4 *Pravda*, 11 July 1969.
5 *Pravda*, 3 April 1964.

9 POLITICAL INSTITUTIONS

1 Karl Radek, *Portraits and Pamphlets*, p. 100. Introduction by A. J. Cummings and notes by Alec Brown.

12 CONCLUSIONS AND SPECULATIONS

1 Alexander Herzen, *My Past and Thoughts*, pp. 112–13. Translated by Constance Garnett, revised by Humphrey Higgins.
2 *Ibid.*, p. 114.
3 Isaac Deutscher, *The Unfinished Revolution; Russia 1917–1967*, pp. 103–5.
4 *Pravda*, 23 April 1970.
5 *Survey*, No. 63, April 1967, p. 162.
6 *Survey*, No. 63, April 1967, p. 163.

Acknowledgments

Intourist, 5; Metropolitan Museum of Art, 4; National Film Archive, 28; Novosti Press Agency (APN), Moscow, 6, 7, 9, 10, 12, 14, 15, 16, 17, 18, 19, 20, 21, 22, 23, 24, 25, 29, 30; Radio Times Hulton Picture Library, 11, 13; Thames and Hudson Archives, 1, 2, 8, 26; Tretyakov Gallery, Moscow, 3; Victor Hochhauser Ltd, 27

Select Bibliography

PRE-REVOLUTIONARY RUSSIA

Hoetzsch, Otto, *The Evolution of Russia* (trans. Rhys Evans), London, 1966.

Portal, Roger, *The Slavs* (trans. Patrick Evans), London, 1969.

Pares, Bernard, *A History of Russia*, London, 1965.

Florinsky, Michael T., *Russia: a History and an Interpretation*, 2 vols., New York, 1969.

Seton-Watson, Hugh, *The Russian Empire 1801–1917*, London, 1967.

Kochan, Lionel, *Russia in Revolution*, London, 1966.

Billington, James H., *The Icon and the Axe: an Interpretative History of Russian Culture*, London, 1966.

SOVIET PERIOD

Kochan, Lionel, *The Making of Modern Russia*, Harmondsworth, 1965.

Carr, E. H., *A History of Soviet Russia.* In progress: a number of volumes published in London, beginning from 1950.

Wolfe, Bertram D., *Three Who Made a Revolution*, Harmondsworth, 1966.

Deutscher, Isaac, *Stalin, A Political Biography*, London, 1949.
The Prophet Armed: Trotsky 1879–1921, London, 1954.
The Prophet Unarmed: Trotsky 1921–1929, London, 1959.
The Prophet Outcast: Trotsky 1929–1940, London, 1963.

Frankland, Mark, *Khrushchev*, Harmondsworth, 1966.

Nettl, J. P., *The Soviet Achievement*, London, 1967.

Werth, Alexander, *Russia: Hopes and Fears*, Harmondsworth, 1969.

Deutscher, Isaac, *The Unfinished Revolution: Russia 1917–1967*, London, 1967.

Fainsod, Merle, *How Russia is Ruled* (revised ed.), Cambridge, Massachusetts, 1963.

Schapiro, Leonard, *The Communist Party of the Soviet Union*, London, 1966.

Mackintosh, J. M., *Strategy and Tactics of Soviet Foreign Policy*, London, 1962.

Zagoria, Donald S., *The Sino-Soviet Conflict 1956–1961*, Princeton, 1962.

Crankshaw, Edward, *The New Cold War: Moscow v. Peking*, Harmondsworth, 1969.

Nove, Alec, *The Soviet Economy* (3rd revised ed.), London, 1968.

An Economic History of the USSR, London, 1969.

Kaser, Michael, *Soviet Economics*, London, 1970.

Zaleski, E., and others, *Science Policy in the USSR*, Paris, 1969.

Lunacharsky, Anatoly Vasilievich, *Revolutionary Profiles* (trans. Michael Glenny), London, 1962.

Mirsky, D. S., *A History of Russian Literature*, London, 1964.

Hingley, Ronald, *Russian Writers and Society 1825–1904*, London, 1967.

Slonim, Mark, *Soviet Russian Literature: Writers and Problems 1917–1967*, New York, 1967.

Houghton, Norris, *Moscow Rehearsals: the Golden Age of the Soviet Theatre*, New York, 1962.

Rice, Tamara Talbot, *A Concise History of Russian Art*, London, 1963.

Gray, Camilla, *The Great Experiment: Russian Art 1863–1922*, London, 1962.

Gregory, James S., *Russian Land Soviet People, a Geographical Approach to the USSR*, London, 1968.

Who's Who

AKHMATOVA, Anna (1889–1966). Pseudonym of Anna Andreevna Gorenko. Her first husband was the poet Gumilev. She was a leading Academist poet who remained silent for decades after 1922. Her later poems, among them the *War Requiem*, still unpublished in the Soviet Union, are noted for their classical severity of form and expression.

BAKUNIN, Mikhail Alexandrovich (1814–76). Theorist of Anarchism and a leading revolutionary, his influence was more felt in Europe than in Russia. He took a leading part in the 1848 revolution in Western Europe. He was in opposition to Karl Marx in the First International.

BELINSKY, Vissarion Grigoryevich (1811–1848). A radical, who changed the course of Russian literary criticism by insisting upon sociological relevance as a criterion of works of art. It may be said that the idea of socialist realism in literature originates from him.

BERDYAEV, Nikolai Alexandrovich (1874–1948). A brilliant philosopher who turned from Marxism to orthodox Christianity. He was expelled from the Soviet Union in 1922 and ultimately settled in France. He was opposed to the post-revolutionary regime.

BERIA, Lavrenti Pavlovich (1899–1953). A Georgian by birth, he made his career in the Soviet security service in the 1930's in Transcaucasia and later rose to be the head of the Soviet security organs, first as Commissar for Internal Affairs from 1938 to 1945 and later as a Deputy Prime Minister from 1948 to 1953. He was dreaded by everybody and shortly after Stalin's death was disarmed, arrested and shot after a trial in which he was accused of being an 'imperialist agent'.

BLOK, Alexander Alexandrovich (1880–1921). The most inspired and the greatest of the Symbolist poets, he combined an eclectic, mystic nationalism with support for the revolution in its early days. His acknowledged master-piece is *The Twelve,* which is unique even in his poetry.

BREZHNEV, Leonid Ilyich (b.1906). He has been General Secretary of the Central Committee of the Communist Party of the Soviet Union since October 1964. He was born in Kamenskoe, now Dneprodzerzhinsk, in the Ukraine. Joined the Komsomol in 1923 and the Communist Party in 1931. In 1938 he became a full-time party organizer and it was during this period that he came to work under Khrushchev. In 1952 he became a member of the Central Committee and a candidate member of the Praesidium. In 1953, after the death of Stalin, he was excluded from it; in 1954 he was appointed second secretary of the Kazakhstan Communist Party and later promoted to be the first secretary. In 1956 he was recalled to Moscow, appointed to the Central Committee secretariat and candidate member of the Praesidium. In May 1960 he was appointed Chairman of the Praesidium of the Supreme Soviet in place of Voroshilov. He was relieved of this post in July 1964. In October of the same year he was appointed First Secretary of the CPSU in place of Khrushchev. The title was changed to General Secretary by the 23rd Party Congress in 1966.

BUKHARIN, Nikolai Ivabovich (1888–1938). A leading theoretician of the Bolshevik Party before and after the Revolution. Took a prominent part in the seizure of power in Moscow after returning from exile in February 1917. Frequently opposed Lenin but remained on good terms and largely co-authored with him the Party Programme adopted in 1919. After Lenin's death he supported Stalin, first against Trotsky and then against Zinoviev and Kamenev. Soon, however, he quarrelled with Stalin, and was stripped of all power in the beginning of 1930. He was tried in a show trial during the Great Purge in 1936 and executed. His economic theories, which brought him into conflict with Stalin, are still interesting, and are best approached in *The ABC of Communism*, which he co-authored with E. Preobrazhensky.

BULGANIN, Nikolai Alexandrovich (b. 1895). Joined the Party in 1917, and steadily rose under Stalin to become a deputy Prime Minister from 1947 to 1955. After the death of Stalin he first supported Khrushchev and was appointed Prime Minister in 1955. In 1957 he joined the opposition to Khrushchev, recanted when defeated, but was gradually edged out of power. In 1958 he was expelled from the Party Praesidium and has lived in retirement near Moscow ever since.

CHAADAYEV, Pyotr Yakovlevich (1793–1856). Precursor of the Western-izers in Russia, who maintained in his philosophical letters that the

223

Russian past was meaningless and the only future was for her to reunite with Europe and the Roman Catholic Church. He was severely persecuted for his heretical views and declared insane. But he was allowed to live in peace afterwards on condition he did not write any more.

CHEKHOV, Anton Pavlovich (1860–1904). Outstanding short-story writer and dramatist, whose style has had great influence upon Russian and non-Russian writers alike. He was son of a grocer and grandson of a serf, and all his life suffered from the tuberculosis which finally caused his death.

DENIKIN, Anton Ivanovich (1872–1947). An officer in the Tsarist army, he joined the anti-Communist forces after the Revolution and became their commander; tried to restore land to landlords. He was defeated in 1919, fled to Istanbul and by stages reached America, where he lived for the rest of his life.

DMITRI DONSKOI (1350–89). He was the Grand Prince of Moscow from 1363 and won a famous victory over the Tatars on the Don in 1380.

DOSTOEVSKY, Fyodor Mikhailovich (1822–81). An outstanding novelist, son of a Moscow doctor, suffered from epilepsy all his life. He was also given to an incurable passion for gambling. Trained as an engineer, he narrowly escaped execution in 1849 for belonging to a secret revolutionary society, and was exiled to Siberia instead. His first great work, *Crime and Punishment*, came out in 1866 and many others followed it. Dostoyevsky lived in dire poverty almost all his life.

DZERZHINSKY, Felix Edmundovich (1877–1926). Born in high-class Polish family, he progressed to Communism through the Social Democratic Party of Poland and Lithuania. He was exiled to Siberia several times during the Tsarist period. After the Revolution he was appointed head of the Cheka, later the GPU. He supported Stalin in the inner-party struggle.

FRUNZE, Mikhail Vasilyevich (1885–1925). Took early part in revolutionary activities and during the Civil War defeated Admiral Kolchak and General Wrangel. For Stalin and against Trotsky, whom he replaced as People's Commissar for Military and Naval affairs in January 1925.

GODUNOV, Boris Fyodorovich (1552–1605). A boyar, who rose to be a powerful but unpopular Tsar from 1598. Earlier he had great influence on Ivan the Terrible and Ivan's son Fyodor.

GAPON, Georgi Apollonovich (1870–1906). Orthodox priest and advocate of Police Socialism. A procession of workers led by him was on the way to the Tsar to present a petition when it was fired upon mercilessly and caused the 1905 revolution. The incident is known as the Bloody Sunday. Gapon was murdered by a Socialist Revolutionary.

GROMYKO, Andrey Andreyevich (b.1909). An economist by training, a party member since 1931, he has held the post of the Foreign Minister since 1957. He has also been ambassador to the United States and Britain.

HERZEN, Alexander Ivanovich (1812–70). A liberal socialist, Herzen exercised tremendous influence in the 19th-century Russia through his writings and editorship of the journal *The Bell*, which he edited from exile. He left Russia in 1847 and never returned, living mostly in London.

KAMENEV, Lev Borisovich (1883–1936). A prominent leader of the Bolshevik movement before the Revolution, opposed Lenin's seizure of power in 1917 but remained prominent in the Party. At first he supported Stalin against Trotsky, later Trotsky and Zinoviev, several times expelled from the party. Finally, he was sentenced to five years imprisonment in 1935, tried again in 1936 and executed.

KERENSKY, Alexander Fyodorovich (1881–1970). Son of a headmaster, he was born in Simbirsk. A moderate socialist, he was known mainly for his association with the Provisional Government in various capacities. His last post was as Prime Minister. He was in favour of carrying on the war and lost all support. After the October revolution he escaped, and in 1940 settled down in the United States.

KHRUSHCHEV, Nikita Sergeyevich (b. 1894). Born in Kalinkova in the Ukraine. Began work as a shepherd boy, became a miner and joined the Bolshevik Party in 1918. Had little education or aptitude for intellectual niceties. Became a Central Committee member in 1934 and held various jobs in Moscow and the Ukraine subsequently. Became member of the Politburo in 1939. Shortly after the death of Stalin he became First Secretary of the CPSU after defeating Stalin and played a momentous role in de-Stalinization. In 1964 he was retired and replaced by Leonid Brezhnev.

KOLCHAK, Alexander Vasilyevich (1870–1920). Admiral of Crimean Tatar origin, became leader of the anti-Bolshevik struggle in Siberia during the Civil War and eventually taken prisoner and shot at Irkutsk.

KOSYGIN, Alexei Nikolayevich (b.1904). Born in St Petersburg in a worker's family. Volunteered for the Red Army in 1919, joined the Party in 1927. He studied afterwards to become a textile engineer and rose to prominence in Leningrad under Zhdanov. 1940–53, Deputy Chairman of the Council of Commissars (Council of Ministers from 1946) and concurrently Premier of the RSFSR. His further rise began after the fall of Malenkov, becoming a candidate member of the Party Praesidium in 1957, Chairman of Gosplan in 1958, First Deputy Prime Minister in 1960, full member of the Party Praesidium in 1960. After the fall of Khrushchev he was appointed Prime Minister, or Chairman of the USSR Council of Ministers.

KUTUZOV, Mikhail Illarionovich (1745–1813). Russian Field Marshal, who won immortal fame for driving Napoleon out of Russia.

LITVINOV, Maxim Maximovich (1876–1951). After early revolutionary activity, a good deal of it in exile in London, he represented the Soviet Government in Britain after the Revolution but was arrested and later exchanged for the British Ambassador. In 1930 he was appointed Foreign Minister (Commissar for Foreign Affairs) and was notable for the tremendous impression he made at the League of Nations and his advocacy of disarmament. He was removed from the post before the signing of the Nazi-Soviet pact in 1939, reappointed Deputy Foreign Minister and later Ambassador to Washington from 1941 to 1943.

LOMONOSOV, Mikhail Vasilyevich (1711–65). Son of a fisherman from Archangel, he ran away to Moscow when 17 in search of education. He became a scientist and poet. Often described as father of modern Russian literature, he founded the Moscow University, contributed hugely to scientific research, and generally did a lot for spread of education in Russia.

MALENKOV, Georgi Maximilianovich (b.1902). Joined the Communist Party in 1920 while in the Red Army. He rose steadily under Stalin, carrying out an important role during the purges, played an important part during the war as a member of the State Defence Committee and became a Deputy Prime Minister and Politburo member in 1946. In 1953, after the death of Stalin, became Prime Minister. In 1955 he was forced to resign and in 1957 he was expelled from the Central Committee for his part in leading the opposition to Khrushchev. He now lives in retirement near Moscow.

MEYERHOLD, Vsevolod Emilyevich (1874–1942). His early career began in the Moscow Art Theatre. He joined the Party in 1918 and for some time was put in charge of all Moscow theatres. In 1920 he founded his own Theatre of the Revolution. He was an original talent and great innovator and in the thirties was accused of formalism. His theatre was closed down in 1938; a year later he was arrested and disappeared.

MOLOTOV, Vyacheslav Mikhailovich (b.1890). Joined the Bolsheviks in 1906 and was a prominent personality in the party before the Revolution. Later he moved closer to Stalin and during his ascendancy was next in importance to him. He held various high-level posts during the Stalin period but will be remembered most in his capacity as a tough Foreign Minister. After Stalin's death, his decline began and he was thrown out of the Central Committee and its Praesidium for being a member of the anti-party group opposed to Khrushchev. Subsequently for three years he was in Mongolia as Ambassador and in 1960–61 Soviet representative to the International Atomic Energy Agency in Vienna. He now lives in retirement near Moscow.

PLEKHANOV, Georgi Valentinovich (1857–1918). An early revolutionary, he was converted to Marxism after his emigration to Western Europe in 1880. He played a unique role in converting the Russian intelligentsia to Marxism. At one stage he collaborated with Lenin but parted company in 1903 and joined the Mensheviks. He left them, too, in 1910 and founded his own group, co-operating with Lenin again. Returning to Russia after the February Revolution in 1917, bitterly opposed the Bolsheviks but died shortly after the October Revolution.

POBEDONOSTSEV, Konstantin Petrovich (1827–1907). A Russian courtier and politician. Appointed Procurator of the Holy Synod of the Russian Orthodox Church in 1880. He was a dyed-in-the-wool reactionary and inspired the thoroughly illiberal policies of Alexander III.

PODGORNY, Nikolai Viktorovich (b.1903). Member of the Party since 1930 and of the Central Committee since 1956, full member of the Politburo since 1960, his early career was mostly in the Ukraine, holding various party and government posts. Since 1965, Chairman of the Praesidium of the Supreme Soviet, i.e. President of the Soviet Union.

PUGACHEV, Yemelyan Ivanovich (1726–1775). A Cossack, leader of a peasant revolt in the Volga region and the Urals during the reign of Catherine the Great. The revolt was ruthlessly crushed and Pugachev brutally executed.

PUSHKIN, Alexander Sergeyevich (1799–1837). Undoubtedly the greatest master of the Russian language and the best Russian poet. He came from the nobility, and had Ethiopian blood on his mother's side. He was well educated and early in his life became a revolutionary, for which he was twice banished. Later a liberal, he was exempted from the usual censorship by the Tsar, who carried out the task himself. But Pushkin had many enemies among the courtiers and they involved him in a futile duel in which he was killed.

RADEK, Karl (1885–1939?). Born in Lvov, of a Jewish family, he was a brilliant publicist and revolutionary. He was active in German revolutionary activity after the war and in 1922 settled in Moscow. He joined the Trotskyist opposition group, was expelled from the Party in 1927 and a year later banished to the Urals. He was accepted in the ranks again in 1930 and became a foreign affairs commentator. Again expelled in 1936, he was tried in 1937 at one of the big show trials and sentenced to ten years' imprisonment. When he perished is not known with certainty.

RASPUTIN, Grigory Yefimovich (1872–1916). A Siberian peasant who exercised tremendous power of a mystic sort over the family of the last Tsar which did much to discredit the Royal family. He was instrumental in dismissing all liberal ministers while the Tsar was at the front. Outraged nobles had him murdered.

STANISLAVSKY, Konstantin Sergeyevich (1863–1938). A greatly talented actor and director, he revolutionized the Russian theatre before the Revolution. He founded, together with V. I. Nemirovich-Danchenko, the Moscow Art Theatre in 1898 and established his own school of realist acting and staging. This later became the authorized method, to the great detriment of the development of Soviet theatre. But Stanislavsky's own contribution to the theatre and his influence on a world-wide scale is undeniable.

STOLYPIN, Pyotr Arkadyevich (1862–1911). He was Minister of the Interior and the Prime Minister from 1906. He did very good work in agricultural reform but his policy was highly repressive in the political sphere. He was shot by a Socialist Revolutionary who was also a police spy.

SULEIMANOV, Olzhas (b.1936). A Kazakh poet and film director, geologist by training. Writes poetry in Russian. First book of poems, *Earth, Bow to Man,* published in 1961. Latest, *The Clay Book,* in 1969. Among discerning readers he is beginning to have a reputation of having his own individual style and voice.

Suslov, Mikhail Andreyevich (b.1902). Member of the Party since 1921. Has always specialized in ideological matters and relations with other Communist parites. He acted as the chief ideologue during Khrushchev's polemic with Mao. Since 1957 he has been a full member of the Politburo and wields great influence in party matters and ideological questions.

Suvorov, Count Alexander Vasilyevich (1730–1800). Considered by many to be the greatest Russian commander ever born. He distinguished himself in the Seven Years Wars and the Russo-Turkish Wars. But his best work was done in Italy, when he defeated the French on a number of occasions and conquered northern Italy. Once, surrounded by the French in Switzerland, he marched through the St Gotthard, a great feat by any standards.

Tolstoy, Count Leo Nikolayevich (1828–1910). A great novelist as well as moral philosopher. Among his masterpieces are *War and Peace* and *Anna Karenina*. He earned the wrath of the Orthodox Church, which excommunicated him, and the government's hostility because he rejected the Church and State.

Turgenev, Ivan Sergeyevich (1818–83). A highly sophisticated novelist, he was most notable for his portrayal of the intellectual urges of the Russia of his times.

Witte, Count Sergei Yulyevich (1849–1915). Minister of Finance from 1892–1903 and Prime Minister 1903–06, he launched on a policy of extensive industrialization of Russia. He was a moderate conservative, disliked by the liberals as well as the extreme right and the Tsar dismissed him because he urged the grant of a constitution with a Duma given the power of legislation.

Wrangel, Pyotr Nikolayevich (1878–1928). Tsarist general who joined the anti-Bolshevik forces and succeeded Denikin. He was forced to evacuate from Sevastopol in 1920 and thereafter lived in Belgium.

Yezhov, Nikolai Ivanovich (1895–1939?). Came from a poor family. In 1936 he was appointed by Stalin to be the head of the NKVD and thus directed the bloodiest of Stalin's purges. The period has come to be known as Yezhovshchina. He was replaced by Beria in 1938 and a year later disappeared without trace.

Zhdanov, Andrei Alexandrovich (1896–1948). Joined the Bolsheviks in 1915 and was First Secretary of the Leningrad Party from 1934 to 1944. He was concurrently a Secretary of the Central Committee. He became full member of the Politburo in 1939. Zhdanov was in charge of ideological matters and enforced socialist realism with ruthless energy and severity. He was later prominent in the defence of Leningrad and in the Cominform in 1947.

ZINOVIEV. Grigory Yevseyevich (1883–1936). He joined the Bolsheviks in 1903, was closely associated with Lenin in exile from 1905 to 1917 and returned with him. He opposed Lenin's policy on the seizure of power but remained with the Party and became a Politburo member in 1921. He first opposed Trotsky and then joined him against Stalin. He was falsely accused of complicity in the murder of Kirov and in 1935 sentenced to 10 years' imprisonment. He was retried in the great show trial in 1936 and executed.

Index

Bismarck, Otto von, 42, 44
Blok, Alexander, 186
'Bloody Sunday' (9 Jan. 1905), 49
Boffa, Giuseppe, 96
Bolshevik Central Committee, 58,
    163; see also Central Committee
    of CPSU
Bolsheviks, 48–9, 148; revolution
    and consolidation of power by,
    54–67; see also Communist
    Party
Bondarchuk, Sergei, 194
Boris Godunov, 20
Boris Godunov (Mussorgsky), 185
Borodin, Alexander, 42, 185
boyars, 19, 20, 21
Brezhnev, Leonid, 107, 109, 110,
    114, 117, 126, 134, 177, 211–12
Brissov, Valery, 186
Buchanan, Sir George, 58
Bukharin, Nikolai, 61, 75, 76–7,
    97
Bulgakov, Sergei, 191
Bulganin, Marshal Nikolai, 94, 99
Bulgaria, 42
Bunin, Ivan, 188
Burma, 174
Byelorussia, 88, 153

CADETS, see Constitutional
    Democratic Party
Cancer Ward, The (Solzhenitsyn),
    126
Catherine the Great, 33–5, 180
censorship, 43, 193
Central Committee of CPSU, 93;
    Stalin eliminates opposition in,
    79; Khruschchev and, 96, 99,
    106–7, 152; role of, 149, 150–2,
    153, 157–8
Central Revision Commission (of
    CPSU), 150
Chaadayev, Petr, 38
Chagall, Marc, 185
Chaliapin, Fyodor, 52
Chamberlain, Neville, 81

Charlemagne, 11
Cheka (security service), 155
Chekhov, Anton, 28–9, 51, 181,
    184, 186, 193
Chernov, Viktor, 56
Chernyshevsky, Nikolai, 183
Cherry Orchard, The (Chekhov),
    184
China, Communist, Stalin and,
    89–90, 167; Khrushchev and,
    103, 104–6, 173; Soviet post-
    Khrushchev relations with, 110,
    116, 117, 122–5, 174; as source
    of conflict to USSR, 169, 170–5,
    205–6
Chingiz Khan, 16
Chou En-lai, 105, 110, 123, 124
Chukrai, 194
Churchill, Winston, 83, 85, 87
cinema, 194
Civil War in Russia, 60, 61–2, 67
Cold War, 87–8, 89, 115, 126, 167,
    179
collectivization, 70–3, 129
Communist Party of the Soviet
    Union (CPSU), post-Stalin
    reorganization of, 93–4, 110;
    role of, 147–53, 156; judiciary
    and, 160; science and, 194–7;
    fundamental ideology of, 204–5;
    see also Bolsheviks
Congresses of CPSU, 2nd (1917),
    58–9; 10th (1921), 63–5; 14th
    (1925), 69; 16th (1927), 70;
    17th (1934), 77; 18th (1939),
    93; 19th (1952), 93, 151; 20th
    (1956), 96–8, 125; 21st (1959),
    106; 22nd (1961), 105; 23rd
    (1966), 114–15, 150, 151
Congress of Berlin (1878), 42
Congress of Paris (1856), 42
Constantine, 37
Constitutional Democratic Party
    (the Cadets), 51, 57
Constitution(s) of USSR, 147–8
Council of Boyars, 14

Kazakhstan, collectivization in, 72; cultivation of virgin land in, 100–1; population of, 153
Kazakov, Yuri, 190
Kennedy, President John F., 104
Kerensky, Alexander, 55, 56, 57, 58, 59
Kerner, Robert J., 18
KGB, *see* State Committe for Security
Khazars, 11, 12–13
Khlebnikov, Velemir, 186
Khodassevich, Vladislav, 188
Khrushchev, Nikita, *134*; elected as First Secretary, 92–3; agricultural policy of, 88, 94–5, 99–101, 102, 110; and de-Stalinization campaign, 90, 96–8, 204; gains supremacy over Malenkov, 95–6; industrial policy of, 95, 102, 111; and foreign policy, 96, 103–6, 115–16, 119; fall of, 106–7, 109–12
Kiev (Kievan Rus), 10, 12, 13–15, 16, 18
Kirov, Sergei, 77
Kochetov, Vsevolod, 115, 125, 192
Kolchak, Admiral Alexander, 62
Kolokol (The Bell), 43
Kolpakova, Irina, *135*
Komsomol (Young Communist League), 150
Koniev, Marshal Ivan, 84
Korea, 46; North, 175
Korean War, 90, 103, 167
Kornilov, Lavr Georgiyevich, 56, 57
Kosygin, Alexei, 107, 110, 116, 117, 118, 123, 124, *134, 138*
Kozintsev, Gregory, *135, 194*
Kreuzer Sonata (Tolstoy), 184
Kronstadt Mutiny (1921), 64
Kropotkin, Prince Petr, 183
Krupskaya, Nadezhda (Lenin's wife), 75
Krylov, Ivan, 38, 181
kulaks, 70, 71, 77
Kuznetsov, Vasily, 124

LAND AND FREEDOM, *see* Populists
Lange, Oscar, 145
Larionov, Mikhail, 186
Latin America, Soviet interest in, 176
League of Nations, 81
Lenin, Vladimir Ilyich (Ulyanov), birth of, 44; pre-Revolution activities of, 48, 51; as leader of Revolution, *31*, 54–55, 199–200; death of, 65; career of, 65–7; Stalin/Trotsky power struggle and, 74–5; foreign policy and, 80, 163, 164; his views on political institutions, 147, 148; minorities problem and, 153–4; Brezhnev on, 212
Leningrad, siege of, 85–6
Lermontov, Mikhail, 37, 181
Levitan, Isaak, 52
'Liberation of Labour' organization, 47
Lissitsky, El, 185
Liszt, Franz, 207, 208
literature, pre-revolutionary, 38, 39, 42–3, 51, 180–4, 186, 187–91, 192–3; Soviet, 113–15, 125–6
Lomonossov, Mikhail, 180
Lower Depths, The (Gorky), 189
Lvov, Prince Georgiy, 55, 56
Lysenko, Trofim, 89, 107, 112

MACHINE TRACTOR STATIONS, 100
Makhno, N. I., 62
Malaysia, 117, 173, 174
Malenkov, G. M., 87, 92, 94, 95–6, 99, 100, 103, 152
Malevich, Kasimir, 185
Mamai (Tatar leader), 18
Mandelshtam, Osip, 186, 188, 191
Mao Tse-tung, 105, 110, 205